HERTFORDSHIRE

The King's England

A New Domesday Book of 10,000 Towns and Villages

Edited by Arthur Mee

Complete in 41 Volumes

NOTHING like these books has ever been presented to the English people. Every place has been visited. The Compilers have travelled half-a-million miles and have prepared a unique picture of our countryside as it has come down through the ages, a census of all that is enduring and worthy of record.

Hertford Castle, Ancient Home of Kings

THE KING'S ENGLAND

HERTFORDSHIRE

London's Country Neighbour

EDITED BY
ARTHUR MEE

With 148 Places
and 108 Pictures

THE KING'S ENGLAND PRESS
1991

First Published 1939 by
Hodder & Stoughton Ltd

This edition published 1991 by
The King's England Press
37 Crookes Lane, Carlton
Nr Barnsley, S. Yorks

ISBN 1 872438 05 9

Printed and bound by
SMITH SETTLE
Ilkley Road, Otley, West Yorkshire LS21 3JP

The Editor is indebted to

STELLA PAWLYN, CLAUDE SCANLON
and HUGO TYERMAN

for their help with this book

For the pictures to

SIDNEY TURNER, ART EDITOR

and to the following :

*Messrs Edgar Bull, Country Life, J. Dixon-Scott,
P. Howard, H. Joel, A. F. Kersting, Newtonian,
K. Reitz, H. J. Smith, E. W. Tattersall, W. F.
Taylor, F. Thurston ; also to the BBC, the
Bishop's Stortford Museum, His Majesty's Station-
ery Office, the Royal Commission on Historical
Monuments, the First Garden City Ltd, Welwyn
Garden City, Limited, and the Father Superior of
the Abbey Folk Museum at New Barnet*

PICTURES OF HERTFORDSHIRE

*Where the pictures are not on or facing the page given
they are inside the set of pictures beginning on that page*

PICTURES OF HERTFORDSHIRE

PICTURES OF HERTFORDSHIRE

ix

London's Country Neighbour

IT is the countryside that London loves, for Londoners have sought it out for centuries, and in our own time it has received as many new people as would make up a great town. It is country as it should be, unspoiled by the heavy hand of industry. Its four hundred thousand people on their four hundred thousand acres are all country folk, loving their small rivers and their little hills, so near to town that they can come to London when they will, always going back.

That was how Charles Lamb felt about this countryside. "I turn my back on thy detested walls, Proud City," he would say, as he set out to leave London behind him, and though the pull of London was with him as he went it was enough that he would think of it:

And I shall muse on thee, slow journeying on
To the green plains of pleasant Hertfordshire.

If it be true that there is something unique in an Englishman among the races of the world may it not be that he is a mixture of the country and the town?

Certainly Charles Lamb's pleasant Hertfordshire has contributed its abundant share to the life of the nation. We may wonder if any other small county has such proud boasts to make of its service to great causes. Its fields and lanes, so near the town, have sown seeds that have yielded infinite harvests of happiness and prosperity throughout the world. It is a wide claim to make, but it is true. Where was the great example of the Garden City given to the world? Where did the idea of freedom for the slaves dawn in Thomas Clarkson's mind? Where was the action taken which blotted witchcraft from the statute book? Where were the seeds of scientific agriculture sown? Where was the idea of our great canal system born? The answer to all these questions is Hertfordshire.

We see that it has been a place for pioneers, for the birth of ideas and the rise of great movements. It was the home of Sir Henry Bessemer whose steel revolutionised the Age of Power. It was the home of William Cowper who changed the course of English poetry. It is the only English county which has given a cardinal and a pope to the Church of Rome, and in its county town of Hertford was held the first Synod ever held by the Church of England. Here (in Hertford Castle) King Richard was deposed; from here Charles Stuart set out to raise his standard at Nottingham and to lose his throne; from here Mary Tudor went to take the throne: from here Queen Elizabeth went to London to put on her crown. They are interesting links with the throne for this county which gave birth to another Queen Elizabeth in our own time, and yet there is still this to say of London's country neighbour—that here began our Tudor dynasty, for it was in a Hertfordshire farmhouse that Henry the Fifth's Catherine gave birth to Edmund Tudor, whose son Harry won the throne on Bosworth Field.

We see that a county full of Nature's quiet places can have a famous place in history. Perhaps we do not wonder that the first aerial traveller in England chose to come down here, or that it was in this natural English paradise that there was born a man who gave his life to spread the English spirit about the world, beginning with South Africa: it was here that Cecil Rhodes was born. As for the history that goes back to the civilisation before the English arrived in these islands, Hertfordshire has a noble share of it in St Albans, one of our first Roman cities; and the hand of the Roman, the Saxon, and the Norman is seen in many of its villages and towns. In this old town of St Albans lies one of the most famous and perplexing Englishmen, the wisest, brightest, meanest of men, Francis Bacon. This old city, the Roman Verulamium, has been for the student of ancient civilisations one of the richest sources of our knowledge of the life the Romans lived. It was a soldier of Verulamium who became the first English martyr, immortalised in the name of St Albans, where, gathered about his shrine, grew up a monastery with one of the chief libraries of medieval England.

Of all the counties that are relieving London of its vast multitude of people we may say that Hertfordshire is relieving London with the least damage to its amenities. It remains essentially an agricultural county, productive in a variety of ways. Its meadows send their dairy produce to the capital. It has great areas of market gardening. Its streams have been haunts envied by anglers since Izaak Walton sat on their banks with his rod and his book.

For the most part Hertfordshire drains into the Thames, a few other small streams like the Hiz, the Ivel and the Rhee making their way to the Great Ouse. The biggest river in the county is the Lea, running for 50 miles and almost dividing the county in two; it enters from Luton's valley in Bedfordshire and makes its way past Wheathampstead to skirt Hatfield Park and pass in two branches through Hertford. The county town is a veritable gathering place of waters, with three tributaries coming down from three valleys: first the Maran from the Waldens by way of Welwyn, second the Beane from Ardeley by way of Walkern and Watton, and third the Rib which rises near Reed, picks up the Quin from the Barkway Downs at Braughing, and passes Standon, Thunbridge, and Ware Park. The Lea flows on through Ware, and soon turns south having received the River Ash from the Hadhams and the Pelhams. At the Essex border the Lea is joined by the Stort (the first river Cecil Rhodes would know). The Stort itself has formed the boundary with Essex, but the wider and deeper River Lea now becomes the boundary as far as Waltham Abbey, where the river leaves Hertfordshire. But from Amwell, hard by Ware, another river has been keeping the Lea company, the famous New River made by Sir Hugh Myddelton for nearly 40 miles to supply London with drinking water from the clear chalk springs of this countryside.

West of the Lea basin we cross into that of the Colne, which from its beginnings near Hatfield runs to meet its tributary the Ver, the name the Romans took for one of their most famous towns in Britain, Verulamium. The Colne is joined at Watford by the River Gade, and at Rickmansworth by the sparkling River Chess; then it makes south to pour itself into the Thames. The third tributary of the Thames from these downs travels much farther to reach it; it is the River Thame, which has three springs at Tring and only glitters at Puttenham before crossing Buckinghamshire and Oxfordshire to join the Thames.

As in the east, so in the west it is an artificial river which impresses us more than Nature's little streams. At Tring the Grand Union Canal has a reservoir and many locks marking the end of its rise of 400 feet from the level of the sea, so that the canal here is higher than the dome of St Paul's. The canal links London with Birmingham and other Midland towns, and if the railways had not come would have been of even greater importance to the county. Actually the two great railways to the North and some of the most important commercial roads in England run through Hertfordshire, and there was a great road here before the Romans came. Made before the Romans made anything we know of was the Icknield Way which runs across the northern hills, coming from the Wash by way of Cambridge-shire, passing through Royston, Baldock, Letchworth, and Hitchin, crossing Bedfordshire and touching Hertfordshire again near Tring before making its way over the Thames. It was the trade route of the ancient Britons, and some of their camps are beside it—Ravensburgh, for example.

Crossing this ancient route are the great Roman roads of Ermine Street at Royston and Akeman Street at Tring. Akeman Street comes from St Albans and is a continuation of the Stane Street which linked Colchester with that Roman town, through which also passes Watling Street. Even more important than these old roads is the Great North Road through Hatfield, Stevenage, and Baldock; it is the A 1 of our Transport Board.

Though these great roads carry mighty streams of traffic there are byways and lanes and grass tracks innumerable, the constant delight of cyclist and walker passing up and down this countryside so pleasantly undulating, with ample shade and many a fine common: most people know Harpenden's and Wheathampstead's and Chipperfield's.

The fact that the county has such magnificent highways, railways, and waterways has attracted certain industries, and brick-making and quarrying have long flourished here. The red brick tower of St Albans Cathedral is an eloquent witness of these age-old industries, for its materials were made by the Romans hereabouts; they fashioned millions of their dark red tiles from the glacial clays of Hertfordshire. These glacial deposits rest in places on the chalk which forms most of the bedrock of the county, almost all the rest being London clay, with gravel beds spreading across the south. In the extreme north are patches of strata older than the chalk, and, like the clay, providing the oak and other vegetation not found on the downs. Yet the chalk country of Hertfordshire is not so bare as downlands usually are. Such bareness is found here only in the extreme north where the Chilterns throw up such heights as Hastoe Hill near Tring, 709 feet; Butts Hill overlooking Hexton, and hills of 400 to 500 feet looking down on Royston. The downs continue to maintain a height of about 300 feet over half the eastern boundary of Essex, but they drop steadily as they come southward towards Middlesex. We see that five other counties touch this, Essex, Middlesex, Buckinghamshire, Bedfordshire, and Cambridgeshire, and a very long boundary line Hertfordshire has for its size. We have found in our tour of England that one of the surprises of our coast is Poole Harbour with so many creeks and inlets that its shore is about 90 miles, and Hertfordshire has a surprise something like it, for to walk round the county would mean a 130-mile journey, so deep are its projections into its neighbours. There are only seven smaller counties in England than this. It has an area of only 632 square miles, and it is striking that it should be so rich in ways of getting about—so much beauty so accessible.

We do not wonder that the county is becoming more and more the Londoner's playground, with London's Green Belt running between Greater London and the North Orbital Road. Much of it is open to us all (as at Knebworth and Tring), and delightful are the parks, with glorious trees and lakes made by widening the rivers. Hertfordshire has about a hundred parks, and it is not to be wondered at that a county so richly endowed should have led the way in solving the pressing problem of our crowded cities. It is Hertfordshire which has seen the fulfilling of Ebenezer Howard's dream.

It must lift up the hearts of every country-planner to see what Letchworth and Welwyn have done; they are among the social triumphs of our time, and Letchworth is a veritable delight. The marvellous harvest that has sprung from the seeds sown by John Bennet Lawes at Harpenden has impressed itself upon agriculturists all over the world, for on his Rothamsted estate has been laid the foundation of scientific agriculture. In one field wheat has been grown continuously for about 100 years, and it is beyond all doubt that Rothamsted has increased the supply of the world's daily bread. Two great schools have come to Hertfordshire from London, Christ's Hospital School for Girls, housed in a magnificent block of buildings at Hertford, and the Foundling Hospital, which is carrying on its work at Berkhamsted, having brought Handel's organ with it.

The fine educational work of the Natural History Museum built up by the Rothschilds goes on at Tring, where the park is open for us all, as is Lord Lytton's park at Knebworth. All these are interesting places playing their part in the nation's life. At North Mimms, the ancestral home of Sir Thomas More, is the Brookman's Park Wireless Station, and at Little Gaddesden is Ashridge Park, the great house in the wonderful gardens which was the home of the Duke of Bridgewater, founder of inland navigation in this country, was long before that the home of all the children of Henry the Eighth, and is in our own time a school for training men in public life. Such towns as Watford (biggest town in the county, fast being changed) and Ware with its old houses, narrow streets, and fine medieval church, are much visited and have great interest; and as for Hertford itself it is a delightful place, with a castle in the heart of the town where, in spite of much change, those who know what it means must still feel the thrill of the past. It was here that the first Synod ever held by the Church of England took place, here that the Black Prince brought home the French king captive from Poitiers, and here that the charges were drawn up against the Black Prince's son Richard the Second—the paper he could not read, for his eyes were full of tears. Here also Oliver Cromwell spent one of his critical days.

We have seen how close have been the links between Hertfordshire and the throne, and in truth it would be difficult to find any English county with more intimate associations with our ruling dynasties; fitting it is that it should have been the birthplace (at St Paul's Walden) of our present Queen Elizabeth, for here have come kings and queens for century after century. We have only to think of Hatfield, the seat of so much power since Queen Elizabeth received the news of her accession under an oak which still flourishes in the park, to realise what one great house has been in the story of our land. Here was Mary Tudor as well as her sister Elizabeth and her brother Edward, and it was at Hunsdon that Mary received Master Ridley, who came down to persuade her to change her faith. Had he succeeded he might have saved 300 of his countrymen from the fires at Smithfield, but he failed, Mary Tudor thanking him for his gentleness, but never a whit for his persuasions.

It was at Much Hadham that there was born the child whose son became our first Tudor king, and at Theobalds Park in Cheshunt that our first Stuart king brought up his sons, one of whom was to set out from here to begin a war against his people and to lose his crown. Strange that in this same small town of

Cheshunt Richard Cromwell should drag out a weary old age. At Hoddesdon still stands the gateway of Rye House, where the plot was hatched to murder our last two Stuart kings, a plot most happily frustrated but most unhappily leading to the judicial murder of Algernon Sidney and Lord William Russell, hounded to their doom by the infamous Jeffreys : thus the worst judge in English history started his career of judicial crime.

But it is King's Langley that must stir great emotions in all who know what happened there. Every king from Henry the Third to Richard the Second knew it. From here Edward the Second rode to the wedding of his friend Piers Gaveston, and here he brought the body when Gaveston was slain. Here was born that Duke of York who comes so finely into Shakespeare's Richard the Second, and here is what remains of a garden in which Shakespeare fixes one of his scenes. This is one of the most pathetic places in the life of any king, for here took place the scene in the garden when the queen overhears the gardener talking; the scene of a queen who comes knocking at the door to save her son (A beggar begs who never begged before); and that most terrible scene of all when Sir Pierce of Exton brought Richard in his coffin and heard those terrible words of doom :

With Cain go wander through the shades of night,
And never show thy head by day nor light.

Here the murdered king was buried and lay for years till the Conqueror of Agincourt took him away and laid him in his noble tomb by Edward the Confessor.

As if these tragedies were not enough for this county so small, Hertfordshire was the home of that Duke of Monmouth who began building the church we see at Rickmansworth, and would probably have been laid to rest in it had he not been dragged from a ditch and beheaded on Tower Hill. At Royston, the town with the romantic cave deep down below the street, is a fragment of a palace in which King James signed the paper which sent Sir Walter Raleigh to the block, and at Standon is the tomb of Sir Ralph Sadler, having over it the pole from which the Royal Standard of Scotland waved on a battlefield where 6000 men were slain. We may think that the men who make our films have chosen well in making them in Hertfordshire, for truly it is a dramatic piece of our countryside. Where else could be found a churchyard with two such dramas for the films as in the film town of Elstree, with the two graves of James Hackman and John Thurtell? Both Bulwer-Lytton and Walter Scott were moved by the story of Thurtell, and Boswell rode with Hackman to the scaffold. Not very far need the Elstree film men go for the Tragedy of a Country Churchyard.

It is interesting to remember an odd distinction that Hertfordshire has in the history of flight. It was here that the first Zeppelin was brought down in England, and it was here that the first aerial traveller landed in England long ago; he landed at Standon, having called at North Mimms on the way and startled a country woman by dropping a cat for her to take care of.

We have become familiar in our tour of England with churches taking us back to Saxon and Roman days, but nowhere else have we come upon so much visible Roman material in church walls. The Roman bricks in the tower of St Albans Cathedral are, of course, a wonder of all time, but we found a chancel arch of Roman tiles at Sandridge and the handiwork of the Romans is to be found at Welwyn, Sarratt, Great Wymondley, and Hemel Hempstead. It is odd that with so much Roman there is so little Saxon, almost none, but there are fine examples of Norman and abundant examples of medieval architecture.

Hemel Hempstead Church is a majestic Norman monument, Redbourn has a fine Norman arcade, Hormead has a Norman chancel arch and a treasure not to be equalled by more than one or two places in England—a Norman door. The county is remarkable for its old doors, for Bengeo has a 14th century door still in a Norman doorway, Pirton has two 14th century doors, Kelshall has a 15th century door, and there is another of the same age in the spacious medieval church of Sawbridgeworth. Little Berkhamsted has a bell which has been ringing for 600 years, and Braughing and Flaunden have bells which rang in the good news that the Spanish Armada was beaten. Flamstead has medieval frescoes, brasses, and sculptures; Sarratt has wall-paintings 700 years old; Digswell has two dozen children on brass, and Ashwell has an ancient drawing of Old St Paul's engraved on its 14th century tower. At Wyddial hangs a white ensign which flew at the Battle of Jutland.

The county's roll of honour is a long one and covers every phase of the nation's life. At Bishop's Stortford two churches stand on their hills facing each other with the town between them, and in the little town is the house in which was born Cecil Rhodes, the dreamer of South Africa. No man has had a nobler vision of the British Empire and its place in the world, and it was from this pleasant countryside that he went out to fulfil his dream. Here was the home of those two brothers, Hamburg Jews who would today have been flung out of Germany, who have carried on his work, Alfred and Otto Beit. Here also was the home of another pioneer, the man who helped to build up Canada, Lord Mount Stephen, and out from Hertfordshire also there went the brave John Eliot, known as the Apostle of the Red Indians for the pioneering work he did among them. To this county belongs Lord Somers, a great pillar of the State in the time of Dutch William, and in one house here (Brocket Hall at Lemsford) there lived and died two Prime Ministers, Lord Melbourne and Lord Palmerston.

As for the Church, Bishop Ken, whose hymns are sung around the world, was born at Little Berkhamsted, Cardinal Manning was born at Totteridge, and Nicholas Breakspear began life at Abbots Langley and ended it in the papal chair as Adrian the Fourth. Macaulay was at school at Aspenden and Cowper at Markyate, he having been born at Berkhamsted. At Anstey was born Thomas Campion, whose poem The Man of Life Upright every Englishman should know. At St Albans, in St Michael's Church, sleeps Francis Bacon, and at Stanstead St Margaret lies Henry Lawrence, Cromwell's kinsman and Milton's friend.

At Hitchin was born that George Chapman whose translation of Homer opened a new world for Keats (Much have I travelled in the realms of gold). At Lilley lived and wrote James Janeway, the only rival to John Bunyan in the nurseries of his day, writer of books for children terrible almost beyond belief. At Welwyn lies Edward Young, the poet of Night Thoughts. At Bushey lies Barry Pain, a humorist of the last generation and a poet of no mean order; he lies with two artists near him—Sir Hubert Herkomer and Thomas Hearne, the painter who inspired Turner. Harry Bates (sculptor of the beautiful Socrates talking to his pupils) lies at Stevenage, and the delicate artist Claud Lovat Fraser lies at Buntingford. Nicholas Hawksmoor, the right-hand man of Sir Christopher Wren, who helped in the building of St Paul's and of the Abbey, lies at Shenley. At Charlton, near Hitchin, was born Sir Henry Bessemer, whose discoveries added new resources to engineering all over the world. Cottered has the grave of the great surgeon Sir James Cantlie, and at Cheshunt (where lies Oliveria Cromwell, the last of the family to bear the name) sleeps Nehemiah Grew, the botanist who gave the world new knowledge of trees and flowers.

All these have contributed to the high place that Hertfordshire has in our history, and there are many more; such men as Thomas Dimsdale, pioneer of inoculation; William Yarrell, whose books on birds and fishes were the best of their kind 100 years ago; and Mrs Humphry Ward should not be over-looked. Yet when they are all mentioned who else among them all counts like Charles Lamb? Of all other counties, this is his. He loved it as a boy and never forgot its fields and lanes and houses, or its people. His life would have been changed could he have married his beloved Ann Simmons, whose memory all his life was linked with Hertfordshire for him. He knew all the old cronies who lie in the graveyard at Widford, and we may be sure that when he came to write his haunting verses on the old familiar faces he was thinking much of this countryside and the happy days of his childhood here before the shadow fell across his life.

The Vast Antiquity of Man

ABBOTS LANGLEY. Here was born 800 years ago the only Englishman to become Pope of Rome. He was Nicholas Breakspear, a poor boy left to fend for himself when his father became a monk at St Albans. The story is told that when he would have entered the monastery as a servant he was laughed to scorn and turned out by the abbot, and that this same abbot was chosen to bear the king's greetings to the new Pope when, after working his way up through the monasteries of France, this Hertfordshire man was received into the Vatican as Adrian the Fourth. A tablet has been put in the church to remind us of this dazzling destiny of a village boy.

It is a beautiful church, one of the most interesting in the county, with a low Norman tower which Pope Adrian may have seen rising in his boyhood. Inside are arcades of Norman arches carved with chevron and other designs, and lit by a clerestory which is 15th century. Stone demons support the medieval roof of the nave, while angels support the new roof of the chancel. A medieval head looks out from the piscina, and a skew arch gives a peep to the altar. There is a 15th century font.

From the chancel an arcade on the south opens into the 14th century chapel, with windows of graceful stonework, the east one filled with a glorious Benedicite in modern glass. On one side of it is the stone figure of Anne Combe, who died in 1640; her husband is well remembered at Cambridge, for he left his library to Sidney Sussex College. Even more delightful is the family group opposite, where an old lady sits reading with three babies in cots beside her. She is Dame Ann Raymond, widow of one of Charles the Second's judges, and the three bonneted babies sleeping so peacefully are her grandchildren, all dying within a few weeks of their birth. Their father, Sir Robert Raymond, is sculptured at the other end of the church, reclining on a cushion with a look of intense self-satisfaction as he receives the crown of his labours as Lord Chief Justice.

A stone to Robert Nevyll, who died 500 years ago, reminds us that

This world is but a vanity,
Today a man, tomorrow none;

but several brasses win a little earthly immortality for some of his neighbours and their successors. We see Rauffe Horwode's two wives and six children, though his own portrait of 1498 has been stolen; and another husband, Thomas Cogdell, is here with his two wives in fine big portraits, the women wearing the broad-brimmed hats of Shakespeare's day. One of these wives may have lived on to notice the curious slip in the Table of Commandments set up a few years later, which leaves out the neighbour's maid-servant from the Tenth. Long afterwards someone broke the Eighth by stealing the Commonwealth entries from the registers here, which go back to 1538.

A fragment of medieval glass in the clerestory shows St Lawrence, who has also reappeared with St Thomas of Canterbury on the walls after being hidden for generations under plaster, 13th century frescoes brought to light by Professor Tristram.

A famous man who lies here has a marble memorial with a portrait medallion by Sir William Richmond. He was one of the most re-markable and industrious men of the 19th century, Sir John Evans. A familiar figure in this countryside, he was nearly all his life asso-ciated with the paper mills at Hemel Hempstead, yet he kept almost daily engagements in London and spent every spare moment he had digging into history, geology, and anthropology, till he had estab-lished to his satisfaction the vast antiquity of man. He went to France with Sir Joseph Prestwich to examine the flint implements found in the river gravels of the Somme by Boucher de Perthes. It was this discovery which stirred the mind of the village grocer of Ightham, Benjamin Harrison, who set to work searching for flints on the old plateau of Oldbury Hill, a mile from his shop. He sub-mitted flints to Sir Joseph Prestwich and Sir John Evans, both of whom agreed that they were human handiwork, like those from the Somme, proving that man was hundreds of thousands of years older than had ever been imagined. Sir John Evans built up splendid col-lections of ancient moneys, on which he was a great authority, and in 1864 he published a standard work on the coins of the Ancient Britons. The house in which he lived near the mills was packed with

books and antiquities, which Evans delighted to show to antiquarians from all over Europe.

On the way to the neighbouring hamlet of Bedmond we pass what
is now a Roman Catholic College, where great cedars stand beside
two enormous chestnuts with branches crawling like snakes along
the ground. Beyond them is the farm belonging to Cecil Lodge, a
picturesque group of old gables, and beyond this again is Break-
spears Farm, part of which is 300 years old, though the name takes
us back 800 years to the village boy who became Pope Adrian.

The Englishman in St Peter's Chair

NICHOLAS BREAKSPEAR was the son of a poor man who
entered the monastery at St Albans and left the boy to his own
resources. Having been turned away from St Albans, Nicholas made
his way to France, was admitted in a menial capacity to the Abbey
of St Rufus near Avignon, and eventually rose to be its abbot. His
reforming zeal caused his monks to denounce him to the Pope, who
summoned him to Rome. Finding that he had an exceptional man
in Breakspear, the Pope made him a cardinal and sent him as legate
to Norway and Sweden, where he converted the heathen, founded
the bishopric of Upsala, and returned in triumph to be hailed as the
Apostle of the North.

It was in 1154 that he became Pope, the first and last Englishman
elected to that position. The outcast of St Albans was now the
supreme prince of Christendom, and among those who came to
Rome to do him homage was the head of the house that had rejected
him, the abbot of St Albans!

Our King Henry the Second sent an embassy to Adrian, with
John of Salisbury at its head, seeking permission to conquer and
annex Ireland; and the villager from Langley disposed of a kingdom
at a stroke. His reason was that the Irish church was reported as
guilty of laxity and heresy. His justification was that, according to
the forged donation of Constantine, which Adrian believed authentic,
the successor of St Peter was made possessor of all the islands in the
world. King Henry was to bring the Irish within the pale, and to
pay a penny a year for every hearth in Ireland!

But Adrian had a seething Europe about him. A forerunner of
the Reformation, Arnold of Brescia, had put himself at the head of

a republican Rome and defied the papacy. Adrian took the unprecedented course of laying the Eternal City under interdict, and later he sent Arnold to the stake. He waged a long battle with the Norman king of Sicily, and came to grips with the emperor of the long-lived Holy Roman Empire, Frederick Barbarossa. In a memorable scene at Nepi Adrian compelled this haughty monarch, in the presence of his entire army, to lead his horse by the bridle and hold his stirrup while he mounted and dismounted. Afterwards, in opposition to the wishes of the Romans, Adrian secretly crowned Barbarossa in St Peter's; but the rival claims of the two were never reconciled. Adrian firmly asserted universal sovereignty for the Pope, and entered on a contest that left him apparently defeated, but in the end destroyed the dynasty of Frederick, whom Adrian was on the point of excommunicating when death laid him low, in 1159.

In private life Adrian was unaffected, just, and kind, and he told John of Salisbury that he looked back with a sigh of regret upon his English life, and that the papacy had brought him no real satisfaction.

From the Battlefield

ALBURY. The River Ash trickles through the valley below, and on neighbouring hilltops are Albury Lodge and Upwick Hall, both with 17th century panelling and oak doorways older still, while the gardener at the hall lives in a cottage 500 years old.

Near the church is a 16th century timbered house with leaning walls, and beyond is an inn with a ready-made text in its sign, The Labour in Vain. In summer the scent of lime and syringa steals into the church, where are also the fresh colour and coolness of trees, for the 13th century chancel, behind its screen of 15th century tracery, has been entirely panelled in white oak, with new seats and an altar rail to match, all set against a carpet as green as leaves. The nave, the aisles, and the chancel arch are 14th century; the pinnacled tower and needle spire and two of the bells were added in the 15th, and the porch soon afterwards. There is an ancient ironbound chest with four locks, some 15th century ironwork on the door to the tower staircase, a 17th century altar table, and a pulpit made up of Jacobean panelling inlaid with the arms of the Leventhorpes.

Thomas Leventhorpe, who died in the year of the Spanish Armada, is pictured in brass with his wife and six daughters; an unknown

Ashwell   The Charm of Thatch

Ardeley   The Corner by the Church

The Village Seen from the Hills

Stocks and Cottages by the Pond
OLD ALDBURY

knight and his dainty lady are shown with their four daughters; and thinly scratched on a rough sheet of brass are John Scrogs, his wife and child, some shields and a skull and the date 1592. Another brass shows the arms of Anne Barley and tells of money left by her to buy bread for the poor. In his armour on an altar tomb lies one of Richard the Second's knights, his wife beside him in the simple dress of the end of the 14th century. He may be Sir Walter de la Lee, but his name is lost, and he remains an unknown soldier, like many of those who knelt before the crucifix in the chapel, for this came from the hospital chapel at Wimereux in France, placed here by the chaplain in memory of all who died in that hospital during the war. The altar cloth was also brought from there, having shared in the last communion of a little host of those who died that we might live.

York and Lancaster

ALDBURY. Through lattice windows the 300-year-old timbered manor house looks on to the village pond, the stocks, and the whipping-post, and the old cottages gather round. Here in the pond the scolds were ducked, and village justice was meted out under an enormous elm unhappily blown down in 1939. It was 400 years old, and five trees in one. A little farther on are the almshouses, three or four tiny black-beamed yellow cottages, weighed down under the thatch of 300 years; and in front of all is the ridge of a beech-clad hill, topped by a column nearly 200 feet high in memory of the Duke of Bridgewater and his Canal.

The old parts of the church are mostly 14th century, with a square tower of the 15th; but there is much that is new. In a glass case is the pipe with three notes blown by the clerk to give the pitch in the days before organs. Older treasures are a 16th century wooden lectern, some fragments of 15th and 16th century glass, a chalice of 1514, some medieval tiles, and a stone coffin lid; but the chief interest of the church lies in the monuments of the knights and ladies from the three big houses of Pendley, the Manor, and Stocks.

The beautiful medieval stone screen round most of the Pendley memorials was brought from Ashridge monastery on the other side of the ridge, and with it the tomb and the perfect sculptured figure of the builder of Pendley, Sir Robert Whittingham, a Lancastrian killed at the battle of Tewkesbury. He lies by his wife, with his feet on his heraldic wild man, with the family shields carved round his tomb and two old helmets hanging on the wall. If he could turn his head he might look through a peephole to the altar, but he gazes at the pompous wigged busts of an ancient couple who owned his house 200 years after him, and at the records of the Harcourt family who who followed them. Four little Harcourts have an imposing collection of godmothers and godfathers, a queen, a princess, a bishop, and two Georgian kings.

The staunch Lancastrian's daughter married a Yorkist, Sir John Verney, and Pendley went with her, York and Lancaster coming here to rest in the same tomb. Their descendants, Sir Ralph Verney, his wife, and their nine sons and three daughters, have magnificent brass portraits rich in heraldic design on an altar tomb in the north chapel. On a pillar is a small brass figure of a 15th century London merchant.

The manor house is represented in the church by a curious monument to Sir Thomas Hyde, who died in 1570, and Stocks, where the Duncombes lived for 500 years, by an inscription to the last of the family, who ordered the black marble top of the table in his bowling green house to be used as his monument. Here it is, and outside is the grave of Mrs Humphry Ward, who also lived at Stocks, and there wrote in her novel, Bessie Costrell, a vivid description of this village where so little has changed since the sundial was put on its carved wooden post in the churchyard 300 years ago. Mrs Ward was the granddaughter of the famous Dr Arnold of Rugby, and was born in Tasmania, though brought to England when she was only five. She grew up to take a deep interest in social work, believing that to be the best form of Christianity, and she expounded her views in her best known novel, Robert Elsmere, which had a tremendous success, being reviewed by Mr Gladstone. With a group of friends she founded a University Settlement, and set on foot many schemes for increasing the happiness of cripple children. She was one of the first women magistrates.

The Gardens and the Church

ALDENHAM. The lovely gardens of Aldenham House, with their rare trees and shrubs and multitude of flowers, are known to every horticulturist. The church and the gardens are Aldenham's Pride.

The laying-out of the gardens was a part of the amazing activity of Henry Huck Gibbs, the merchant and banker who adopted politics and architecture with equal zest, found time to write many articles for the Oxford Dictionary, and was helping with its editing when he died in 1907, first Lord Aldenham.

He inherited Aldenham House, which had been almost entirely rebuilt a century before, and he added to it without disturbing the older treasures it still retains, including 17th century panelling and a fireplace of 1529. He also made the park and the gardens among the most renowned in England. Three churches owe much to him. He gave time and money in abundance to restoring St Albans Abbey; he gave new life to the church of Clifton Hampden, one of the loveliest villages of Oxfordshire, which was his, too; and he maintained the beauty of Aldenham's splendid church and gave it its fine oak screen. It is pathetic to remember that his youngest son died within 24 hours of his father, and they were laid in the grave together.

Filled from end to end with beauty and interest is the church, set so proudly in the centre of the village, with a cross designed by Sir Arthur Blomfield and three great sycamores stirring up the graves with their roots. That the Normans had a hand in its building is shown by the west window of the south aisle; the church grew throughout the succeeding building centuries, the 13th adding the chancel, the south chapel, and the tower; the 14th the south arcade with its carved capitals; the 15th an arcade to the north, the top of the tower with its shingled spire, the tower arch, and the clerestory which lights the stone angels supporting the nave roof. After 450 years this roof still reveals traces of its old colour. The chancel is curiously out of centre with the nave, owing to a 16th century widening.

The font is 700 years old, with a Jacobean cover of fine craftsmanship, and by its side is one of the biggest chests in England, hollowed out of an oak beam 10 feet long 600 years ago, and strengthened with iron and 17 hinges. The south chapel screen is 500 years old, and through a little iron gate in the south wall we see the stairs by which in the old days singers would climb up and walk across this screen, passing through an opening in the chancel wall on to the rood screen, which has now been displaced by Lord Aldenham's magnificent gift. The little Tudor vestry is a miniature museum, with fragments from Roman and medieval days in a glass case, with oak shutters 400 years old, and a corner fireplace. On its walls are portraits of the Carys and other great families of the neighbourhood, including William and Mary's powerful friend John Holles, Duke of Newcastle. Ben Jonson's friend Henry Cary, the first Lord Falkland, lies under the chancel, and his grandson Lorenzo was baptised at the old font. Lorenzo was the son of the second Lord Falkland, Lucius Cary, who fell at Newbury, perhaps the most pathetic figure in the story of the Civil War.

Outlined on a floorstone in the north aisle is John Robinson of 1674, and there are numerous portraits in brass, many only fragments now, though on the chancel floor we see Edward Brisko and his wife of Shakespeare's day and Lucas Goodyere of 1547 in her shroud; while in the south chapel are several other 16th century folk in brass, all nameless except Jane Warner. The beauties in this chapel are two nameless ladies of the 14th century, stately figures sculptured under rich stone canopies, with the arms of William Crowmer, twice Lord Mayor of London, and many other devices on their tombs.

When the church was restored a century ago many of its tombstones were put to new use in the cottages near by, and we were told that one enterprising baker used one or two for paving his oven, with the result that loaves appeared on tea tables inscribed *Sacred to the memory*, or *aged 34 years*.

The grammar school stands proudly on its hilltop. Founded in 1596 by Richard Platt, a London brewer, it was greatly enlarged a century ago, and again this century, when a library was added in honour of the 160 boys and masters who fell in the war. A new chapel of great dignity, designed by Mr W. G. Newton, was dedicated in 1938 when (after the style of the House of Commons with Black Rod) the bishop knocked three times before the headmaster called on him to enter. A headmaster specially remembered for his genius was Dr Alfred Hands Cooke, who died in 1934. He received a collection of medals at Cambridge for Greek and Latin poetry, was senior classic when Frazer of the Golden Bough was second classic, and was a great footballer and an authority on zoology. He was a lecturer at King's for more than 20 years before he came to Aldenham, where stories are still told of his kindly wit, his unfailing courtesy, and his brilliant scholarship.

For England

AMWELL. Through the park and down the valley flows the
New River, its waters divided by an island on which stands the
statue of its creator, Hugh Myddelton. It was his indomitable will
which carried the waters from these chalk hills to the London of the
Stuarts. London had long been running short of water, but nobody
did much but complain about it till this London goldsmith, Sir
Walter Raleigh's friend, bestirred himself. With the blessing of the
City Corporation he made a new river for London, turning the
waters round Amwell and Chadwell into a channel which twisted for
nearly 40 miles and emptied itself into a reservoir at Islington. On
Amwell's monument to Myddelton are these lines by John Scott,
the Quaker poet who lived here a century later:

> *Amwell, perpetual be thy stream*
> *Nor e'er thy springs be less*
> *Which thousands drink who never dream*
> *Whence flows the boon they bless.*
>
> *Too often thus ungrateful man*
> *Blind and unconscious lives,*
> *Enjoys kind Heaven's indulgent plan,*
> *Nor thinks of Him that gives.*

It was John Scott, hater of war, who wrote these familiar lines:

> *I hate that drum's discordant sound,*
> *Parading round and round and round.*

He was not Amwell's first poet, for in the churchyard lies William
Warner, who wrote of Albion's England, "a poetical history of
England from the time of Noah till the reign of James the First."
He may have been a friend of Shakespeare, for in London he visited
the same haunts, and it is even thought by some that Shakespeare
saw his translation of Plautus's Menaechmi before it was published,
and in this way got hold of the plot for his Comedy of Errors.
Warner lies in the churchyard, and not far from his grave lies Isaac
Reed, a London solicitor better known as an editor, who brought
out two editions of Shakespeare and died among his books at Staple
Inn, soon after the "drum's discordant sound" had rung out at
Trafalgar.

The old church, with a new spire rising from its 15th century
tower, was here before the first poet wrote in King's English, for the

walls of the nave and chancel, and the chancel arch itself, are Norman. We enter by a 15th century oak door, and find among the church's antiquities a brass of a friar of 1400 and another of a 15th century man with two wives and seven children. A new tower screen has the traceried doors from the lost medieval chancel screen. There is a Jacobean altar table, and an oak pulpit with six heads carved on graceful pilasters by an unknown craftsman of 1696. On each side of the chancel arch is a peephole to the altar.

The village stocks stand by the church, and at Amwellbury is the squire's old pigeon house, with wooden cots and new brick walls safeguarding it after nearly 300 years.

A mile or two away is the modern church of Little Amwell on Hertford Heath, which flanks the grounds of Haileybury College. Haileybury arose in 1862 out of an 80-year-old college for Civil Servants of the East India Company, and it has become one of the public schools of England. An avenue of tall chestnuts leads to the fine classical building designed by the architect of the National Gallery, William Wilkins, and a dome conspicuous for miles rises over the handsome chapel. In the chapel is a tablet to 40 Old Boys who fell in the Indian Mutiny, some under the command of those famous Haileyburians, Sir John Lawrence and Sir Henry Outram. In the chestnut avenue is an obelisk in memory of Old Boys lost in the South African War. But the school's greatest sacrifice was its bitter loss of 577 boys in the Great War. Hundreds were awarded the DSO, and four the Victoria Cross, some of them fighting under the command of the most famous Haileyburian in the Great War, Lord Allenby.

The four heroes of Haileybury who won the VC were Clifford Coffin, Clement Robertson, Cyril Frisby, and Rupert Hallowes. Colonel Coffin, when the troops were on the point of being beaten back, walked through a deadly storm of bullets from shell hole to shell hole, in full view of the enemy, talking cheerfully to his men, who, inspired by his example, achieved what seemed to be impossible and held a line of supreme importance. Captain Robertson won his VC in a world of earthquake and fire, for the ground had been blasted by explosions, and in the midst of the inferno appeared a number of demoniacal Robots, rocking slowly and relentlessly toward the German lines. They were British tanks, but Captain Robertson saw to his consternation that they were losing their way.

There was only one means of saving them, and he took it; he walked
with them and guided them as far as he could before he was shot
down. Captain Frisby captured a bridge near Graincourt, held by a
strong machine gun post; unless it fell the whole British advance
must fail. With sparks shooting from the ground all round he and
three men climbed down the bank into the canal as the bullets hit the
earth. They were in the midst of intense fire, but the swiftness of
their attack took the machine-gunners by surprise and the four
Guardsmen captured the post from a dozen Germans with two
machine guns. Rupert Hallowes, during an intense battle of several
days, made many daring inspections of the German positions and
risked his life by taking supplies behind the lines. He knew no fear,
wrote one of his men; he never sent a man where he would not go
himself. On the seventh day of the battle, when shells were raining
on the trenches, he went to cheer his men in the most dangerous
part of the line, and fell.

Here Thomas Campion Was Born

ANSTEY. A Norman knight chose to settle at Anstey, and built
here his castle and his church. It is one of the places where we
hear the old legend of the Fiddler and his Dog, for it is said that
Blind George the Fiddler disappeared in a subterranean passage
from a chalk pit to the castle, his fiddle getting fainter and fainter
until it stopped, the dog reappearing like a hairless ghost, but Blind
George being never seen again.

The great moated mount in the grounds of the hall is all that is
left of this castle, which Henry the Eighth gave to his first three
wives in turn; but the Norman church still stands, its central tower
on four strong arches, and here is the font in which all the babies of
Anstey have been baptised since his day. It is a curious one with a
merman at each corner. A small stone figure in a recess may be
Richard Anstie, who added and altered much in the 14th century,
building the transepts with turret steps leading to a priest's chamber,
and giving a view of his new chancel from these transepts through
windows in the flying buttresses of two pillars. Even the blocked
priest's doorway, with a kind of dog-fish carved at the end of its
arch, he cut on the cross so that the altar lights could be seen from
the sacristy. And here are some of the stalls put into his chancel 600

years ago, seven with misereres worthy of a cathedral, two jesters exchanging quips among their leafy carvings, and a man putting out his tongue.

The beautifying 15th century added a needle spire to the tower and built the handsome porch with eight trefoil windows and doorways with carved spandrels. In the vestry are two wooden chests, one still in use after 700 years, the other covered 500 years ago with skin before being bound with iron. Here also are two tally sticks, and a register filled with the neat notes of the man who was clerk in 1541.

Two years after that Thomas Campion, the poet and musician who wrote masques and songs for the court of James the First, was born here and baptised at the curious font. His best known poem is the familiar one beginning, The man of life upright. Perhaps he was thinking of this Hertfordshire village when he wrote

> Jack and Joan they think no ill,
> But loving live, and merry still,
> Do their weekday's work and pray
> Devoutly on the holy day.

Those who answer the call of the two 500-year-old-bells in the tower pass through a medieval lychgate, which has served two purposes, one bay having been turned at some time into a lock-up for unruly villagers.

At the rectory is an altar frontal of purple velvet with the date 1637 among its embroideries. The most famous of the rectors was James Fleetwood, who took an active part in the Battle of Edgehill as a soldier and ended as Bishop of Worcester. He was tutor to Charles Stuart's son, who made him his chaplain at the Restoration.

A Village Boy for Harvard

ARDELEY. From this village went out a Hertfordshire boy to be first President of Harvard University in 1656. Charles Chauncy and his brother Henry were born at Ardeley Bury, and though their Stuart home is now much altered it keeps its dry moat and some of the panelling of the rooms where Henry compiled his Antiquities of Hertfordshire. Perhaps he was out searching for information for this book when he heard of Jane Wenham of Walkern; he took sides with those who accused her of being a witch, and at his instigation the last trial for witchcraft was held in England in 1712, the case leading to the abolition of this superstition from the Statute Book. Not far off is the small hamlet of Cromer with one or two cottages and a farm, all 16th century, and a great postmill without sails. At Wood End are two more farms 300 years old.

Ardeley itself has a 17th century vicarage, but its new houses and the new village hall in a horseshoe round the village green, all white-walled and thatched, are charming. No stark memorial keeps alive the names of the 13 men of Ardeley who never came back from the war, but theirs is a garden filled with flowers and a small shrine by the churchyard gate. The churchyard was also bright with flowers when we came this way, and on the church door a notice greeted us saying, You are very welcome.

We could well believe it, for this is a church where great devotion has clearly striven to replace old glories that have gone. A screen with a canopy background to its coloured statues of Calvary, Mary, and John, is exquisite in grey-white oak, and compares in workmanship with the 12 angels spreading wide wings below the old roofs of the nave and the aisles; but the screen is new and the angels are 500 years old. Of the stone steps to the roodloft only one was left, but this has been copied and now a complete newel stair is here for the children to climb to the top of the screen and sing carols at Christmas.

The nave is 700 years old; the north aisle, some carving over a piscina, and a recess in the chancel are 13th century; the south aisle and the tower are 14th, and the clerestory and the north porch are 15th. The font is the oldest thing the church possesses, the rough work of some country mason long ago, with only two of its jutting-out heads left. A few 15th century pews still have their poppyheads, much worn. The Lord's Name be Praised is written on the oldest bell, which may have sounded the news of Agincourt; and another, made later in the 15th century, says, My name is Mary.

Another Mary is remembered in this church, a young woman whose beautifully sculptured head and shoulders are framed in the wall by the roodscreen. She was Mary Markham, who lived at the 17th century farm of Wood End, and died there when she was 24. A fine brass of 1599 shows Thomas Shotbolt with his wife and six children, and a small brass portrait of Philip Metcalff, a 16th century vicar, looks across to a 19th century vicar who also has his portrait in brass, a striking likeness of a grand old man, William Malet. It was left to our own generation to put up a monument to Sir Henry Chauncy, and we may think he deserved something more interesting. The modern windows are more successful. One is crowded with little pictures showing the Seven Sacraments; another is beautiful with a blue-robed Madonna and Child sitting on a green throne.

Pride of the Village

ASHWELL. Set among trees in a countryside of open fields on the Cambridgeshire border, it is one of the pleasant surprises of this part of the county. As we look down from the low hills about it, it is a charming picture with its roofs clustering round a weather-worn church. Some of the many old houses have overhanging storeys and roofs of thatch and tile; some are timbered, and one has remains of ornamental plasterwork. Deep down below the road the River Rhee, a tributary of the Cam, comes to life, springing from the bank like the fingers of a hand and going on as a robust stream. The ash trees growing about the spot, spreading their branches on a level with the road, are said to have given the village its name.

One of the old buildings near the church is the 17th century Merchant Taylors School, now part of a larger school. Another is a timbered medieval cottage with gabled roof, quaint windows, old fireplaces, and huge oak beams—charmingly restored as a little museum for housing the collection of local relics of bygone days which was begun by two enthusiastic schoolboys, who collected antiquities and conducted excavations as if they had been learned professors on a happy hunting ground. A hundred years ago the cottage was a tailor's shop, and before that it was the Tythe House. In the museum are some bits of wool and a few wheat grains that were left in a crevice of the old building from the harvests of years ago. Old Ashwell is represented here in all its ages. There is a rare specimen of a polished Neolithic tool, coins from Roman days down through history, old straw-plaiting tools, and a long metal harvest horn which woke the men of Ashwell from their beds at four in the morning. The museum is the pride of the village, and we heard of labourers hurrying off to it with fresh finds turned up by their ploughs. South-west of Ashwell are the entrenchments known as Arbury Banks, a vast circle of ploughed field, half-surrounded by broad deep banks, now cared for by the Office of Works. Once it was a Roman settlement, and earlier still the great banks protected the pit dwellings of an ancient people.

Reached by a worn lychgate, which may be 15th century, the great church reminds us of the time when Ashwell was a prosperous market town with four fairs a year. Very striking is the tower, with rough and heavy stepped buttresses climbing nearly to the top, and crowned with a slight leaded spire set on an octagonal drum. Records of days gone by are cut on the wall of the tower and on the pillars of the nave, a Latin inscription telling of the days when terror fell upon the people of England and the Black Death struck dead one man in three: "Miserable, wild, and distracted, the dregs of the people alone survive to witness; and in the end a tempest." Ashwell tower stood out against the tempest, but the tower of neighbouring Bassingbourn crashed to the ground. Below the inscription on Ashwell's tower is a fine though much worn drawing of 1350 showing a cathedral, very like Old St Paul's, which was completed that year and must have been in every architect's mind. It is scratched on the wall of the tower and the drawing of a simpler church is on a pillar of the north arcade. A sheet of lead in the tower, once on the roof, has an inscription saying that Thomas Everard laid it here to lie 100 years; he would be glad to know that it lay 200 years, and has only had to be replaced in our own time.

The church is as long as the tower and spire are high, and is chiefly 14th century, with porches added and some of the windows altered a century later. The clerestory is partly 16th century. The original east window of the north aisle has beautiful butterfly tracery, with quaint heads of a man and a woman at each side. The high tower of diminishing stages has fine windows, and striking double buttresses stepped and gabled. The south porch, higher than the nave, has a niche in the gable, and modern vaulting. The old door within it opens to a stately interior full of light from clear glass. The nave arcades have clustered pillars on high bases, and among the figures of men, women, and animals between their arches are two men grimacing, and a man thoughtfully stroking his beard. The walling at the west end of each arcade is carved with tracery like windows, reaching from floor to roof.

Bright as a summer noonday, the beautiful chancel has fine sedilia and a piscina with only half a bowl, a stone panel carved with the

Last Supper under the great east window, a niche in a window splay with an animal carved under the bracket, and the base panels of the 15th century screen, with poppyheads of a griffin and a quaint fish at each side of the entrance. Rich medieval screenwork encloses the north chapel. The pedestal pulpit is 1627, and a 17th century chest has carving and iron bands. A floorstone to John Sell of 1618 has these words: To God a Saint, to Poore a Friend.

Tom Macaulay Goes to School

ASPENDEN. The road ends here, and we found it all so quiet that even the old school was empty, the books mouldering in the cupboards where the children had packed them years ago when they changed their school for Westmill. Sad to see it would have been for that warm-hearted Mary Cator, who saved £210 in her 30 years as servant at the hall, and left it for teaching the children of the village. That was 150 years ago, a generation before young Tom Macaulay was learning his lessons at the same hall, where a clergyman kept a school.

There cannot have been a more wonderful scholar in any school in England at that time than 14-year-old Tom Macaulay, who started to be a historian so early that before he was eight he had written a compendium of Universal History from the Creation to the year of his own birth. Of books he always had a great store, and, reading with lightning speed, he packed away all knowledge as it came into his capacious memory.

The church, with a tiny 18th century spire on its medieval tower, has the mark of most centuries since the 11th, and memorials of many generations. Here is the tomb of Sir Robert Clifford, knight-of-the-body to Henry the Seventh but unfaithful to him when Perkin Warbeck would have seized the throne. He lies in a chapel filled with box pews and cut off behind a rare arcade of two dainty 17th century arches and a wooden rail six feet high. At the back of his tomb, under a crested canopy, we see him in brass with his wife and two daughters, the colours still shining on his heraldic coat. A man and his wife in 15th century dress have their brass portraits by the north door. On another memorial are sculptured half figures of Ralph and William Freman with their hands clasped and holding skulls. Ralph was Lord Mayor of London, and this memorial is of special interest because it survived the Great Fire, having been in St Michael's, Cornhill, when the fire was burning.

There are timbers 500 years old in the roofs, there is a solid bit of 17th century craftsmanship in the almsbox, and from the same century comes the charity of an Aspenden boy who became a bishop and President of the Royal Society. He was Seth Ward, who left £12 for apprenticing village boys, set up the almshouses at Buntingford, and put a stone to his parents outside the chancel wall. In the opposite chancel wall is a tiny window framed in rough flint, the only fragment of Norman work left; and beside it is a curious low window of the 16th century with a grinning face and a fleur-de-lys in the spandrels.

Many of the windows are in memory of the Lushingtons, who have lived for generations at the hall in the park, a 19th century house with 17th century panelling. The rectory is much older, for it has 16th century timbers in its walls and an overhanging storey.

ASTON. Its thatched cottages and barns stand on high ground away from the main roads, and the church is a little way off, with a giant elm near it. The nave and chancel are 13th century, with roofs set over them in the 15th, after the bold west tower was finished. There is a grand double piscina of 600 years ago, a little white and gold glass 500 years old, a chancel screen of 400 years, a panelled oak pulpit and altar table of the 17th century, and the brass portraits of a woman and her husband John Kent, who was steward in the household of Edward the Sixth, Mary Tudor, and Queen Elizabeth.

In their day the brick house named Aston Bury rose a mile away with gabled wings and ornate moulded chimney stacks, and part of an older building in its walls. It is an almost perfect example of an Elizabethan home, with oak-framed windows crossed by mullions and transoms and with two staircases of solid oak. Three ponds still mark the line of the old moat.

A Hoard of Coins

AYOT ST LAWRENCE. The ancient and the beautiful, the quaint and the curious, all come near each other in this quiet place. In Prior's Wood was found a hoard of 230 Roman coins. There are black and white timbered cottages, a 14th century ruined church in a garden of roses, and a Georgian church with a classical colonnade which seems to have dropped from some 18th century town into a field by a Tudor manor house.

In the bird-haunted tower of the medieval church is a panelled tomb on which lie a 15th century knight and his lady. In a niche are kneeling figures of Nicholas Bristow, who died in 1626, with his wife and four children. On a modern gravestone we read the simple words, "Fell asleep in his garden." The Georgian church was designed by Nicholas Revett, whose book on the Antiquities of Athens led Englishmen to appreciate Greek architecture. At each end of the colonnade are open vaulted pavilions with memorials to the builders, Sir Lionel and Lady Lyde. The interior is a simple hall with panelled roof and Greek ornament on pilasters, and on the altar in the apse is a modern painting of the Adoration of the Lamb.

AYOT ST PETER. The nightingales love the woods round this hilltop village, where is a green dotted with old trees and a 19th century church which has surrounded itself with yet more trees of all kinds, a silver birch shimmering among the sombre evergreens. The church's iron screen and stone pulpit with five saints are modern. In the park of Ayot Place is a timber and plaster farmhouse with a tiled roof and twisted chimneys, and in its hall is part of a crested roof beam decorated in classical design, and the date 1615 on a frieze of family shields to tell us when this Jacobean house was finished.

Samuel Pepys's Six Small Books

BALDOCK. It has a piece of the Great North Road for its fine main street, lined with grass banks and trees, and it has at Quickswood Farm a clock which has been going with very few stoppages since the year Charles Stuart came to the throne. On the street look the dormer windows of a charming row of almshouses, telling their age with a syllable under each window: An No Do Mi Ni 1621. John Wynne, who gave them, also wrote on the wall that he left money to carry them on "to the worldes end." Close by is a stalwart pair of panelled gates 500 years old, and down every side street we find old homes and old inns, many with overhanging storeys.

Baldock's church has as spacious an air as its highway, and is almost complete from the 14th century, with nave and chancel, two aisles and two chapels, and a clerestory added in the 15th century. Inside is a pillared font 100 years older than the church itself, and much fine carving in wood and stone. Niches and sedilia and piscina show the art of the medieval mason, and the 15th century woodcarver has a grand display in the screens stretching across the nave and aisles, three in a line, each different. The middle screen has its original doors, and over the patched doors of the north screen is a laughing face. Other faces in stone catch our eye wherever we look up, and there are 22 quaint little oak figures between the beams of the north aisle roof. The staircase door to the priest's room (now made one with the porch) is 500 years old, and some of the roofs are medieval, but, like the screens, they have needed patching, and we found a strenuous battle going on with the death-watch beetle. Fragments of medieval painted glass are in the north chapel, which has a 17th century altar table.

There are several brass portraits, one picturing a nun kneeling in prayer in the nave where she would kneel 500 years ago. Another shows a woman with her husband, whose dress proclaims him a 15th century forester. His horn hangs from his belt, but his dog has gone from his side. Two other men from the 15th and 16th centuries are here with their wives, and beside them hang two ancient deeds, one of 1289 telling of a yearly payment of twopence. Such deeds were probably kept in the little medieval ironbound chest, and there are two other chests with Jacobean carving. Over the north door hang two old breastplates and a sword.

There lies in the church a man with a simple name famous for a great achievement. He came here as rector, but was known long before he came for his work at St John's College, Cambridge, where he toiled for ten thousand hours over six small volumes of closely-packed and mysterious shorthand, fully 3000 pages. They had lain in Pepys's library at Magdalene for 95 years, unregarded, when Lord Grenville looked into them and deciphered some of the arbitrary signs. These he handed to John Smith, an undergraduate of St John's, who promised to decipher the whole and at the end of three years produced the immortal Diary of Samuel Pepys. It was an extraordinary piece of work, and a remarkable fact concerning it is that among the books in Pepys's library at Magdalene was a small volume which would have given John Smith the key to the mysterious characters he had to work out, for in this volume was a shorthand account, written by Pepys from the dictation of Charles the Second, of the king's escape after the Battle of Worcester, with the longhand translation of it. John Smith, who became rector of Baldock, lies in the church.

The broad road leads into Icknield Way, and where this pre-historic track crosses Stane Street the Romans settled in the second century. Their cemetery was in Wall's Field, where hundreds of urns, lamps, beakers, jugs, dishes, and cups have been unearthed; we have seen them in Letchworth Museum, a truly remarkable collection of elegant vessels of all shapes and sizes. Most curious of all the discoveries is a lead tablet with an inscription which has been translated: *Tacita, or by whatever other name she is called, is hereby cursed.* Some vindictive person placed this in Tacita's burial urn, and sent her with a curse into the unknown world.

Mouse and Hare Show the Way

BARKWAY. The way over the hill the Saxons called it, and we found their way from the North a lovely avenue of beeches and chestnuts. The long wide street has some old houses and thatched cottages 300 years old, with steps leading to their doorways raised out of danger of storm-filled gutters. One cottage with 1687 over the porch has been restored and presented to the National Trust; its interior is typical of the best cottage craftsmanship in the country. Several inns remain from the days when Barkway was a convenient stop for coaches from Ware to Cambridge. At the south entrance is the turnpike house and clock and at the north a worn milestone six feet high, one of those set up in 1725 to show the way to Cambridge. They were all marked with the crescent of Trinity Hall, for they were paid for with money left for this purpose by two Elizabethan Fellows of Trinity, Dr Mouse and Robert Hare.

The medieval church, surrounded by trees and a high yew barricade, makes a fine group with the Jacobean manor and its barns. It is one of those rare churches fitted with a medieval system of amplifiers, acoustic jars being embedded in the chancel walls to add resonance to the voices. Its aisles were added in the 15th century at the same time as the tower which has been rebuilt stone for stone. The old font rests on a tree stump and a new one has taken

Benington   **Timbered Houses**

Barkway   **The Street**

Ashwell

Aldenham

Ayot St Lawrence

THREE OLD HERTFORDSHIRE CHURCHES

its place. There is a 13th century piscina, some fragments of a 15th century Jesse window, an Elizabethan family in brass (Robert Poynard, his two wives, and four daughters), and some extraordinary stone figures which, after 500 years, continue to support the new roofs, angels and crouching men and grinning faces, and here is a great toad, and here a rabbit half scuttling down one of the pillars. Over his elaborate marble tomb is Rysbrack's bust of Admiral Sir John Jennings who helped Sir George Rooke to capture Gibraltar in 1704.

The moated mount on Periwinkle Hill is now a little wood in a ploughed field, and in another wood close by was found the Roman statue of Mars which we have seen in the British Museum.

Let Envy Say Her Worst

BARLEY. We turn a corner and look up the hill, and there are the hounds and huntsmen in full cry, with the fox just creeping into a hole in the roof of the inn. They are painted figures spanning the road on a beam, the delightful sign of a 300-year-old inn. At the top of the hill is a wooden lock-up where many an unruly villager spent the night during those 300 years, and beside it is a wooden smithy where good ironwork was still being wrought when we looked in. Some old cottages by the church looked as though uncertain whether to fall backwards or forwards, and may have fallen altogether by now, but the Town House, built in the days of the Tudors, with a jutting out porch at each end, stands firm enough for dances to be held under its great oak beams, above the small ground rooms which once were almshouses.

The church was already old when these houses were growing up round it, for its foundations were laid by the Normans, though only the lower part of the tower with its strong arch is left of their work. Three of the arches in the nave arcade are 13th century, and there is a window and a blocked doorway of the 14th in the south aisle where are also some fragments of 16th century glass. The rest has mostly been made new. Carvings from the 15th century screen are used in the stalls. There is a covered chalice from the time of James the First and a pulpit richly carved in the time of Charles the First. A brass of 1621 pictures Andrew Willet, who published numerous books during his 23 years as rector here, out of which

D   33

Bunyan borrowed ideas for his Pilgrim's Progress. Two other rectors of Barley became Archbishops of Canterbury: William Warham who crowned Henry the Eighth and his first Catherine, and Thomas Herring.

Some of Barley's wealth in old houses and thatched cottages has overflowed into Shaftenhoe End, where a house of 1624 has an overhanging gable supported by two half-animal figures blowing trumpets, while the builder blows his own in these delightfully complacent lines written on the beam between them:

> *So God may still me blesse,*
> *I care the lesse,*
> *Let envy say her worst,*
> *And after burst.*

James Ravenscroft's Charity

BARNET. It is famous for a Battle and a Fair—for the battle in the Wars of the Roses which set Edward the Fourth on the throne, and for its great horse fair, one of the few fairs which have survived from medieval England. Officially it is Chipping Barnet, named after its market; popularly it is High Barnet, because it is set on a hill, so that we see the fine tower of its church guarding one of the historic approaches to London. It lies on the Great North Road, and was long ago a famous town with many inns at which the coaches stopped.

At one of these within the shadow of the church, the Mitre, a man called one day on his way to do business which was to change our history; he was General Monk, who might have been King of England after Cromwell but thought it best for the nation to bring the Stuarts back. He rested at the Mitre when leading his army to London for the restoration of Charles the Second. David Livingstone lived at Hadley Green close by, and Pepys would often come to the famous Barnet wells, one of which has now a graceful wellhouse built over it in the midst of a housing estate. In the old days the site of this well was on Barnet Common, and along the ridge of the hill are now gay public gardens with a pond where old inhabitants of Barnet would see elephants taking their morning bath when Barnet Fair was held on the common. Set back from the road here are several groups of almshouses and red-tiled cottages.

Six old couples live in the houses left by Eleanor Palmer in 1558;

the houses have been made new and are as neat and trim as could be. Six poor Freemen of the Leathersellers Company and widows of others live in a group of white houses, with a cedar, a pine, and a flagstaff on their charming lawns. Six poor women live in the pleasant range known as Jesus Hospital, to which they come through a gate with lions on the posts and the initials of James Ravenscroft, who founded the hospital in 1679; his portrait and that of his wife are indoors. Six old ladies live in another red brick group founded two centuries ago by John Garrett. Queen Elizabeth's Grammar School has fine modern buildings, but the Tudor Hall, with octagonal stair turrets and wooden frames to its windows, is still used for lectures, and in the middle of it rises the solid oak post which supports its roof, and was often used as a whipping-post. In the school kitchen is the original 17th century chest of the Ravenscroft family. The brick gateposts through which so many thousands of children passed into the old grammar school, have carved white stones set in them with a much-worn mitre and the date 1753, and two chestnut trees stand on guard at the gate.

The Norman church has gone and there is little to see outside of the medieval church John Beauchamp built in its place. The flint and stone tower with its draught-board pattern, and the tall and slender spire on the nave roof, are modern. We come in, however, to find the graceful arcades of Beauchamp's church with their clustered columns forming an aisle of the new nave, enclosing the clerestory windows on one side so that they are no longer glazed. In one of the spandrels a red tablet with yellow letters records John Beauchamp's work and the date 1453. The corbels that supported the ancient roof are still in their place, though the roof has gone. What remains of the old tower is now part of the new nave, one of the ancient arches leading into the new tower. On these old stones are mason's marks, and set in the thick walls are two niches, one with a grimacing head in its tracery, the other with something of its original gold tinting the carved flowers. The medieval chancel has become a vestry, and its old piscina is reset in its east wall; there is another piscina at the end of the medieval north aisle. We come into the vestry through a 15th century doorway with the old door still swinging on its hinges, keeping its ancient ring and its massive lock. The old font of the church has had a strange adventure, having been thrown away for a new one, found after many years in a garden at Totteridge, and returned to duty in the mission church of St Stephen a mile or two away. The new font here has a cover rising ten feet high with eight little statues delightfully carved.

All the woodwork of the church is rich in variety and interest. The Gothic pulpit is by Mr J. C. Traylen, the architect, and on it are figures of six missionaries and preachers: Hugh Latimer, John Wesley, Canon Liddon, St Augustine and St Aidan, and Hugh of Lincoln. The canopy is richly carved, and there is more elaborate carving on the choir stalls, while on 159 pew-ends are scenes or devices in relief, among them Christ in the Carpenter's Shop, the Good Samaritan, the Stoning of Stephen, and the Vision of Paul.

The new south aisle leads us into the Ravenscroft Chapel in which Thomas Ravenscroft lies on a huge canopied tomb, a dignified figure in ruff and puff sleeves, with much painted heraldry about him and the heads of three angels. He was the father of James Ravenscroft, and is declared to have been a man of untarnished integrity, of a happy disposition, exceedingly well known for the greatness of his mind. In the wall above the vestry doorway is a tablet to his wife, who died in 1611, and

> *Whom Nature made a lovely modest maid,*
> *And marriage made a virtuous loving wife.*

James Ravenscroft's bust is on the wall of the chapel with that of his wife, beautifully carved little portraits set in niches; he was the founder of Jesus Hospital in this town.

The east window with its fine tracery looks out on the rush and roar of the traffic of the Great North Road; the tower looks down on a lovely garden of peace from which rises the peace memorial set among trees, a tall slender column with a cross and the names of 246 Barnet men, who are supposed to be saying: See that ye conquer by living as we conquered by dying.

By this lovely oasis is the Hyde Institute, founded towards the end of last century by a lady who left £10,000 for a library. Not far away is the museum, with prints and drawings of the Barnet which has passed away, yet lives and grows and is fast becoming the biggest town in Hertfordshire. It has gathered within its bounds the villages of Totteridge and Arkley, so possessing Arkley's windmill.

The Fish and Bird Man

BAYFORD. From the village pond the road bends down to the handsome lychgate of a churchyard where junipers, pines, and yews show up darkly against the elms in the meadows and the lofty oak across the way. Here under the churchyard trees lies William Yarrell, whose books on British fishes and birds were long the best books of their kind. This London bookseller took every opportunity of accumulating knowledge about our birds and fishes and in writing about them with such accurate simplicity that his books are still read after a century. He was born in 1784, and he lies here in his mother's village, while his medallion portrait is in the Piccadilly church of St James's, and his oil portrait is treasured by the Linnean Society, whose treasurer and vice-president he was till he died. Those who make this naturalist's grave a place of spring-time pilgrimage will hear a grand chorus of birds from the deep woods stretching for miles behind these cottages above the Lea Valley; but they can scarcely hope for his good fortune in seeing, as he did at Therfield, the rare rock thrush. It came in the spring of 1843, but has never been seen wild in England since.

Bayford's church is new since Yarrell's day, but it keeps the rose-carved Tudor font, the brasses, and a marble figure from the old one. Two of the brasses are portraits of 16th century knights, the palimpsest one sketched on the back of part of a shrouded figure being thought to be John Knightson, whose descendant George appears in the same recess, a white armoured figure of 1612 in ruff, trunk hose, and jackboots. In his day the manor house was built, and though many alterations were made last century the old stairs still climb the three storeys in six flights, one above the other, and in one of the rooms is some painted panelling.

Bayfordbury, the great house here, stands in grounds remarkable for their trees, three cedars forming a magnificent group about 100 feet high. The house has classical porticos on both sides and is famous for its portraits of members of the Kit Cat Club, which were painted by Sir Godfrey Kneller.

The Old Door in the Norman Doorway

BENGEO. The hillside road to this quaintly-named village (a little walk out of Hertford and now brought within the borough for civic purposes) passes through some of the finest scenery in the county. From the sandy slopes above two rivers (the Beane and the Rib) flowing past to join the Lea in the valley below, spring larches and firs in rich profusion. With a cottage or two and a 17th century house stands the little church of St Leonard, one of the oldest buildings in Hertfordshire, overlooking the valley. Its inheritors for 800 years or more treated the little building not too well, blocking up or replacing Norman windows and doorways; but except for an 18th century porch and a modern bell-turret the church keeps the plan of its Norman builders. With its round apse it is 68 feet long and 21 wide. An ancient mass dial is on a wall and the doorway is plain Norman, with a door of the 14th century, one of the oldest in the county, still on its hinges. On one of the capitals of the chancel arch is a Norman head, and above the altar is a narrow Norman window below which are 14th century tiles. There are traces of painting and masonry patterns at a window and on the walls. The small font is rough and plain, part of a coffin lid forms the sill of a piscina, and the portrait of Humphrey Hall in a medallion held up by two angels has been looking down on it all since 1695.

Bengeo has a 19th century church of Holy Trinity to which we come through an attractive avenue of limes, and in it is a reredos interesting because its central panel is the work of George Tinworth, one of the pioneer potters at the Doulton works. He did much relief work for churches; his panel here has on it a relief showing the miraculous draught of fishes.

The Hidden Keep

BENINGTON. The road climbs up a green and pleasant hill to where a tall willow weeps over a pond behind the green, while a timber and plaster row of 16th century cottages looks on, and an attractive old inn cheerfully declares itself twice as old as it is.

We see the little medieval church on a steep bank by the roadside with a yew collapsed from old age beside it; but what stranger would guess that behind the tall trees topping the church hides the keep of a Norman castle? It stands four-square on a moated mount, the only one of its kind in Hertfordshire, but the water has drained from the moat and the strong walls have crumbled. This forgotten place came early into history, for here lived the kings of Mercia, and on this hill Berthulf held a council in 850 when news came that the Danes had captured Canterbury and London, and that their fleet was in the Thames. He met the invaders in battle, but failed to stop them.

All this is written in the ancient chronicles, but much more of Benington's story is set forth in the church. The chancel and the nave were finished about 1300, the chapel and the porch were added in the 14th century, and from the 15th come the tower, the clerestory, and the roof of the nave. A battered St Michael continues his 600-year-old fight with the dragon in a niche over our heads as we push open the 14th century south door, and inside and out are numerous other small stone carvings, many of them grotesque. But the most beautiful stonework is the row of three magnificent arches between the chancel and the chapel built about 1330 by Petronilla, the widow of Sir John de Benstede, who was one of the envoys sent north to draw up the peace treaty between Edward the First and Robert Bruce. We see his knightly figure lying on a tomb under one of these lovely arches, his wife in her long veil beside him and their feet on lions. The third arch, panelled and pinnacled, was added during the next century as a canopy for another knight and his lady sculptured on their tomb, an angel in the point of the arch holding miniature copies of their figures.

These were the Benstedes, whose arms are with the Moynes on the buttresses of the tower and on the bosses of the nave. There are some 16th century benches, a chair and an altar table in the chapel are 17th century, the excellent screen and rich gilt reredos belong to our own day, and there is one brass portrait, a small figure of a 15th century priest with a rose badge on the shoulder of his cope.

A stone on the floor of the chancel describes Sir Charles Caesar, a judge of Charles Stuart's reign, as an equal distributor of unsuspected justice, but the man who lies beneath it seems to have been a far less capable figure than his father, Sir Julius Caesar, the great legal light of the reigns of Elizabeth and James. The epitaph, as epitaphs will, unduly flatters the judge, who bought his position of Master of the Rolls for £15,000 and a loan to the king of £2000 trust money left by an uncle to found university scholarships. The loan was never repaid, and though Jesus College, Cambridge, received annuities for these scholarships from the family till 1668, that was all that was done about it. Sir Charles Caesar died of small-pox in 1642.

The 17th century rectory has seen many changes, but keeps the old staircase leading up to elegant rooms with powder closets.

The Castle and the Foundlings

BERKHAMSTED. Through this small town of 10,000 people come the road from Aylesbury to Watford, the Grand Union Canal, and the little River Bulbourne on its way to join the River Gade. The green valley belongs to the Chilterns, and there are glorious hills around, with a breezy common 600 feet above the sea to the north, and to the south the Ashlyns domain in a lovely park, high above the town.

In a group of fine buildings only a few years old, standing by Ashlyns Park, is now being carried on the great work begun by Thomas Coram in 1739. He was, of course, the extraordinary man who started the Foundling Hospital in London, and in our own time this great institution has moved from the heart of Bloomsbury and come here, leaving London children a wonderful playground in its place, and giving Berkhamsted a handsome block of buildings and the pride of housing a famous hospital. There are lawns and playing fields, and the buildings are set round a green court which we see from the colonnade at each side of the chapel, which has four columns supporting a pediment and a domed belfry with a lamb for a weathervane. The Foundling has kept its chief treasure, the organ on which Handel used to play to Londoners on Sunday afternoons, and which he himself gave to the hospital. The new home has cost a quarter of a million pounds, but its work is worth it, for it has the proud record of having placed 50,000 children on the way to health and opportunity in the world.

The story of the town is a long one, and its name has changed half a hundred times from the ancient Beorchehamstede. The mile-long High Street is on the line of the old Roman Akeman Street, and the famous British earthwork, Grim's Ditch, can still be traced on the common. Ancient and modern meet across the river, where the railway made a hundred years ago encroaches on what is left

Amwell   The Chestnut Avenue of Haileybury College

Amwell   Haileybury from the Playing Fields

Great Gaddesden   The Ancient Church by the River Gade

Berkhamsted   **Earthworks of the Castle**

Berkhamsted   **A Beech Wood near the Town**

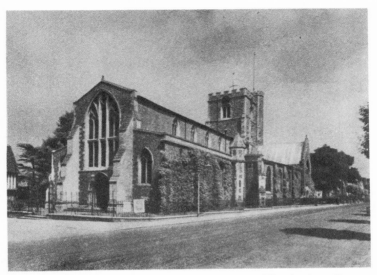

Berkhamsted   **The Ancient Church**

Bishop's Stortford   **The Town of Cecil Rhodes**

North Mimms   The BBC Masts at Brookman's Park

Broxbourne   The Medieval Church by the Lea

Braughing   Houses Gathered About the Ancient Church

of Berkhamsted Castle, sheltering on the lower slopes of the hillside. The Conqueror gave the manor to his half-brother, and the earthworks, a fine example of a Norman military fortress, are believed to date from his time, though a Saxon fortress may have stood on this spot.

The earthworks are still impressive, though little but ragged walling is left of the castle itself. It has been razed to the ground and rebuilt. It became the home of Thomas Becket, who lived here in state, and was a favourite place of Henry the Second, who gave the town a charter. King John gave it to his Queen Isabella. In 1216 it was taken by Louis of France and the English barons. Henry the Third gave it to his brother Richard, Earl of Cornwall, whose marriage with the queen's sister was celebrated here with a great banquet, and there was another historic banquet here when Piers Gaveston owned the castle and married the niece of Edward the Second. Edward the Third restored the castle for the Black Prince, when he was made Duke of Cornwall, and Berkhamsted is still part of the Duchy. King John of France was a prisoner here after Poitiers. Chaucer was clerk of the works here under Richard the Second. Edward the Fourth gave it to his mother, who died here. After her death it fell into decay, though it was held by three of Henry the Eighth's six queens, and in Elizabeth's time Sir Edward Cary used much of its material for building Berkhamsted Place, the great house on the hill.

The house once belonged to Prince Henry and passed on his death to his brother Charles Stuart. It is odd that after this it should have been the home of Daniel Axtel, a grocer's apprentice who was converted to the Parliamentary cause by a sermon he listened to on a fast-day. It was he who made the arrangements for the king's trial in Westminster Hall, and who called out threatening to shoot Lady Fairfax when she interrupted the proceedings. At the Restoration he was arrested and sentenced to death. He made a remarkable speech on the scaffold, in which he mourned the general depravity of the nation, but declared that he suffered as Our Lord had suffered. His head was set up on Westminster Hall.

A green lawn now marks the site of the outer court, which is 450 feet long and 300 wide, surrounded by a steep fosse and a wet moat. At its north-east corner is the fine conical mound 45 feet high, with a diameter of 180 feet at the base, and 60 feet at the top, where, within the circle of low walling of the keep, is the well the Normans made. Another bank and ditch surround the inner earthworks, and on the north and east sides is a third bank, which is further strengthened by eight great bastions of earth. The fragments of walling still to be seen (high and low, in long and short stretches) are chiefly of flint and rubble, having been robbed of their facing. The remains on the west side of the outer court are perhaps part of the chapel. The oldest of all this masonry may be of Thomas Becket's time; the outer walls with their towers and the keep on the mound are from 1186. The banks rising from the moat are gay in spring with daffodils, and we walk round the rampart under the shade of trees. Slumbering peacefully in its old age, the site of the castle is cared for now by the Office of Works. In the Great War the grounds were used as a gunnery school by the Inns of Court Training Corps, and on the common is an obelisk set up in memory of 2000 of them who were in training here.

The High Street has a sprinkling of old houses, shops, and inns; at its most charming corner stands the old church of St Peter in company with a few Georgian houses, older houses with gables and dormers, and the Court House standing back from the road. In this fine old house, built of brick and flint and timber in the 16th century and now partly new, the manor courts were held; later it was a school, and now is a Church House. Another 16th century building is the charming timbered Incent House with an overhanging storey: now a place where we may have tea, it is said to have been the home of John Incent, Dean of St Paul's, who died in 1645. He founded Berkhamsted Grammar School, which after a long period of stagnation has become a source of pride for the town. The dean planned for 144 boys; now there are over 500. The fine old school, of red brick with stone mullioned windows, mellowed with four centuries of time, stands on the north side of the churchyard. Since its addition of two wings last century, the buildings have grown round two courts. Near the fine timber entrance to the south court is the school chapel, with the altar 19 steps higher than the nave, and much stained glass. The west window is a tribute to those who fell in the Great War, and shows Our Lord in Glory, saints, and knights carrying the flags of the victorious nations. The school library is another memorial to 212 Old Boys, one of whom, Major G. R. Pearkes, won the VC. In spite of being wounded, he captured and held a vital point, making possible an important advance, and throughout the War he showed a supreme contempt of danger and wonderful power of control as a leader of men.

In the cemetery in Rectory Lane, shaded by fine avenues of Irish yews and trimmed yews by the path, lies another soldier who won renown in our wars, General Richard Mildmay Foot, who was wounded in the Great War, during which he was mentioned in dispatches five times. When wounded in the head on the Tugela Heights during the South African War he was called on to surrender by the Boers, had replied "No, I'll die first," and was carried in by a rescue party from his regiment.

The rectory standing by the cemetery is not the house in which Berkhamsted's most famous son, William Cowper, was born in 1731. The old house was a little lower down the hill. His father was rector here for 34 years, and in the church where he preached are memorials to his wife, Ann Cowper, and their poet son. Cowper wrote these lines about this place:

> *Where once we dwelt our name is heard no more,*
> *Children not thine have trod my nursery floor;*
> *And where the gardener Robin, day by day,*
> *Drew me to school along the public way,*
> *Delighted with my bawble coach, and wrapt*
> *In scarlet mantle warm, and velvet capt,*
> *'Tis now become a history little known,*
> *That once we called the pastoral house our own.*

It is a striking church, and one of the biggest in the county, measuring 168 feet from east to west, and 91 feet across the transepts. A fragment of an ancient arch in a wall of the north transept suggests that there was a church here before the Conquest, but the one we see began early in the 13th century as a simple cross-shaped building of chancel, nave, transepts, and central tower. Later in the same century aisles were added to the nave, and the north transept was given its eastern aisle with a vaulted roof; in the 14th century this transept was lengthened and received its windows enriched with ballflowers. Other 14th century additions were St Catherine's chapel and the chapel of St John the Baptist. The 15th century porch has become part of this chapel, which was used by the grammar school till their own chapel was built. Over the leaning arcades in the nave is the 15th century clerestory. The two lower stages of the tower are 13th century, the heavy arches resting on clustered shafts, but the top storey was added 400 years ago. In the original lancet windows still in the chancel is old glass showing two royal coats-of-arms and fragments. The glass of the modern east window is Cowper's memorial, showing Our Lord Risen, the women and disciples going to the tomb, and a portrait of the poet at a prayer desk, with his tame hares. The register tells of his baptism. His mother's memorial has a rhyming inscription by Lady Walsingham.

The massive arches and clustered pillars between the south transept and St John's Chapel are 14th century, and the fine oak pillar between the chapel and the south aisle is believed to be as old, though the rest of the chapel detail is modern. The tie-beams of the nave roof rest on arches with arcaded spandrels. The 15th century screen has a new vine cornice, and 14 new figures on the base panels, among which we see Nicholas with three children in a tub; Patrick with shamrock and a staff, lizards and a serpent about his feet; Jerome with a lion at his feet; Gregory with a bird on his shoulder; George slaying a dragon; and Peter holding keys and a church. A fine carved chest with drawers is over 300 years old; the 19th century pulpit has five angels with outspread wings, and a pew is Elizabethan. Four heads under the tower, and a bearded head at the east end of the north aisle are among the many carved corbels to be seen.

On a richly arcaded tomb lie a 14th century knight and his lady, he wearing armour, she in a fine netted headdress; they are believed to be Richard and Margaret Torrington. Over the tomb hangs the funeral helmet of Sir Adolphus Cary, who lived at Berkhamsted Place after his brother Sir Edward, who built it. Sir John Cornwallis of 1544 has a marble tomb with his arms in brass; he was a member of the Council of Edward the Sixth and died at Ashridge. By his tomb is that of Charles the Second's chief cook, John Sayer, who lived at Berkhamsted Place and founded for his poorer neighbours the quaint row of alms-houses at the west end of the town. Under one of two rich recesses in St Catherine's Chapel is a fine medieval coffin lid, carved by a medieval craftsman, with a floral cross.

The oldest brass here is of Richard and Margaret Torrington of about 1356, wearing long robes and holding hands; two dogs are at her feet and a lion at his. Others are the bust of a priest of about 1400; Richard Westbrook, a civilian of 1485; 14th century Margaret Briggs with netted hair and draped headdress; and John Raven, squire to the Black Prince, as a knight in armour. A palimpsest brass is on a swivel so that we can see both sides; one with a 16th century inscription, the other side with fragments of the figures of Thomas Humfre of about 1470, his wife and children, and also part of a representation of St Michael weighing souls. In the first letter of Thomas's inscription is an engraving of St Jerome as a cardinal. There is an inscription to Robert Incent of 1509, and his wife Katherine is a shrouded figure in brass.

In monuments and glass we see the names of Smith and Dorrien, whose union by marriage gave us a famous name. One window is to Colonel R. A. Smith-Dorrien, who succeeded his uncle, Augustus Smith, in the Ashlyns estate. The lantern cross in the churchyard was set up in 1910 in memory of Mary Ann Smith-Dorrien.

Some of the cottages in Castle Street have the very small rooms used by the village folk for straw-plaiting in days gone by.

Cowper's Place in English Literature

IT was the poet Cowper, born at Berkhamsted, who led the way of escape for English poetry from the dead world such men as Pope were making of it. Such poets as he were writing bookish verse made in a library according to rules laid down, but Cowper would have none of it; he did what Wordsworth was to do after him, he found his poetry in the fields and lanes. He put his feelings into it, and not mere words.

Nothing was too homely for his pen. He would write of mankind as a whole, or of men as individuals, of the friendly world of animals, or of the changeful beauty of outdoor life. His gentle spirit was invincibly humane, and yet his life was cursed by doubts about his soul. It is one of the tragedies of genius that this man who was so kind, so gentle that he could not hurt a fly, was driven insane by the thought that God would punish him.

One of the most pathetic love stories was that of Cowper and Mary Unwin. He lived with the Unwins in their home at Huntingdon and thought them the finest people in the world. It was to please

Mrs Unwin that he wrote much prose and poetry, and it is thought she inspired his famous poem on Boadicea, and the famous one on Alexander Selkirk.

Mary Unwin became a widow, and it is believed they may have become engaged, but Cowper's mind broke down and the woman who should have been his wife became his nurse. She saved him in his hours of despair, turning him to writing poetry and hymns, but at last she herself broke down under the long strain and was stricken with paralysis. Now the poet was able to repay in some measure the debt he owed to her, but her death was the last blow to him, and left him a wreck with one fine gloomy poem to write before he followed her to the grave.

As a poet his interest is singularly wide and varied. He loved a frolic, as we know by John Gilpin. He was an ardent patriot, a thoughtful politician, a humanitarian fired with the love of freedom, and he brought poetry down into the homely ways of men. Some of his lines belong to our daily speech, and he lives because he shares our common sympathies and touches a chord deep in the hearts of men.

A House for Empire Pilgrims

BISHOP'S STORTFORD. The greatest thing it has done for the world was to give birth to Cecil Rhodes, and we may believe that the time will come when the house in which he was born will be a place of pilgrimage. Yet this small town had its place in history centuries before young Rhodes sat in the pews at St Michael's listening to his father preach. In the public gardens is a mound on which it is believed a castle stood, Waytemore Castle, the fortress of Bishop Maurice of London, into whose hands the Conqueror entrusted this key position by the ford over the River Stort. It is supposed that the castle had deep and dark dungeons, and it is said that the terrible Bishop Bonner kept prisoners here in Mary Tudor's day. The outer works and moats can be traced among the walks and flowerbeds, and a charred stump has been found which was probably the remains of a stake at which Bishop Bonner burned a man. One man was burned in the marketplace and another who was to suffer the same fate at Saffron Walden was dragged out here to witness his martyrdom.

The hilly streets of Bishop's Stortford set off to advantage the fine old buildings among the new, many of them inns from the 16th to 17th centuries with overhanging storeys; the Boar's Head and the timbered Black Lion still carrying on, the White Horse, with its plastered heraldic front of Italian work, an inn no longer.

Two fine churches, an old one and a new one, look to each other across the roofs of the town, both set on hills. The new church is All Saints, the old one is St Michael's. The new one, looking out over the town from Hockerill, was designed by Mr Dykes Bower, and is one of the best modern churches we have seen. It has a magnificent rose window in the east with Christ in the centre surrounded by dazzling colours, rings of little suns, flames, and symbols. The west window has three great plain lancets in the tower. There are four high arches on each side of the nave, supported by round columns, the stone roof is spaced out in 125 compartments, and there is a charming oriel in the sanctuary.

But the eye turns first and last in this town to the splendid 500-year-old church shooting up its pinnacled tower and spire from among the houses on the top of the other hill, summoning its worshippers with a peal of ten bells. They enter today by the very door people pushed open five centuries ago, and in one spandrel of the doorway is the same strange carving of the All-Seeing Eye, the Angel of the Resurrection sounding his trumpet in the opposite spandrel. The door opens on the six great bays of the spacious nave and aisles, where corbels of angels and apostles and medieval folk turn on us their stony gaze; we noticed a gardener, a cook, and a woodman among them. Save for a few changes and additions the church is wholly medieval, and has a Norman font which has been buried, having probably belonged to the church before this. There are 18 rich choir stalls, making a grand show with their traceried backs and panelled fronts, and misereres crowded with 15th century faces and fancies, men and animals, one of them a rare early carving of a whale. It is believed that some of these misereres came from Old St Paul's before the fire. The fine chancel screen is mainly 15th century, but the vaulting is new. The pulpit and a remarkable chest are Jacobean, the chest having an inside lock of 14 bolts as long as the lid.

There is a tablet in this fine church to a man who made the River Stort navigable up to Bishop's Stortford. He befriended

Captain Cook, who showed his gratitude by making him known to navigators all over the world, naming after him Port Jackson in New South Wales and Point Jackson in New Zealand. The man whose name thus lives on the map was born George Jackson at Richmond in Yorkshire, but he died Sir George Duckett; here in the church is his memorial. We find no memorial to a butcher's son born here in 1813, who did much to help photography by proving the use of collodion in developing films. He was Frederick Scott Archer, and his children were pensioned by the Crown because his invention brought him no profit but yielded vast profits for others.

Much happier in his fortune was the famous physician who lies in the Quaker burial ground; he was Thomas Dimsdale, an Essex man who adopted Hertfordshire as his county, practised as a doctor in the county town, and sat in Parliament for it. He is remembered for his pioneering with inoculation for smallpox, and especially because Catherine of Russia invited him to her capital to inoculate herself and her son. It was in 1768, when the adventure was fraught with some peril, and the empress arranged for relays of horses from the capital to the border to aid the doctor's escape in case of disaster. Happily all was well, and Dimsdale received £2000 for expenses, a fee of £10,000, and an allowance of £500 a year. He was laid in the burial ground of the Quakers here on the last day but one of last century, when he was 89 years old.

One of the windows of St Michael's is in memory of the old vicar Francis Rhodes, who was laid to rest here eight years after his delicate son had left for South Africa. He lived to hear the good news that his son had found health and strength and was working in the diamond digging, and he saw him home again entering on a graduate's life at Oxford; but he died in 1878 before Cecil entered the Cape Parliament, and before he had formed his great plan of a British South Africa. In the birthplace we see his portrait looking down from the wall on the bed in which Cecil Rhodes was born.

Bishop's Stortford has been long in paying homage to its great son, but it has made amends, has bought the house he was born in and the house next door, and is developing both as a Cecil Rhodes Museum. The house is refurnished with pieces that either belonged to the family or belonged to the time, and it is an attractive place for any pilgrim interested in Rhodes of Rhodesia. In addition

Hemel Hempstead   **The Slender Steeple and the Norman Nave**

Hemel Hempstead Norman Doorway **Bengeo**   Norman Chancel Arch

The Cecil Rhodes Museum

The Room where Rhodes was Born
THE PRIDE OF BISHOP'S STORTFORD

to the bed he was born in, one of eleven children, there is here the Bible his mother gave him, a fine old clock which was ticking in those days, a picturesque native drum used for communicating signals, a water colour he painted of a windjammer, and the uniforms he wore on ceremonial occasions—and never again. It is gratifying to see that at last the prophet has honour in his own town, and it is good to know that the old grammar school where he learned his first lesson is still a flourishing concern, though what was the school then is now the parish hall.

The Dream of Cecil Rhodes

ON the lips of Cecil Rhodes when he was dying were the words, "So little done, so much to do." A future generation will say whether the purpose of this man was greater than his achievement, greater than his failures. He saw all Africa waiting for the White Man, and he resolved to stamp the British Empire on it. He pursued this purpose all his life, scornful of indifference, contemptuous of opposition. He met disaster and even catastrophe with unflinching serenity.

He began life with some of the handicaps that have often beset heroes and saints, though he would never have called himself either. He was sent to that land of Africa which so seized his imagination when he was a youth with indifferent health, and it was thought the open air life might benefit him. It did. It made a man of him physically and created in him an empire builder.

Africa had restored the health; it should give him the gold with which to win her. This visionary young man had no illusions about the lever to move the world. When General Gordon told him that the Chinese Government had offered him "a roomful of gold" and he had refused it, Rhodes replied that he should have taken it, and as many more roomfuls as the Chinese would have given him, for big ideas were of no use to a man without money to carry them out. Rhodes got his money in the rough-and-tumble struggle for grabbing the spoils of Africa. He had gone back from Africa to take a degree at Oxford. Oxford was his city of dreams. The other side of him, his ruthless financial genius, his power to manage men, were fostered under other skies. They came to fruition in the environment, both good and evil, of his associates in South Africa.

The good predominated for long years. In them he developed with the magic of his golden wand the first part of his idea for taking hold of Africa. This was the development of the vast territory of Rhodesia on which his name is set. It was at this period of his career that he disclosed one of the secrets that accounted for his greatness. His Chartered Company of South Africa was formed and was not immediately prosperous. There was a great meeting of shareholders in London and Rhodes came to address it. It was a meeting eager to see this inscrutable man but rather anxious about its dividends, and not altogether friendly. Rhodes faced them as he faced any crisis, but this time the inspiration of a profound belief filled his mind. He painted for them a picture of Africa as it might be, and of the imperial burden and tribute that it must share. As he spoke, not with eloquence but with power and conviction, he won the minds of that matter-of-fact audience to follow him and see the vision that his own eyes beheld. That was one of the great moments in the life of Rhodes, as courageous as when later he faced unarmed the hostile Matabele chiefs in the Matoppos.

The wilder spirits of the Matabele, who for three years had been living peacefully while the face of their country was being changed by wholesome labour, had rebelled. There was fighting for four months; it might have lasted much longer but for the pluck of Rhodes. The Matabele forces had been driven into the Matoppo Hills, a rocky region in which they could not be attacked without serious loss. Rhodes resolved to try persuasion. For six weeks he camped in a place near the hills and let it be known that he wished to come to them unarmed to hold a conference. The Matabele invited him, and Rhodes went with three friends. They knew they might be killed at any moment, but they rode into the heart of the enemy country, dismounted, and sat down. The chiefs filed in and sat down solemnly in a half-circle. Then one of Rhodes's companions said: "Tell your troubles to Rhodes, your father. He has come among you, unarmed, with peace in his heart." They told him all their grievances, and Rhodes promised to remove many of them, admitting that they were reasonable. He then asked what the future was to be—was it to be peace or war? One of the chiefs stood up and threw a stick on the ground in front of Rhodes, declaring that it was a symbol of laying his weapons of war at the feet of a generous chieftain. As Rhodes rode away he was heard to say that was one of the scenes which make life worth living.

But this event happened at a time when his wider vision of Africa had dissolved in murky clouds. At first Rhodes, recognising the worth of the Cape Dutch, had been minded that their race should be joined with the British in extending the white man's influence throughout South Africa; but the gold brought him into conflict with the northern Dutch, the Boers of the Transvaal, and led to the ruin or the postponement of all his hopes. The Jameson Raid, which sought to wrest political power from President Kruger, was a crime, a blunder, and a disastrous failure. If Rhodes could not be held responsible for the failure, he could not dissociate himself from the attempt, and the end of a story England would like to forget was that he was summoned to appear before a Commission at Westminster. He faced doubt, suspicion, and enmity with unflinching courage. On the first day he seemed disconcerted by finding himself, he who had been an acknowledged dictator, in something of the position of an accused person; but he quickly rallied, and from the second day onward it is hardly too much to say that he took charge of the Commission and emerged from it eventually, if not with colours flying, at any rate with unlowered crest.

There was something in the appearance of Cecil Rhodes that was half Roman consul and half East Anglian farmer. The Roman consul served not himself but Rome. Cecil Rhodes, who would have taken the whole world for the flag, sought not to serve himself but to consolidate his country's influence, for he felt that our race stood for the three essential needs of humanity—Justice, Liberty, and Peace. The English-speaking man, he wrote, was the type who did the most practical effective work to establish Justice, to promote Liberty, and to ensure Peace over the widest possible area of the planet. He appreciated, however, that other white races could help his great ideal. He imagined a future when the northern races would march to world leadership together. When he died he embodied this hope and aspiration in the creation of Rhodes Scholarships at his beloved Oxford, where the young manhood of Greater Britain, of Germany, and of the United States should meet, and, learning to know one another, would garner the traditions of the white race and enable it to march forward and achieve the vision.

The Post Office and the Farm

B OVINGDON. A more attractive shop-window for his stamps and postal orders the Postmaster-General could scarcely have than we found here, a little old house with crooked chimneys and casement windows. Another pretty picture is Renstreet Farm, black and white against a background of red-roofed barns, with a projecting storey on Elizabethan foundations. Long, straight avenues of shaped yews lead through an immense churchyard. There has been a church here since the Conquest, but this one is only a hundred years old. Its high bench-ends catch our eye, and then we notice the stone figure of a man who may have fought at Agincourt. His name has vanished with his fame, but his jewelled belt still proclaims his rank, and a hound still guards his feet. Little hands smoothing his stone pillow are all that remain after 500 years of the angels that were once at his head.

B OXMOOR. Its houses are linked, none too attractively, with those of its growing neighbour Hemel Hempstead, but there is charm in its stretches of green, its long lines of chestnut trees, and the occasional glimpses through the willows of gaily-painted barges gliding along the Grand Union Canal. Here, too, the tiny river Bulbourne is made to spread out and cover one of the biggest watercress beds we have seen. Two deep yew paths show where the porches of the old church used to be, but a church twice as big has taken its place, designed last century by Norman Shaw. The east window is in memory of the rector, Thomas White, and his sister, who paid for it, and a screen honours Henry Balderson who was churchwarden for 50 years.

The foundations of a Roman villa were dug up in the station-master's garden some years ago, and here, too, was found a beautiful Saxon brooch made of bronze.

Thomas Becket, Rector

B RAMFIELD. It has green verges by the wayside, an old well under a canopy on the green, one or two finely thatched cottages, a rectory with gables and dormers and clustered chimneys, and a church to which clings the memory of a famous man. We reach the church by a fine avenue of limes.

Thomas Becket's name heads the list of rectors in the church.

According to Matthew of Westminster, Bramfield was his first living, and, though many a village in the 12th century never saw its rector, it is a moving thought that the voice once sternly raised against a king may have been here subdued to the service of a humble congregation. The church of his day was made new in the 13th century, and much restored a hundred years ago, when the low tower and spire were built on the site of an old well. There are several 14th and 15th century windows, and old tie-beams with timbering above them. Over the beam between the nave and chancel is open arcading in stone. At the two sides of the porch are a man scratching his chin and a woman holding a cross and a rosary in her crossed hands. The chalice is Elizabethan, the chest is 17th century, and one of the two bells was made at the time Chaucer was writing his Canterbury Tales. One other reminder of the Bramfield rector whose murder at Canterbury set Chaucer's pilgrims on their way is the pond in the rectory garden still known as Becket's pond.

A mile or two away, on a hill by lovely woodlands, stands Queen Hoo Hall, still much as it was in Elizabeth's day. A tall house of red brick, patterned with blue on the front, it has clustered chimneys and mullioned windows from which is a magnificent view.

The Armada Bell

B RAUGHING. The world does improve; we found here a memorial to an MP who died after being attacked by highwaymen on Hounslow Heath. Of the old church of this pleasant tree-girt place above the River Quin, set 700 years ago in a sloping churchyard where cottage roofs are on a level with the church doors, only some windows remain, for the 15th century built anew the nave and the aisles, the porch, and the tall lead-spired tower with its grinning gargoyles. They built on a noble scale, and it is all here still, though patched with new stone. Higher than the nave roof rise the turret stairs to the vanished roodloft, and higher than the aisle stands the pinnacled porch with its upper room floorless so that we look up to the vaulted roof. Queer stone faces watch outside the walls, and there are wooden angels in the nave and stone angels in the aisles to hold up the 500-year-old roofs. Modern woodwork makes a good show in the elaborate screen, and on the wall hangs a 17th century painting of the Resurrection, thought to be part of the old altarpiece. A modern font of Caen stone has taken the place of the 14th century font, which has been brought back into the church after having been cast out. Five of the bells average nearly 350 years, the oldest having rung out the defeat of the Armada.

One who was living at that time, Augustin Steward, appears here in Elizabethan armour in an alabaster bust, but it is two soldier brothers, Charles and John Brograve, who take pride of place, lying in alabaster on their stately Stuart monument. Simeon Brograve has his name painted inside the chapel he bequeathed before he died in 1638, and many others of the family are remembered here. There are also little brass portraits of an unknown 15th century man and his wife.

Several old homes add their testimony to the fact that long generations have found Braughing a pleasant place to live in. On the hills a mile away is the 17th century Upp Hall, with a huge barn of older red and blue brick beside it; and farther still is Rotten Row, a timbered farmhouse still staunchly Elizabethan, though the past three centuries have changed it much indoors. That at least one Roman made his home here is proved by the discovery of such oddments as the shells of the oysters he ate, and a few coins from his purse, as well as a stone sarcophagus.

The Dragon Slayer

B RENT PELHAM. Through all its changes (and the church has seen much rebuilding in our own day) Piers Shonks the dragon slayer has slept undisturbed. We find his tomb in the church among great trees, with the stocks and the whipping post beside it and one or two old thatched cottages. The nave and the chancel are 14th century; the tower with a small leaded spire is just as it was added in the 15th, and in it hang three bells 300 years old. Two deep crosses cut on a nave buttress may be the original consecration marks. There is a new porch worthy of the fine building, with some 14th century tracery from the old door fixed on to the new. Some later medieval tracery is used again in the screen to the high tower arch. Near the tower are the brass portraits of Mary and Anne, the young wives of Francis Rowley, pictured exactly alike with wide-brimmed hats and ruffs. The first died in 1625, the second two years later, and the disconsolate husband wrote over their grave:

Thy sting, O death, most sharply here appears,
To take them both away in their prime of years.

Then we come to the curious tomb in the wall, which looks 13th century, though an 18th century inscription painted behind it says it is the tomb of Piers Shonks, a noted dragon slayer of 1086. To give reality to the legend, here is a dragon breathing out fire, carved in relief on the black marble top, together with the winged creatures of the evangelists and a dog peacefully asleep on its side. Tales of this dragon-slayer were told for centuries in the village and his name has been given to one of the moats in the neighbourhood, Shonks's Moat. We may wish the true story of this village St George could be found in some old record.

To the east of the church is Brent Pelham Hall with a stone giving its date as 1608. The patterned chimney stacks prove its age, but its timbering was cased in with brick later in the 17th century. The hall stretching from wing to wing has a Tudor arch for a fireplace. The mantelpieces and panelling are Jacobean, some brought from The Beeches, the 17th century farmhouse about a mile off which used to be the manor house.

Portraits in Brass and Stone

BROXBOURNE. Its church, its priest's house, and its giant yew have been here on the bank of the River Lea for about 500 years, and every year sees more homes collect around them. The Jacobean church porch, with a trapdoor leading to a priest's room above, has become the vestry, and we enter by the tower doorway, which is 15th century, as are the striking arcades running the whole length of the church, and the roofs of the nave and the aisles. The panelled chancel roof is 16th century. A Norman arcade decorates the font, one of the earliest in the Purbeck marble fashion of the 13th century. A great treasure is the arcaded 14th century chest nearly six feet long, very much like one we have seen in Hereford Cathedral.

But it is the people of Broxbourne here in brass and stone who interest us most. Two priests who must have lived in the old gabled house when it was new have their portraits in brass. One is Robert Ecton, who died in 1474; the other preached his last sermon here about 1510. Another brass shows Sir John Borrell in armour holding

55

a mace, for he was sergeant-at-arms to Henry the Eighth. Finest of all are the brasses on the altar tomb of Sir John Say, the Lancastrian who died a Yorkist in 1478, after having been Speaker of the House of Commons during the Wars of the Roses. He makes a fine figure in elaborate armour and short heraldic coat, with his wife in a butter-fly headdress and with traces of colour on her heraldic mantle. Gone from his tomb is the brass of Sir William Say, who lies under a fan-vaulted canopy in an arch leading to the chapel he added in 1522.

Exquisitely sculptured in his Elizabethan armour lies Sir Henry Cock, resting his bearded head on his hand on a ledge behind his wife who reclines with upward gaze. Their children and their grandchildren appear in relief, some big, some tiny, two of the girls wearing curious halo-like headdresses. Adding to the splendour of this monument are many delicate carvings of fruit and flowers. A tablet recalls a famous figure of a hundred years ago, John Macadam, the Scottish engineer who taught us how to make good roads and whose English home was at Hoddesdon, close by.

There lies in the chancel here Marmaduke Rawdon, who won fame for himself while on his uncle's business in Canary Islands in the 17th century by climbing the Peak of Teneriffe. The British Museum has a collection of notes by him on life in 17th century England. Because he was born at York, Rawdon left to that city a gold loving cup and money to buy a gold chain which is still worn by every lady mayoress of York.

A Chantrey Portrait

BUCKLAND. Cutting through the broad harvest fields comes the Romans' Ermine Street, and where it climbs this village hill is the church Nicholas de Bokeland built in 1348, recording his deed on the glass of a chancel window; it is one of the few Hertford-shire churches of which the exact date is known. Though Nicholas's glass has gone a few fragments of 14th century glass remain in other windows. The font is old enough to have served for the baptism of this church-builder's children, though its bowl of Barnack stone has been recut. The tower, the aisle, and the porch were added in the 15th century, and several people who saw them new are here in brass—Alice Boteler, the wife of a Sheriff of London; John Gyll

with his six sons (his four daughters have been stolen from him);
William Langley, the rector who died in 1478, pictured in his robes
with the chalice he held out to the villagers 500 years ago. Under
the altar is an inscription to a rector's wife who died the year before
Charles Stuart, and close by is Chantrey's beautiful medallion
portrait of William Michell, son of another rector. An 18th century
rector, Dr Thomas Morrell, made for himself another kind of
memorial, compiling the words for some of Handel's oratorios.

Claud Lovat Fraser

BUNTINGFORD. A small town on the River Rib, it has a wide
stretch of a Roman road for its High Street, full of quaint
houses with gables, overhanging storeys, deep archways, and red
roofs turned yellow here and there with creeping stone-crop.

By a group of lime trees are the 17th century almshouses, standing
round a court filled with flowers; they are the homes of four old men
and four old women, founded in 1684 by that famous man of his
day, Seth Ward. His portrait hangs inside, and outside are his arms
and mitre, carved in stone. He was born at Aspenden, and walked
over here every day to the free school till he left for Cambridge.
He lost his fellowship there by refusing to take the Covenant, but
later was made Professor of Astronomy at Oxford, and, branching
into philosophy, started his long controversy with Hobbes. After
having been Bishop of Exeter, he became Bishop of Salisbury,
and one of his first acts there was to call on his friend Christopher
Wren to survey the cathedral. Wren's report is now in the possession
of the Royal Society, of which Seth Ward was the second President.

Close to his almshouses is a red brick chapel 300 years old, for it
was built about 1625 to gather in more of the people of Buntingford
than could attend the old church on the hill. Inside is a picture
drawn on brass soon after the chapel was finished, showing it, with
its vicar Alexander Strange in the pulpit, as it was before the apse
and porch were added; and hanging in the vestry is a charter giving
the town permission to hold a market. It has a portrait of Henry the
Eighth on the seal hanging from it.

In a garden farther down the street is a Roman Catholic chapel
and priest's house, with roses climbing up the walls. Robert Hugh
Benson lived and wrote many of his novels close by, at Hare Street,

and now lies in the graveyard. Son of the Archbishop of Canterbury who died in Mr Gladstone's pew at Hawarden Church, he became private chamberlain to Pope Pius the Tenth.

All round are fine old houses. Hare Street has many and near it is the 17th century Alswick Hall. The Court was the Grammar School 300 years ago, and the Old Manor is a little way out at Corney Bury. In the main street are many 16th and 17th century houses and hostelries, one with its sign hanging from magnificent ironwork. An old turret over the archway of the Angel Inn has a clock with one hand and a bell which the Charity Commissioners (who own the inn) used to have rung whenever there was a service in the chapel down the street or in the church on the hill.

The church on the hill is still called Layston, though nothing else is left of that lost village. For years the church was a ruin, but now its bells ring out again in the 15th century tower. There are Roman bricks in the thick walls. The font is 15th century. The beautiful doorway to the porch and the sinister face on the chancel wall are also 15th century. The pulpit belongs to the 16th, being decorated 100 years later with its panelling and linenfold. As we leave the church we read these words painted round royal arms:

Fear God, Honour the Queen, and meddle not with those who are given to change.

This lonely place knows little of change. Every year the grass grows higher round the stones in the churchyard, the leaves fall and rise green again, the fields are sown and harvested, another stone crumbles in the walls; and that is all.

Close by, in a new little graveyard which we found as bright with flowers as his own decorative work, lies Claud Lovat Fraser, a delightful artist of our time. He was the son of a Buntingford solicitor, and he loved beauty over all. Very early he began to make drawings for books and rhyme sheets—long slips of paper with a poem or a ballad printed on them. People loved them partly because of the verses and the artist's work, and partly because many hundreds of years ago the same kind of sheets were printed, and ballad-mongers walked the streets selling them as fishmongers sell fish. Looking at these works of art, some of them not much bigger than a postage-stamp, it would seem that the artist's greatest genius lay in drawing minute head-pieces and tail-pieces for poems. They look as if he did them with one hand while he was waving the other about, telling a story; they look as if he had just thought about them that minute, and must put them down before he forgot. They are little images of people and places, not as ordinary people see them but as Mr Fraser saw them. He knew that at night tree trunks become "little old men with twisted knees." He knew what a lovely colour a highwayman's cloak ought to be. He knew exactly, down to a spar, the kind of ship that went a-sailing, a-sailing on the sea.

But Claud Fraser was not only an illustrator of poems. He designed book-covers, posters, advertisements, costumes and scenery for plays; he drew beautiful pictures of houses and towns, studies of characters in books, of dancers; and he painted marvellous interiors, where fantastic people walk about great halls looking brave and gay and sad. He had a very strong sense of colour, and, though he was fond of clear, bright tones, he never made his pictures gaudy. He dared to do what no one else dared, and he was always right. He was only 31 when he died, and his death was the lingering result of his four years of active service in the war.

Two Artists and a Poet

BUSHEY. Each year its houses spread a little farther, but the panorama from Bushey Heath remains a fair reward for climbing the hill from Watford, and an old inn hangs out its sign of The Merry Month of May as a reminder that that is the best time to come, when even the birds in the aviary of old Hartsbourne Manor park are chattering about spring.

The view has had its artists, for old Thomas Hearne, the painter who had something to teach Turner, lived and died here at the beginning of last century, and at the end of the century came Hubert Herkomer, followed by the younger artists flocking to his famous school. Two artists and a storyteller poet this village has known, and they lie in the churchyard of Bushey's oldest church, St James's, shaded by the park trees where the hill dips down to a deep valley. Perhaps no village in Hertfordshire has a more interesting group of graves in its churchyard than those of Thomas Hearne, Hubert Herkomer, and Barry Pain.

Thomas Hearne, an 18th century water colourist who lived on till after Waterloo, did much to revive interest in Gothic architecture, and it is known that his work was an inspiration to the immortal Turner. There are fine collections of his drawings in the British Museum and at South Kensington. The first great experience he gave himself may seem to us extraordinary, for he went out to the Leeward Islands and spent three years sketching the life of the islands and their people. Then he came home and became one of our forerunners, for he made a grand tour of England, spending four years on it and making a great collection of drawings of our antiquities.

Sir Hubert Herkomer was the son of a Bavarian craftsman, who went out to America and then came to England, sending his son Hubert to the School of Art at Southampton. A picture of a Gipsy Encampment started him on his way, and in 1870, when he was 21, he was doing successful water colours. He took a cottage at Bushey, married, and in 1875 was a great success at the Academy with his famous painting of the Chelsea war veterans in their scarlet coats, The Last Muster. He settled down at Bushey in a house like a mountain schloss to which he brought his father and his grandfather, who enriched the house with their woodcarving. A delightful man, he longed to be not only a painter but a craftsman, and he wrote music and operas, designed scenes for the stage, took an interest in the early films, lectured everywhere, and died while holidaying in Devon, just before the war which would have broken his heart. In the years of depression that have followed the war his palace of art has been pulled down because nobody wanted it.

Barry Pain was one of the bright writers of the last generation, humorist, poet, and storyteller. He wrote one of the most famous poems of the Great War, addressed to the Kaiser, who had telegraphed that God had magnificently supported them. These were the lines of Barry Pain's poem:

> *Impious braggart, you forget;*
> *God is not your conscript yet;*
> *You shall learn in dumb amaze*
> *That His ways are not your ways,*
> *That the mire through which you trod*
> *Is not the high white road of God.*
>
> *To Whom, whichever way the combat rolls,*
> *We, fighting to the end, commend our souls.*

HERTFORDSHIRE

On his grave in Bushey churchyard, in which Barry Pain was laid in 1928, are the last words of another of his poems. He was dreaming that up in the sky he saw the army of the dead go by, and he called upon us all to pay homage in these words which are on his stone:

Look upward, standing mute; Salute.

On another tomb in Bushey churchyard 12 loaves of bread used to wait for 12 poor people every Sunday morning, the gift of Dame Fuller of Queen Anne's day who also endowed the Free School at Watford. A stone in the vestry, and his daughter's stone outside, remind us that here, too, was laid to rest that humorous, vigorous Presbyterian Silius Titus, the Parliamentary colonel who turned Royalist and plotted to release Charles Stuart while guarding him at Carisbrooke, though Cromwell grew suspicious and moved him from his post. Even then he continued to correspond with the king, and we can still read the letters the imprisoned king wrote to him. Throughout the Commonwealth he was everlastingly plotting to bring the Stuarts back, even planning the assassination of Cromwell and perhaps having a hand in that notorious tract, Killing no Murder. In the end he saw the return of the Stuarts and survived till the reign of the last of them.

Though most of the church to which all these folk made their last journey was made new at the end of last century, the fine open roof of the nave and the tower remain from the 15th century; there is an original bell. In place of a chancel arch is a 500-year-old beam supporting the arms of Queen Anne painted on plaster, and the side windows of the chancel are framed in shallow 13th century wall arcades. The Jacobean pulpit, with its sounding board, is a mass of rich carving which must have delighted the old wood-carvers from Bavaria.

Bushey saw the Royal Caledonian School grow up at the beginning of this century, and another famous school here is the Royal Masonic Institution for 800 Boys, with a lofty tower and chapel. The Caledonian School was designed by Sir William Emerson; the Royal Masonic Junior School is another fine building, standing at the end of Bushey High Street.

A little way off lies Bushey Heath, long noted among botanists for its wild lily-of-the-valley. From the stately tower of its modern church the valleys of the Thames and the Colne lie spread before us, and on a clear day we may see the red walls of Hampton Court and the round tower of Windsor Castle. It is from here, at Merry Hill, that Watford draws some of its water supply, a great reservoir 500 feet above the sea, holding two million gallons.

The impressive church has an attractive interior with windows from the workshops of William Morris, paid for largely by children who collected farthings. The Morris windows are in the baptistry and represent the Children of the Bible surrounding the Child of Bethlehem. There are two other windows by Henry Holiday, the west window one of his masterpieces, strong in design and beautiful in colour; it is in memory of Basil Hicks, who gave his life for England at Loos, and it has symbolical scenes with figures of Wisdom, Power, Truth, and Love. The window over the altar is of the Crucifixion, with the two Marys, the Roman Centurion, Joseph of Arimathea, and St John. In the memorial chapel to the men who fell in the war are several lancet windows of saints, the two central ones representing Christ Triumphant and St George of England.

The Black Death Days

BYGRAVE. A rough lane from the Icknield Way leads to this quiet little place on a saddle of the Chilterns, where is a church, a rectory, a manor farm, and little else. Round the farm are ditches and banks dug to protect a huge double enclosure, 17 acres in all, perhaps the defences of some British tribe before the Romans tramped down Icknield Way. All that is known for certain is that about 550 years ago Sir John Thornbury, who lies at Little Munden, had his manor here, and made the ditches into moats round his house filling them with water for better protection from the bands of marauders wandering the country in those days, the miserable days when men still remembered the Black Death which halved the population of England.

The church was two centuries old when Sir John entered its Norman nave, as we do, through a doorway with scalloped capitals, much patched after 800 years. The font is 500 years old and is the loveliest thing here, with angels round its stem and reminders of the Crucifixion round the bowl, among them the cock that crowed and Judas's bag of silver. The windows, like the turret leading to the bellcot, are mostly 15th century. The chancel is 14th. The altar table and altar rails were made in the 17th century, and about that time someone put the coat-of-arms on the top of the rood screen, which is 15th. The choir stalls with poppyheads and the screen tracery used on the new pulpit are also 15th century. The pulpit has still the iron stand which held the hourglass 300 years ago. One who preached his last sermon watching it while the sands of 1725 were running out was Peter Feuillerade, a Huguenot who found sanctuary here from French persecution. His name is on a gravestone in the chancel. The graves in the smooth turf outside are like flower beds, with only a metal disc on each to show who lies beneath, no more than the label a gardener puts in to remind him of the seeds he has planted.

Between the Ancient Ways

CALDECOTE. Here, between the Roman Way and the Icknield Way which meet at Baldock, are wide hedgeless fields of oats and barley, wheat and hay, waving blue-green or gold against the horizon; and planted among them, without street or wall, is the church, the farm, and a group of cottages. There is no road through, and few come this way, but many must have lived here under Roman rule, for several urns and 500 Roman coins have been found hereabouts. Great thatched barns stretched along two sides of the churchyard, dwarfing the little 15th century church which wears its red brick restorations so charmingly. By the ancient door is a holy-water stoup with a high decorated canopy, one of the finest in Hertfordshire, a strange find in this rough and lonely place. The font, carved with emblems of the Passion, is 500 years old, and the church has other ancient possessions—some 15th century glass with part of a kneeling figure, an Elizabethan chalice, and a bell hung in Charles Stuart's days. The Old Rectory of timber and plaster keeps traces of its 16th century builders.

Old Temple Bar and Old Mr Clarke

CHESHUNT. We should come to it in rose time, for its roses are not to be forgotten; but indeed it is a place to draw the traveller any time. Old Temple Bar for one of its gateways, the hall of Cardinal Wolsey's old home, a noble 15th century church, several timbered houses from the past standing out among hundreds of new ones, all these it has, and more, for on its outskirts is Waltham Cross, raised by Edward the First to mark the place the body of his beloved Eleanor rested on its last journey from Nottinghamshire to Westminster.

Hertfordshire has gathered to itself this famous relic, though Waltham Abbey, with which the Cross is historically linked, is over the Essex border. This is perhaps the best of all the crosses set up to mark the place where the body of Queen Eleanor rested on its way to Westminster, where she lies in the Confessor's Chapel, her lovely tomb protected by the beautiful grille made by one of the famous craftsmen of this countryside, Thomas of Leighton over the border. Twelve crosses were set up to mark her resting-places, the first at Lincoln, the last at Charing, and Waltham Cross and one outside Northampton are still monuments of splendour. It is believed that Waltham Cross was designed by William Torel, the goldsmith who made the queen's tomb. The cross stands on modern steps and is fashioned in stone with three stages, the first stage being original 13th century work, and all above it rebuilt twice in the 19th century from the old materials. The first stage has six panelled and traceried sides with slender buttresses at the corners and a charming sculptured cornice. The second stage is an elaborate piece of carving, with three statues of Queen Eleanor under canopies with carved finials; the queen is holding her sceptre and all the statues are original and complete except for the loss of one head, which has been made new. Rising above the third stage is an elegant pinnacle set on a dainty base and crowned with a cross.

The most ancient of Cheshunt's national monuments is the church, but curiosity takes most of us first to Theobalds Park to see old Temple Bar. For two centuries it stood across Fleet Street, the gate to the City, and even today the King must wait where it stood to receive the sword of the City and give it back to the Lord Mayor before he enters. It has been decked with gold for royal processions and hung with black for Nelson's funeral, and many a gruesome head has been stuck on it for the wind to batter and the rain to beat. But it got in the way of the traffic, and towards the end of last century it came down. Its stones were numbered and after it had lain some time uncared for the owner of Theobalds, Sir Henry Meux, bought it and set it up here. Christopher Wren designed it,

Cheshunt   **The Famous Waltham Cross**

Cheshunt   **Old Temple Bar in Theobolds Park**

An Arcade of Old Shops

A Congo Native Hut

In a 16th Century Witch's Cottage

THE REMARKABLE FOLK MUSEUM AT EAST BARNET

with its central gateway and the smaller round-headed doorways through which six generations of Londoners passed, but the statues in the niches were the work of John Bushnell. Between these statues of three kings and a queen are windows into a room in which a City bank long stored its records.

Only a few fragments remain of the old palace of Theobalds, built by Queen Elizabeth's Lord Burghley and accepted by James the First in exchange for Hatfield House, for the palace was demolished and three houses have been set up in its place; but we may see part of the old garden wall, and farther afield (at Aldbury Farm) is a bit of the wall which ran ten miles round the royal park in which King James and his children lived. By an irony of fate it was within this wall that James the First's son Charles grew into manhood, and from Theobalds he went to Nottingham to set up his standard on Castle Hill, signal for the Civil War; and it was outside this wall Oliver Cromwell's son Richard dragged out a weary old age in lodgings for which he paid ten shillings a week.

Cheshunt Great House, once the home of Cardinal Wolsey, is a shadow of its former greatness, with only a fragment left of its moat, but it has still the panelled hall with a splendid 15th century timber roof under which the cardinal sat down to dine.

The common, which once covered acres of the high ground to the north, has dwindled to the little green where Goff's Oak, a venerable tree 22 feet round, stands dead under a pall of ivy, near to another pathetic old figure, a windmill bereft of its sails. The cawing of the rooks among the chestnuts guides us to the handsome church begun in 1418 and completed after 30 years of devoted care by its rector Nicholas Dixon, whose brass inscription is under the altar table. There are brass portraits of some of his flock, William and Ellen Parke and two other 15th century women without names, and the kneeling figure of Elizabeth Collen on a brass of 1609.

Apart from two chapels and the south porch, the church is much as Parson Dixon built it, and we may wish he could see it with the beauty of the painted angels in the nave. The new roof resting on the old stone corbels is also painted, adding to the splendour. Here is a big armoured coffer with three locks which has served the church for nearly four centuries, and an old barrel organ with ten tunes

F

on each barrel, still treasured though its day is past. The chancel stalls are a memorial to the men of the war, whose names are recorded in gold. By the altar is a great tomb of the Dacres family, the first name on it being that of Robert, Privy Councillor to Henry the Eighth. The monument to Henry Atkins, physician to two Stuart kings, has been moved to one of the chapels, and near it is a graceful tribute in white marble to a young wife of 24, Margaret Whatton "fair as an angel, virtuous as a saint."

One of the curates here, John Tillotson, son of a Puritan clothier, rose to be Archbishop of Canterbury. Though his marriage with Cromwell's niece was no recommendation in those Restoration days, his merit was not to be denied, and men flocked to hear him preach. There lies in a vault in the church one of the half-forgotten great men of that time, whose father also knew Cromwell; he was Nehemiah Grew the botanist, who crowded into his 71 years of life, which ended here, many botanical discoveries which revolutionised the knowledge of flowers and plants and trees. There lie in the churchyard, also, under a square tomb in the north-west corner, some members of the Cromwell family, one of them an Oliver Cromwell (great-great-grandson) and his daughter Elizabeth Oliveria, the last of the family to bear the surname of the great Protector. The Cromwells had long been familiar figures in Cheshunt, and Richard Cromwell himself here lived out the end of his days when his romance was over.

On stepping down from his high office as Protector, Richard Cromwell went into exile and wandered on the continent for 20 years, when he came back (his wife having been dead five years), took the name of Clarke, and lived with his friend Mrs Pengelly at Cheshunt. There was trouble with his daughters, and an appearance in the courts, but in due course they were reconciled and Richard divided his time between Cheshunt and Hursley in Hampshire, where his daughter Elizabeth lived. At Cheshunt he paid Mrs Pengelly ten shillings a week for his board and lodging, but there were evidently extras, for we find among a bundle of accounts charges for tobacco, brandy, pipes, and a loan of £2 "when you had your feast." A charge of sixpence is for "repairing your breeches," 30 shillings for a new hat, and there is an entry for £3 18s. 0d., "money you were pleased to give Tommy on his entrance at the

Temple, and a guinea towards buying his law books." Richard appears to have spent half-a-crown on mourning gloves in honour of the memory of Queen Mary. One of the most pathetic things ever seen in Cheshunt must have been the little shagreen trunk of Richard Cromwell, which he gave into the care of Mrs Pengelly with orders that it should be very carefully treated. It was probably the trunk which contained the addresses of congratulation on his accession to power, sent to him from all parts of the kingdom.

Another notable figure in Nonconformity Cheshunt knew in those days—Isaac Watts, who spent a quarter of a century preaching in the town, and here preached his last sermon in a meeting-house which has now vanished. The Crossbrook Street Congregational church is named after him.

The Wonderful Botanist

NEHEMIAH GREW, who lies in Cheshunt church, came of a family rich in brains and character; his father, a schoolmaster parson who had suffered bitterly as a Parliament man, personally interceding with Cromwell for King Charles's life. Nehemiah passed from Cambridge to Leyden, where he was admitted doctor of medicine at 30, practised at Coventry and in London with much success, and began investigations on the digestive system that led to important results.

He was a good astronomer, one of the little company watching the stars from the top of the Monument at London Bridge, till its vibrations made observations useless. But it was as a botanist that Grew astonished his generation. He first recognised system, design, and function in trees, plants, and flowers. He began his study of vegetable anatomy when he was 23, and five years later his first paper on the subject was read before the Royal Society. At 36 he was elected secretary of that unique fellowship of learning. Watching the stars, curing his patients, and devoutly applying himself to religious practices, he studied the growths of field and garden as if he had had the leisure of a dozen men. He had a marvellous eye; only by the aid of the microscope were others able to verify the discoveries he made with his unaided sight.

He first revealed the sex of flowers and explained the purpose

THE KING'S ENGLAND

of stamen and pistil. He explained the growth of roots and the way Nature builds tree trunks, and he pointed out the resin ducts in the pine. He anatomised leaves and seeds, the composition of fruits, the nature of plant hairs, the sap channels in the vine. In book after book, laboriously written and lavishly illustrated, he poured out new and astonishing knowledge.

Still his professional work went on, still he attended the Royal Society, classifying and describing its rarities in terms of delightful quaintness. He was one of the lesser great men of an age of giants. We sometimes get a peep of him in company with Prince Rupert and John Evelyn, but he could have had little spare time for social relaxation. He worked to the end, and died visiting a patient.

Oliveria Cromwell

ELIZABETH OLIVERIA CROMWELL, lying here, was the only daughter of Oliver Cromwell, great-great-grandson of the famous Oliver. Her father had begun life as a solicitor practising in London. In 1792, when his cousins Elizabeth and Letitia Cromwell died at Hampstead, they left him their family estate at Brantingsay, a mile to the north of the church and now known as Cheshunt Park.

Sorrow came to little Elizabeth when she was eight years old, for her little brother Oliver, the very last Oliver Cromwell, died, and she was left to play alone in this lovely park and to wander through the great rooms on whose walls were many family portraits. She learned to love them, and knew the story of every one, for this was her home for 57 years. Each Sunday she would accompany her parents and Aunt Susanna to chapel. Her grandmother would often go with them, a splendid old lady who lived to the great age of 104 and lies with Aunt Susanna in Bunhill Fields.

In 1801 Elizabeth married Thomas Artemidorus Russell. Her father had devoted himself to the study of the Cromwell family, and before he died he published the memoirs of his ancestors. It was a source of sorrow to him that he should be the last to bear the name of Oliver Cromwell, so with his son-in-law he approached the Heralds College asking them to obtain permission for Thomas Russell to receive the name and arms of Cromwell. Such a change of name, provided the appropriate fees were paid, is usually sanctioned without question, but when the request was mentioned to old King

George the Third he started up and paced the room, saying, "No, no—no more Cromwells!" So there was nothing more to say.

Mrs Russell had nine children, the eldest of whom (also called Elizabeth Oliveria) married Frederick Prescott of Theobalds, James the First's old home, and had a host of descendants. So had her eldest son Artemidorus, and most of the boys among those descendants received the Christian name Cromwell.

Mrs Elizabeth Russell passed away at the age of 72, and James Waylen, who in 1880 published his famous work on the House of Cromwell, records in it his recollections of her over 30 years before. "To watch her passing from portrait to portrait through the Brantingsay gallery (he wrote), and to hear her with tremulous voice dwelling on the virtues of each successive representative of the house from the Protector's parents down to her own father, was to become for a while a passive recipient of very pleasant sensations—sensations, it may be, too thronging for description, too complex for analysis, but bathed in an aroma such as no other legend of English domestic life was capable of kindling." So passed away the old lady who was the last of the Cromwell family to bear the famous name.

The Trees on the Common

CHIPPERFIELD. It is country pure and simple, chiefly village green, a wide and lovely stretch of Hertfordshire, with a background of wood and common, a place for cricket with a good view from the old inn, or for a stroll into woods and high bracken and sweet-smelling gorse. Among lime trees at one corner of the green stands a small church of last century, not unattractive within; on the far side a road leads in one direction past the dignified manor house (seen through fine gates), and down the hill another road leads to Pale Farm, a timbered brick building with an overhanging storey 400 years old.

Chipperfield is not the place for antiquarians; it is fresh and green and young, one of the best bits of country within easy reach of London, and we found it rejoicing in another gift from its generous Blackwell family, who had just given 113 more acres of wood and heath to the public on condition the elms in front of the manor house are not cut down. On the common is the Apostles' Pond, encircled by eleven beautiful limes, which used to be twelve until Judas Iscariot was blown down. A Spanish chestnut is said to be 300 years old, with a trunk about 21 feet round.

An Actor and a Lady

CHORLEY WOOD. It is the nearest Hertfordshire village to the Chalfont country, whose loveliness it shares. Here is a beautiful and extensive gorse common, and there are wide views over the valley of the Chess. In this village William Penn married the beautiful Gulielma Springett, whose charming personality lives in Thomas Ellwood's story of the early Quakers and their sufferings under the tyranny of the Restoration. The marriage took place in 1672 at King John's Farm, a brick and timber house of exquisite charm, still keeping the room, with its exposed beams, in which the event took place. In it hangs a copy of the portrait of Penn in armour, showing him as a soldier before he was a Quaker.

The church, with its shingled spire and shingled gables, is by the great common, with cedars in the churchyard. In a niche in the sanctuary is a statue of St John holding a chalice, in memory of John Gilliat, who died in 1912. A flat wreath of bronze marks the grave of Sir George Alexander, the famous actor who was laid to rest here in 1918. There are three bronze fawns beside it, and we read on the inscription:

> Do thy duty, that is best,
> Leave unto thy God the rest.

There is a bronze portrait of Sir George Alexander on the wall, the work of Mr G. L. Hartwell. Sir George was born at Reading in the middle of last century, and as a manufacturer's son had a short business career before he turned actor. Then he joined Sir Henry Irving's company and played under that great man's wing for eight years. For most of the rest of his life he was actor-manager at St James's theatre, which must always be associated with his memory. He was admirable in comedy parts and most successful as a producer, a man of sterling character and great personal charm who added lustre to the English stage.

There is also remembered in this village a woman who died in a cottage encircled by flowers on Chorley Wood Common. She was born as Jessie Butler, and was one of the American girls painted by

Sargent. Marrying an Englishman, she became Mrs Phipps, settled
down to educational work in Chelsea, and was the first woman to
be Chairman of the Educational Committee of the LCC. She
gave the energy of a lifetime to helping London's schoolchildren,
and when her sight failed she became Chairman of the Central
Council for the London Blind. She was charming, and everybody
loved her, and when she died a friend said of her that "she lived
by a few plain principles, and had the strength of her convictions."

The Prehistoric Terraces

CLOTHALL. It is a lonely spot that any traveller must love
to see, with a few old thatched cottages and a wonderful
little church on a hill, looking over cornfields red with poppies when
we called. It is only here that they have crept in, for all round we
found fields with some of the finest wheat in England, and there are
terraces still to be seen on which men were growing their food in the
days before history.

We come into the church by a door studded with the nails of
hundreds of church notices, and painted with the name of John
Warren—perhaps the name of the proud man who made it in the
14th century. The door opens on a quaint group of old seats raised
in tiers to the back of the church. Among their poppyheads stands
the little panelled font on pillars, 800 years old with a cover made
300 years ago. The chantry chapel is now the children's chapel and
is 14th century. They saved their pennies to buy vases for it and
they keep them filled with flowers. The images have gone from the
brackets, but here is still an Old French inscription to a man who
died when the chantry was new. The children must love the east
window, for it is filled with birds of the countryside, all in glass of
the 14th and 15th centuries. There are six heads of saints in the
window and every inch of space between is filled with hawks and
peewits, ducks and partridges, and all the birds from the fields
around. One of the bells has been ringing while all these birds
have been singing.

Yet more treasures has this small place, five brasses. They show
four priests of the 15th and 16th centuries, and a mother with her
16 children. The oldest rector here is John Vynter of 1404, shown
in his robes, and the three other priests are John Wright of 1519,

Thomas Dalyson of the 16th century, and William Lucas who died in 1602. Unfortunately his brass and that of Anne Bramfield, with her very big family, are hidden by the pews.

CODICOTE. One house catches our eye in the long village street, as it is meant to do, for this pleasant gabled inn has halted travellers on their way for more than 300 years. It has a contemporary not far off in Codicote Bury, which still keeps its Jacobean panelling, staircase, and carved overmantels. The lower part of the church tower has walls five feet thick, probably part of the church dedicated here 800 years ago when the Conqueror's second son was on the throne. For the rest, the church is mainly 14th century, its age disguised by restoration, but with some iron-work probably old enough to be Norman on the door, a Jacobean pulpit, and an Elizabethan chalice.

John Bunyan, Pilgrim

COLEMAN GREEN. It must surely be the only place in England that has a chimney stack for a monument. We found ivy hiding it; the birds had built their nests in it; but it is a link with the immortal tinker, and so it remains. Its buttressed bricks are all that is left of a 300-year-old cottage where the tinker came on his pilgrimage, where, as a stone here tells us, "John Bunyan by tradition is said to have preached and occasionally to have lodged." Where the voice of the preacher was heard is now a group of allotments, and when we came this way a thrush had the pulpit to himself, carolling from an apple tree beside the chimney; but we did not find it hard to picture the great little man riding down the lane to this common, having crossed the ford at Water End like one of his own pilgrims, and having seen the fine chimneys and the three steep gables of the Jacobean manor house which are beside the Lea to this day. It is actually in Sandridge, as indeed this hamlet is. At one time it belonged to Sarah Jennings, and when her husband was raised to the peerage it was as Lord Churchill of Sandridge.

COLNEY HEATH. Here oldest and newest England meet. The Colne flows across the wide heath unchanged since the last grey wolf stole by; dark pines and oak frame the wildness; and to the north the masts and spidery network of a wireless station break the horizon. This 20th century miracle is the newest of all things here. The 19th century gave the village its church, designed in ancient Byzantine style, and of last century too is the Hertfordshire Agricultural Institute, whose avenue of chestnuts and neatly planned surroundings signify the coming of cultivation to the wild.

A Surgeon in the East

COTTERED. It gathers about its green, on which cows and donkeys graze in the shadow of tall elms. There is an ancient farmhouse and a church 600 years old. We open the 500-year-old door of the church and find the faded figure of St Christopher greeting us, the background of the scene like a medieval map, with castles and roads, a horseman riding, and a countryman stepping through the meadows, like a picture of our countryside when this church was built in the middle of the 14th century. The lofty nave has a 15th century timber roof, and is lit by six medieval transomed windows, some with fragments of their original glass. There is a second old door to the vestry with 16th century ironwork, and the vase-shaped marble font is 18th century. The chapel was built 500 years ago by Edward Pulter of Broadfield Manor, a house that has been made new but keeps the 17th century stables.

Here is one of the oldest houses in the county, a farmhouse known as The Lordship, built 500 years ago and interesting as showing the changes of the 17th century. It has many of its original doorways and much 17th century panelling, but the front door which the village knew for nearly five centuries is now in America.

There died in this village in 1926 a brilliant surgeon who spent his life in public causes, Sir James Cantlie. Here he lies in the churchyard, and on the wall of the church is a white tablet with a bronze medallion showing his kindly face, with the words: Blessed are the merciful, for they shall obtain mercy. Merciful indeed he was, a Scotsman who went out to China in 1887 as a surgeon, and also spent many years in India, mastering the mystery of tropical sickness and founding the Royal Society of Tropical Medicine. The tablet was set up by the Chinese Minister in London, Dr Alfred Sze, in appreciation of the noble services Sir James Cantlie rendered to China. In the critical days when Dr Sun Yat Sen was kidnapped and held a prisoner in the Chinese Legation in London it was Dr Cantlie who saved his life and enabled him to become the Christian

President of the Chinese Republic. Sir James was knighted for his work in the Great War.

CROXLEY GREEN. It is a rapidly growing place by a big green on a hill near Watford. Down in the valley the Grand Union Canal runs beside the River Gade, with papermills along its bank, and behind the village rises the tower of an old windmill. The church is modern but has one gracious memorial, a bronze tablet to Leslie and Nigel Newall, who fell in the Great War. It is bright with the painted arms of their school and their regiments, and on a pedestal at the top is a miniature copy of Michael Angelo's immortal sculpture of Lorenzo de Medici.

The Poet Forgotten

DATCHWORTH. Ivied elms and a lonely church spire brave the winds that sweep across this high ledge. The fine modern spire is set on a 14th century tower. The nave may be Norman, but the aisle and the arcade are 13th century, a 15th century arch opening into a patchwork chancel of various ages. The nave roof and the font are both 500 years old, and there is a chair, a chest, and a poor-box which have served for 300 years. In a recess is a gravestone carved 600 years ago with a flowery cross, perhaps to cover the body of John de Burgh, the church's patron, whose widow founded Clare College, Cambridge.

Half a mile to the south is Datchworth Green, where an old whipping post six feet high, still with its iron handcuffs, stands by some cottages which have been here 300 years. Not far off are two pleasant 17th century homes, timbered Hoppers Hall and Cherry Tree Farm. Under Datchworth's yew trees Edward Young, the 18th century poet then living in retirement at Welwyn, wrote some of his Night Thoughts, his best remembered poem, though by now he might say, as he said of himself in his lifetime "I've been so long remembered, I'm forgot."

Two Dozen Children in Brass

DIGSWELL. Here, in the church which for more than seven centuries has overlooked the valley of the Maran, men who fought for England when much of France was her province are joined with those who came from a young Dominion to fight with France and England against a common enemy. Their country's flag hangs on the church wall, given on behalf of all the Australian officers nursed during the war at Digswell House and Digswell Place; and near it is a memorial to 73 whom no nursing could save.

It is 500 years since those other soldiers were brought here whose brass portraits are among the shining array in front of the altar. Almost lifesize is that of John Peryent, the squire of three kings whose last battles were for Henry the Fifth. We see him in his armour with his feet on a leopard, and by him the wife who died in the victorious year of Agincourt, imposing in her high headdress with her crest of a hedgehog at her feet. The armed knight next to them is believed to be a later John Peryent who died about 1430. Their family coat-of-arms is carved on two brackets in the chapel. The other brasses show Thomas Hoore, a mercer (as one of his shields shows) in the quieter reign of Henry the Seventh, his wife and 12 children with him; then Robert Battyll with his wife and ten children, their portraits all made the year before Mary Tudor lost Calais; then William Robert with the wife who died in 1484 and his two sons (the date of his own death was begun but never filled in); and last come an unknown couple lying in their shrouds.

This brass portrait gallery of 11 grown-ups and 24 children is a proud possession for this little church, whose nave and chancel walls were raised by Normans masons, though none of their doorways or windows remain. The tower out-topped by the yew beside it was added in Tudor days to the 13th century aisle, where is a rich recess arch with a dove carved on it. There are 15th century beams over the nave, and 16th century oak panelling roofs the chancel. Parts of several Tudor screens are left. The patterned chalice was made when Elizabeth was queen, and two of the bells just after her death.

The new world is pressing close about the old church on the hill. The great house beside it is now used by people from all over the country as a Conference Hall.

Bestriding the valley like a Colossus is a mighty range of 40 arches over which the trains pass like toys, a giant viaduct 100 feet high, 1490 feet long, and noble from sheer magnitude. Passing under it we find a group of Digswell's oldest homes, and beyond them the big house and grounds of Tewin Water, where the two brothers Alfred and Otto Beit died, leaving vast sums to many good causes and a family fortune from the diamond mines of Kimberley. The elder brother, Alfred, was right-hand man to Cecil Rhodes.

The Wonderful Outdoor Museum

EAST BARNET. Like its neighbour on the hill it comes into Greater London, and thousands of houses cover the land where 800 years ago the woodmen and swineherds of the monks of St Albans were busy in the valley and worshipping in the Norman church standing on a knoll. But though Greater London swallows up East Barnet its public-spirited authority has saved for it much open space, Oak Hill Park, Hadley Woods, Waterfall and Everleigh Walks, with a common and a green, giving hundreds of acres and delight to nature-lovers. At Hadley Green (where tradition says the Battle of Barnet was fought) are charming houses looking across the turf where David Livingstone used to walk, and on one of these houses (a white one) is his portrait in bronze, for he lived here on his first return to England after 16 years in Africa. It was in this house that he wrote his Missionary Travels and the Cambridge lectures which led to the formation of the Universities Mission.

Down in the valley three spires rise in a row, all from Nonconformist churches, and between one of these spires and the town hall is a winged figure in bronze, on a stone pedestal carved in relief with a lion victorious over a winged dragon. It is the tribute of East Barnet to the 279 men who fell in the Great War, and their names are here.

A mile away, standing like a rock against the rising tide of red brick houses, is the church on the hillock, still with walls the old monks of Norman England knew, three feet thick. It is only the nave that is old, the rest of the church having been rebuilt, but a queer head shaped by a Norman craftsman watches us as we enter, and on the north side are the splayed windows through which the light dimly entered the Norman church. There is a magnificent cedar among the yews and ivied stones of the old churchyard, and in its shade lies John Hadley, who thrilled astronomers in the 18th century by producing the first reflecting telescope powerful enough for studying the stars. It was a great help to seamen, so improving the reflecting quadrant that it became their sextant.

There lies here also a gallant Swiss, General Augustine Prevost, who lies here with his more famous son Sir George, Governor-General of Canada during the last war between England and America, in 1812. Sir George had fought against the French in the West Indies in the early days of the struggle with Napoleon, and had been rewarded for attaching their French colony to the British flag—perhaps because he had French blood in his veins. He made an unfortunate intervention, however, in the military operations, having once or twice to sound the signal for retreat, and he was recalled and condemned by a naval court, his health being ruined by the anxiety of these events.

Two benefactors of our seamen lie in this churchyard, for there came to East Barnet as vicar a Huguenot refugee whose son was the Daniel Beaufort who helped to found the Royal Irish Academy, and prepared a map of Ireland and an account of the country which is of historic value. Daniel's son became Admiral Sir Francis Beaufort, and it was he who made valuable charts and drew up a table of winds well known to sailors all over the world as the Beaufort Scale.

What will seem to most people the most captivating possession of East Barnet is the remarkable Abbey Folk Park built up by Father J. M. S. Ward, whose energy and enthusiasm have brought together one of the most remarkable outdoor museums within an hour's reach of London. It is packed with treasure.

We begin with it in the summer hut of a caveman of 20,000 years ago; it is made of grass and turfed with pieces cut with small flint flakes. By it is a pit dwelling of Stone Age men with the dim beginnings of the four-post bedstead, the post having a skin stretched over it to keep off the rain from the grass roof. Five other prehistoric dwellings show the march of men till Caesar came to Britain, and as such primitive races still exist in the world we come next to an African village, the home of such people now. Here is magic and witchcraft, a witch's cottage from 16th century England with a stuffed crocodile and other monsters hanging from the beams, and, of course, the witch's broom.

Among more human things is an interesting group of homes and workshops including a wheelwright's shop, and a farrier's shop found in Barnet itself. There is one of the last woad wagons used in England, with wide wheels for marshy ground. There is an

Elizabethan armourer's shop, a weaver's shop, and a china shop of the 18th century; a Victorian toyshop and a genuine old curiosity shop. There are rooms such as the Elizabethans and Victorians slept in and dined in. The wealth of Victorian objects is surprising; many treasures and knick-knacks have been given by Queen Mary.

The museum is full of surprises. It has an arrow from Marathon with its point bent by the armour it struck, a Roman helmet on which the owner has punched his name with a nail, Roman shoes and English wooden clogs, and an axe-head which is known to have belonged to the bodyguard of Queen Bertha, the woman who should be for ever sacred in our history as inspirer and founder of the first Christian church still existing in England—St Martin's at Canterbury. Many things here illustrate the rise of Christianity and most of them are housed in a tithe barn which once stood at St Nicholas in Thanet. Built in a marvellous way to resist the wind from the North Sea, this barn stood from the 13th century to our own on its original site and was then taken down and set up here. In it now are over 200 interesting things.

It is difficult to exaggerate the appeal that this captivating place makes to a traveller. It has crude things and splendid things, historic things and curious things, terrifying things and beautiful things, and a walk round it is one of the most interesting hours a traveller could have in this countryside, and probably worth a month of schooling to any boy or girl.

The Lady and the Knight

EASTWICK. Behind its few cottages are meadows with high and solitary trees and a distant gleam of the River Stort as it turns south into Essex. The church, reached between walls of clipped yew, has changed much; but, though it was rebuilt last century, the richly moulded stones of its first chancel arch were set up again as they were 700 years ago and the old gargoyles are back on the tower. In the tower hang two medieval bells, and a third which was new when it tolled for Queen Elizabeth; and below them is the portrait of an Elizabethan lady, Joan Lee, looking down from her brass on a stone knight of the 13th century who lies cross-legged in chain mail with his long sword. They are an interesting couple, both showing in detail the costume of their time.

Drama at Elstree

ELSTREE. It is the home of the English film, and if it would put a thrilling story on the screen it needs only to turn its cameras on to the story of Elstree. Along old Watling Street came stones from the Roman city of Sulloniacae for building the old church, but, alas, it has been rebuilt, facing a row of black and white cottages in the narrow street. The 600-year-old gargoyles are back on the walls, and the pillars of the south arcade bear the mark of the 15th century mason, but mostly the church built with Roman stones has been made new. It has an elaborate iron chancel screen designed by Sir Arthur Blomfield, and has something which will greatly interest the traveller who is sorry to have lost the old church. It is a collection of fragments kept in a case here, so old that they carry our thoughts back to St Paul, for they are from the temple of Diana of the Ephesians, expressive little heads and some vases, one of them marked with the bee we find stamped on Ephesian coins by silversmiths like Demetrius, who, fearing that his trade in idols was threatened, roused the people of Ephesus against Paul so that they cried out for two hours, *Great is Diana of the Ephesians.*

It is in the graveyard that we come upon the drama so appropriate for an Elstree film. Here lie Martha Ray and William Weare, whose deaths stirred all England in the 17th and 18th centuries.

Martha Ray was an attractive young woman, elegant and musical, who became the mistress of the fourth Earl Sandwich, who lived at Hinchingbrooke, Huntingdon. There a young soldier named James Hackman met her one day in 1772 and fell in love with her, although she had given the earl several children. Hackman became a lieutenant, but eventually left the army to become a priest, yet for six or seven years he paid his unwanted attentions to Martha Ray, in spite of her refusing his offer of marriage. One night he waited for her outside Covent Garden Theatre and shot her dead, being less fortunate in his attempt to kill himself. Within a week she was buried in the chancel here, and within a fortnight he was found guilty and hanged at Tyburn, Dr Johnson's friend Boswell riding with him in the coach.

William Weare was a solicitor who had been accused of cheating by John Thurtell, a ne'er-do-well son of the Mayor of Norwich, who, having failed in his father's business, became the associate of a low sporting set and was well known as a boxer. George Borrow mentions him in Lavengro. He opened a tavern in London, and managed to get £2000 insurance for a mysterious fire, and began gambling it away. He lost heavily to William Weare, but after a quarrel and charges of trickery they became reconciled, and Thurtell arranged to pick up Weare and take him to the house of a friend at Elstree for a shooting party. Thurtell drove him in his gig, and between Elstree and St Albans suddenly took out a pistol and shot him, then stunning him and cutting his throat. He threw the body into a swamp two miles away, but he had two associates who turned king's evidence, and in spite of an eloquent appeal before the judges he was hanged. The case attracted wide interest. Even Hazlitt was impressed by Thurtell's rhetoric, and Sir Walter Scott made a commonplace book of the newspaper accounts and visited the scene of the murder. Bulwer Lytton is said to have used some incidents of the crime in one of his novels, a drama based on it was given with success in the Surrey Theatre, and a ballad writer made £500 out of it.

On the church porch are the old arms of St Albans Abbey, whose towers may be seen from one end of the village, while Aldenham reservoir gleams 200 feet below to the west. Also within sight from here is Brockley Hill, where the Royal National Orthopaedic Hospital stands on what was a battlefield 20 centuries ago. An obelisk has been put up to mark the site of this historic event, for it was here, in the second Roman invasion of 54 BC, that our British ancestors checked the Roman advance on what is now St Albans, a victory of much significance in itself, and of great interest because the British tribesmen were led by Cassivellaunus, who by virtue of this triumph became the first Briton living in these islands to have his name in history. We hear of him in the writings of Julius Caesar, and we know that his people were warlike and powerful, and that his Kingdom was in the area now known as Buckinghamshire, Berkshire, and Hertfordshire.

Elstree has become the chief centre of British films. A mile and a half beyond Elstree station lies Boreham Wood, where stand the great studios. The trek of the film men to Elstree began in 1913, in the days when a good natural light was essential for film work. The high position of the village gives it a clear atmosphere. We found still standing a small brick studio built in that year, now entirely dwarfed by the gigantic white structures with green roofs built for the modern films. These can be seen beyond the shops and houses on the Shenley road, but on the main road itself lies the group of iron buildings which maintain a steady output of film plays, giving employment to hundreds. When a big production is in hand, calling for crowds, these normally quiet roads are scenes of great excitement. The passer-by may be intrigued to see the funnels of an Atlantic liner over the roofs of houses here, or a medieval castle suddenly appearing on the skyline; odd it is suddenly to pass to the side or the back of such a place and realise that it is all unreal. We are in the land of make-believe.

A Dark September Night

ESSENDON. The village will not soon forget the dark September night in 1916 when a German Zeppelin was brought down in flames at Cuffley, not far away, for before this ghastly blaze lit up the sky this Zeppelin, one of the first criminals of the air, had emptied what was left of its load of bombs on this peaceful village, shattering cottages and wrecking the chancel of the church. The tower of the church alone is as it was in the 15th century, but inside are various memories of the past. One, a melancholy reminder of English justice not so very long ago, is a stone high on the west wall on which is written that a young man who suffered at Hertford for theft in 1785 "begged a grave in this churchyard and prayed to God that his suffering might prove a warning to others."

The church has a delightful christening bowl which has the distinction of having been made by the famous potter Josiah Wedgwood. On a brass is pictured an Elizabethan family, William Tooke, his wife, and 12 children, all kneeling, the father having died in 1588, Armada year. Many of their descendants lie here, and towards Hatfield Park is their old home, Pope's Farm, where George Tooke retired in 1635 after having taken part in the ill-fated attack on Cadiz. Thereafter he spent 40 placid years in writing prose and poetry which tells us much about the military tactics of his day.

The church, which has a noble cedar in the churchyard, stands in the centre of this pleasant village, and a road from the south approaches it between two big estates, Bedwell Park with its collection of pictures (to be seen for a fee) and Essendon Place with its handsome iron gates and luxurious trees, the home of several Baron Dimsdales since the physician of that name was summoned to Russia in 1746 by the Empress Catherine to inoculate her and her son against smallpox. So satisfied was the Empress with the skilful Thomas Dimsdale that she loaded him with gifts and created him a baron. His grave is in the Quaker burial ground at Bishop's Stortford.

Down in the valley by the River Lea is a mill still vigorous and strong after 300 years of work; it has the same mighty timbers.

The Pictures on the Wall

FLAMSTEAD. The River Ver ripples and winds by the unbending Watling Street, and above it lies Flamstead and its old cottages, a church with a Norman tower crowned by a medieval spire, and gabled almshouses of the 17th century.

Lilacs and red and white chestnuts, with two giant sycamores among them, surround the church, and at the entrance, in memory of those who did not come back from the war, are John Bunyan's immortal words, So he passed over and all the trumpets sounded for him on the other side. Inside is a wealth of medieval frescoes, brass portraits, and sculptured figures. The 15th century added a high clerestory to the church, so that we have light to admire the 500-year-old roof with its carved stone corbels, the exquisite leafy capitals of the 13th century arcades, and the old paintings, which were the picture Bible of the village folk in the Middle Ages; they have appeared in our time from under centuries of plaster. Most curious of all these finds under the whitewash was an oil painting of the Stuart arms surrounded by cherubs and prophets, completely blotting out the older painting now revealed over the chancel arch, where Christ sits in judgment on a rainbow with an angel towering on one side and the windowed walls of heaven on the other. Elsewhere we see barefooted Apostles ten feet high, the Last Supper, the Crucifixion, the Entombment, and the Risen Christ. Several of these originally decorated a chantry chapel of the Beauchamps, one of whom left his name to the Beauchamp Tower in the Tower of London, where he was imprisoned for conspiring against Richard the Second. Here is a font from those days and a screen with a new beam taking the place of its vaulted roodloft. The altar table and rails are 17th century; the bit of oak ceiling in the aisle is probably 600 years old, and the six bells average over 250 years each.

Portrayed in brass are John Oudeby, the rector who died in 1414, and a couple from the end of that century with their four children. In stone we see a nameless 15th century couple lying on their tomb under a canopy; the resplendent red and gold kneeling figure of Sir Bartholomew Fouke, the Master of Elizabeth's household who lived to see James on her throne; and the tomb of Thomas Saunders, the almshouse founder, with his five children kneeling below it, and in front the odd dwarfed figure of his widow striking a dramatic attitude. He lived in Beechwood Park. But best of all we like the inscriptions to humbler folk cut on the chalk pillars. One is dated 1598 and says

> *In this middle space and at this seat's end*
> *There lieth buried our neighbore frind*
> *Olde John Grigge of Cheverill's End.*

The Little Church Lost

FLAUNDEN. The view from the church gate over the fields and woods is delightful, but the old church has given way to a new one built at the beginning of the Victorian Era by Sir Gilbert Scott. The three old bells have been hung in the tower, one of them old enough to have sounded the good news of the Armada, and here is the Elizabethan chalice, and the bowl of the 15th century font. But all that remains of the old church is the broken wall about a mile away among nettles and pine trees by the cress-beds of the River Chess. We see the outline of the tiny church, not more than 12 yards long, and piercing the wall is a low 700-year-old arch and a three-light window of the 15th century. Yet here services are sometimes held for the sake of other days, and the little congregation lifts up its eyes to see all about it the wide fields rolling on to the horizon.

Marching with the Sword

FURNEUX PELHAM. "Time Flies, Mind Your Business," announces the church clock for all to see; and a swarm of bees seemed to be taking the words to heart when we called, flying in and out under the clock. For the rest, time and business seemed merely to saunter by in this pleasant village off the highway.

Yet 800 years have passed since the Norman family of De Furneux gave the village its first name, and 700 years have gone since the chancel of the church was built. It still has its three stone seats for the priests. The tower where the bees make honey was added in the 14th century, and the 15th left the greatest mark, enlarging the church by two aisles, a clerestory, and a two-storeyed porch, with sundials scratched on its walls. The finest sight here is also from the 15th century, the altar tomb with two figures cut in brass, a man and his widow under canopies. Another brass of a very small knight kneeling with his wife and five children is thought to portray Robert Newport, whose money built the south chapel, where an Elizabethan helmet hangs over the altar tomb of a later lord of the manor, Edward Cason.

The low-pitched roof of this chapel and the angels supporting it seem to have been modelled on the finer 15th century roof of the nave, borne up by wooden angels holding shields, two painted with coats-of-arms. The font is 700 years old. Built into a wall are two stone coffins, and in the chapel we found the lid of another. The royal arms on the screen at the west end of the south aisle mark three new kings with the dates 1634, 1660, and 1831. It is indeed a Royalist church, and a story told here is that the vicar Richard Hancock marched up and down the churchyard sword in hand to prevent any Puritan making away with the altar rails or with the first of these royal arms.

The village street sinks into a hollow, then rises to the green verge and gates of the hall, a big Elizabethan house with curving Stuart gables among the older ones. We get a glimpse of it from the road through a window cut in a thick yew hedge.

The Good Squire

GILSTON. It has homes on the highway near the River Stort and others on the byway skirting the park of the great house, once the home of the Plumer family, described with such charm by Charles Lamb in his essay on Blakesmoor. It was one of the kind hearted squires here, Colonel John Plumer, who befriended poor Jane Wenham of Walkern, the last Englishwoman sentenced to death for witchcraft.

In the gently undulating park is a lake through which the Fiddlers

Brook plays its way to the river in tune with the surrounding calm, and high up beyond a group of giant walnut trees is the church, much changed with the centuries but well cared for and still keeping a fine doorway (now blocked up), a combined table and piscina, a coffin lid with a cross, and a font bowl, all 700 years old. Just as old, but of a rarer beauty, is the oak chancel screen with roses carved above its trefoil arches and graceful pillars only an inch wide. In the tower window is a coloured shield of Sir William Estfield, Sheriff of London in 1429, and in the chancel are monuments to the Gores, forerunners of the Plumers at the great house, among them being a tablet to Sir John Gore who sat in Cromwell's Parliament, and a quaint figure of his four-year-old Bridget who fell asleep two years before him.

The village inn, 300 years old, boasts the proud name of Plume of Feathers, but stands humbly at Pye Corner.

The Conqueror Gave It Away

GRAVELEY. The Conqueror gave this village to his friend William Ewe, and the Normans built a church here. We find it up a country lane with two 17th century farms and a few attendant cottages, while the rest of Graveley's houses keep to the main road. Only the nave is left of the Norman church, and its doorway was removed to the chancel when the aisle was added last century. If we may judge by the beautiful double piscina this chancel must have been a lovely place when it was rebuilt in the 13th century. The chancel arch, its oak screen, and the nave roof are 500 years old. The modern pulpit has panels of carving a century older still. In the 15th century tower hangs a bell made the year after the Armada.

A short distance from this church a narrow road leads up to another which is now in ruins. Ivy clings to all that is left of its 600-year-old walls, and nettles and grass grow where men and women once knelt in prayer. Beside it is the manor house of Chesfield, still with its old boundary wall and the big chimney stacks which boldly proclaim its Stuart origin.

What a Man!

GREAT GADDESDEN. Londoners off to Whipsnade see its church and the cluster of cottages on the other side of the River Gade, and they will see no fiercer animal at Whipsnade than the gargoyles round the church tower. But it is the Roman bricks that are the marvel here, seemingly as long-lived as the phoenix. The Normans who built this church 800 years ago made use of these bricks, which were then 800 years old, and, though the church changed through the Middle Ages, the flat red bricks of the Romans still buttress the chancel and form one corner of its walls. On the other side of the chancel is the chapel added in 1730 to house the memorials of the Halseys, whom we found still living at Gaddesden Place, the 18th century house glimpsed among the trees on the opposite side of the river. Drear and bleak is this chapel where the white busts of six 18th century Halseys look down on us, secure with their estimable epitaphs. The Latin epitaph of an earlier one, whose handsome bust is niched over an elaborate monument in the chancel, culminates in the ecstatic exclamation, What a husband! What a father!

Two older couples are portrayed in brass, both bereft of their little children: William Croke of 1506 with his wife on the chancel floor, the other couple by the north door. The altar table and the table in the tower vestry are 17th century, and there is a small medieval chest hollowed from a solid log, and an extraordinary narrow one over eight feet long. The south arcade has capitals deeply carved with leaves by 13th century masons; the plain north arcade is 14th century; the clerestory, the porch, and the tower are 15th; and the roofs are all 500 years old, the handsome nave roof having carved bosses. The chalice was made shortly before Charles Stuart lost his throne, and four of the bells shortly after his son got it back.

The Gade flows on and reaches Waterend, a charming hamlet of a dozen brick and timber cottages from the 17th century; then, emerging from under a pretty bridge, it widens and sobers to match the stateliness of the green slopes up to Gaddesden Place. On the high ground beyond is Gaddesden Row, which provided the British Museum with a fine collection of flints, the tools and hunting weapons of the first of our Stone Age men.

The Scholar and the King

GREAT MUNDEN. It is little more than a farm, a duckpond, a cottage and a church. The cottage is a frail-looking wooden one, yet it has lasted 300 years, as long as High Trees Farm, which has 17th century stacks and a heavy screen carved in Cromwell's day.

The church proclaims its Norman ancestry with a blocked doorway, a deep window, and a pillar with a carved capital left in the chancel arch, but succeeding generations have obliterated the rest of the Norman work and left their own windows, doorways, arches, and the four stone angels holding up the nave roof, two playing lutes. The aisle was added in the 14th century, and for years its small niched reredos was hidden beneath plaster. The worn tower with fantastic faces outside its windows was added in the 15th century, and in 1621 Robert Oldfield made for it four bells which are still ringing here. It is almost within living memory that one was rung as a gleaning bell each morning and evening during harvest time, to call the gleaners to the fields.

Two choir pews have poppyheads which have outlasted 15 generations of choirboys, and in the small arcaded Jacobean pulpit John Lightfoot, whom some consider the greatest Bible scholar of his day, preached his first sermon as rector here in 1644, and his last 31 years later. He was often to preach before Parliament during the Commonwealth, but when he wrote down the entry of the execution of Charles Stuart in Great Munden's register he added the word *Murdered.*

A little way down the road is quite a pleasant hamlet known in olden days as Munden Furnival, but now called Nasty, as if in sympathy with the little Essex village of Ugley across the border.

Cardinal Wolsey Comes This Way

GREAT WYMONDLEY. Facing a row of thatched cottages is Delamere House with three storeys rising to Elizabethan gables. But there was a finer house here before it, where Cardinal Wolsey entertained Henry the Eighth. Great Wymondley indeed had a permanent link with the kings of England, for the lord of the manor, who lived in the timbered 16th century house to the north west of the church, held the right to be cupbearer at their coronation.

If Wolsey did not hear mass in his private chapel, he must have gone to this ancient village church which was here so long before him and has so long survived him. In imagination we may follow him in his red cardinal's robe past the pond and up the green slope to this church where Roman tiles dot the flint walls built by the Normans. The Norman work is also well shown in the round windows and the arch of the chancel, while their humour looks out from the sharp-featured faces on the capitals of the doorway with its starry tympanum. On the south wall is scratched an ancient sundial.

Supporting the 500 year-old roof of the nave is a medieval portrait gallery in stone—scowling barons, a king, a patient nun, and women in curious square headdresses, a shaggy lion among them resembling the beasts on the 15th century tower. The plain font and a few of the patched benches were made 500 years ago, and one of the bells is old enough to have tolled for Queen Elizabeth. Steps inside the wall lead to the vanished roodloft, and on one side of the Norman chancel arch is a peephole to the altar.

The ground falls away behind the church, where is the mound of a fortified enclosure which covered five acres in Wolsey's day. Beyond it lived a Roman farmer who sowed pottery, tiles, and coins for our own generation to harvest. The farmer probably built the rich villa buried a mile or so away on the bank of the River Purwell, where an almost perfect tessellated pavement was found half a century ago. Still older inhabitants raised their huts beside the lake which then covered this valley, and their flint knives and scrapers prove that Great Wymondley was a village even in the Stone Age.

Lo, Now His Glory

HADLEY. Its green was a famous battlefield; its common was a royal hunting ground; its church has a beacon that signalled the coming of the Armada, the only one left in the county.

Linked by Barnet to Greater London, its houses still look on the green where on Easter Sunday in 1471 Edward the Fourth overthrew in battle the earl who had overthrown kings or put them on the throne. So misty it was that one could scarcely see friend or foe, but when the battle was lost and Warwick the Kingmaker tried to escape on horseback, he was followed into these woods and slain. Shakespeare imagines him saying:

> *Lo, now my glory smeared in dust and blood!*
> *My parks, my walks, my manors that I had*

The Imposing South Front

Queen Elizabeth's Court (Carved on a Seat) and her Cradle

The Oriels of the North Front
HATFIELD HOUSE AND ITS TREASURES

The South Porch of Hatfield House

East Gallery of the Great Hall of Hatfield House

King James's Drawing Room

The Wonderful Carved Staircase

HATFIELD HOUSE IN ALL ITS SPLENDOUR

Even now forsake me, and of all my lands
Is nothing left me but my body's length.
Why, what is pomp, rule, reign, but earth and dust?
And live we how we can, yet die we must.

An obelisk set up in 1740 by the Great North Road marks the scene of this battle.

Hadley's Common was made from 200 acres of Enfield Chase, once the king's hunting ground, and it has still its woodland glades, the brook and bridle paths, copper beeches, chestnuts, oaks, and pines, stretching across the valley to Cockfosters and open to all.

The copper beacon which took its share in the flaring ring round England when the Armada sailed is on the tower roof of the church, which, with its aisles and chapels and font, is all mainly 15th century with 19th century alterations. The date 1494 with the curious Arabic 4 is over the tower door to tell when the 15th century finished this rebuilding, and inside are the brass portraits of folk who were here at the time. One of them, John Goodyere, has left his crest of a partridge and a wheat ear carved on two of the pillars, but only his wife's portrait is left. There are two women of the 15th century; a husband and wife of the 16th; William Turnour with his wife and four children in costume of about 1500; and a Jacobean couple, William Gale and his wife, all portrayed in brass. Sir Roger Wilbraham, Solicitor-General of Ireland in Elizabeth's time and founder of almshouses here, appears with other family busts on a marble monument designed by Nicholas Stone.

The Fame of a Country Town

HARPENDEN. It is the country town of great delight, unspoilt by the Industrial Age, with a touch of gold forever on its gorse-clad common, lovely walks through woods and fields, trees in its streets, and an air as sweet and pure as any corner of the British Isles. Its very name means Valley of the Nightingales, and it is worthy of it.

It has little to tell us of history, but Nature has endowed it richly with her bounty—commons, woods, and No Man's Land; streets like avenues, with roofs of houses peeping through the trees; and one of those broad High Streets that have come straight down from Old England, with a strip of green turf along the middle. In the heart of the village, just off the High Street by the green, stands the medieval tower of the church built with flint and plaster in 1470. The church itself was new last century, but it has kept a few memorials from the ancient church, and the font at which Harpenden's babies have been baptised since Norman days; it has a panelled bowl. There are brass portraits of two married couples, William Cressye and his wife in Tudor costume, and William and Isabella Annabull, worn out by being in the floor of the nave for about 500 years. A brass tablet pays tribute to a man who must have been delighted to make this country town his home, for he was one of the most painstaking students of Nature who ever lived, Richard Lydekker. Here he died in 1915, an immense loss to the science of Natural History, for he knew as much as any man about the structure of mammal, bird, and reptile, whether fossil or alive.

The churchyard slopes pleasantly with its limes and cypresses, and pines as high as the tower, and beyond are greens where pink chestnuts, may trees, and copper beeches flaunt themselves gaily as a background to a group of timbered cottages which have been here since Stuart days. On the outskirts of the town, at Hatching Green, is an inn with a Tudor rose and crown on its rough plaster front, and away towards Flamstead is Turner's Hall with the date of 1665 somewhere about it and one wing 400 years old. The memorial to the men who did not come back from the war is a cross in the middle of the green.

A fitting place is Harpenden for natural research, and it has become the home of the greatest agricultural experimental station in the world. It is in the beautiful Rothamsted Park which lies beyond Harpenden Common. Here there was born just before Waterloo, in an old gabled house with medieval timbers and Tudor bricks, Sir John Bennet Lawes, whose family took over the house in the early days of Charles Stuart. He profited little at school or at Oxford, but, being of a purely scientific train of mind, he had a laboratory fitted up in a bedroom here and made himself a master of chemistry. At 21 he inherited the estate, and it happened that his attention was turned to the value of bones as a fertiliser of the soil, and prolonged experiments led him to set up a factory for the production of fertilisers, from which he derived much profit.

All the money he made he spent on his experiments for enriching the soil, and in time he came to develop food for cattle on new and revolutionary lines. He was laying the foundation of scientific agriculture, and men came from all over the world to look into his work. He studied various kinds of drainage, the varying results of fertilisers on different soils, and watched the evolution of new varieties of corn and vegetables. With a chemist friend, Sir Joseph Henry Gilbert, he brought about a great increase in the world's daily bread. They divided the land at Rothamsted into special plots to experiment in all problems of soil, fertility, and crops, and it may be said that nearly every improvement in fertilisers, in wheat selection, or in rotation of crops, was first worked out at Rothamsted.

There is one field here where wheat has been grown continuously since 1843. Lawes carried on his splendid work for more than 50 years, and his jubilee was honoured as that of a man famous throughout civilisation. He was a man of liberal mind, a social reformer, and took great interest in furnishing the village folk with allotments and amenities in those early days. His admirers built him a new laboratory for his jubilee.

In order to ensure the future of his work Sir John founded the Rothamsted Trust, embracing the laboratory and 40 acres of land, and enriched with an endowment of £100,000. All over the world farmers are grateful to Rothamsted, and if that man has blessed his fellows who makes two blades of grass grow where one grew before, John Bennet Lawes must be counted among the incalculable benefactors of mankind. One thing we noticed which gives us an insight into the detail of the work at Rothamsted; we found a bright light shining at night, and discovered that it was meant to trap for examination the insects which play so great a part as friend or foe in agriculture. We were told that as many as 6000 have been caught in the single summer's night.

A Stately Home of England

HATFIELD. It gathers itself about one of the greatest houses in the land, the home of the Cecils, built by the son of Queen Elizabeth's Burghley, whose life was the heart of English history for 40 years. He himself had built the great house of Theobalds, which James the First took from Robert Cecil, giving him Hatfield in exchange. Sir Robert began the building of this marvellous place but never lived in it, for it was no sooner finished than his life was over and they laid him to rest in Hatfield church.

Here is a quiet little street where the old houses seem to mount in steps. It brings us to a delightful group of old buildings, clustering about and within the park. Picturesque cottages and a Georgian house look across to the church in its delightful setting of lawn and trees, carpeted in spring with crocuses and daffodils. At one corner of it is a timbered house, at another are iron gates which have a history, for they stood round St Paul's, the iron having been foundried in Sussex in the days when iron founders were burning down forests instead of digging up coal. These gates were part of half-a-mile of iron railings ordered by Wren for St Paul's, 200 tons of them. They stood in the heart of London till last century, when they were taken down to be sent to Canada. Only a few arrived, for the ship was wrecked and most of the railings now lie in the bed of the Atlantic.

Ending the vista of these buildings along the road is the brick gatehouse of the palace once occupied by the Bishops of Ely; what is left of the palace itself is across a lawn, a fine long range of mellowed brick with gables and a central tower, all 15th century. But a few steps away rises the great Hatfield House, nearly 100 yards long, with two wings projecting to the south, enclosing three sides of the great courtyard.

In Saxon days the land hereabouts belonged to the monks. Here in a few more generations grew up the home of the bishops of Ely, and in the 15th century Cardinal Morton began the building of Hatfield Palace. Brick had then become a popular material for builders, and in this great group of buildings no stone was used. What remains of the palace today is delightful. The gatehouse has ancient beams over its archway and a fine mullioned window above it, and the heavily buttressed west front of the palace itself is impressive, with a square tower, and a charming stepped gable at the end, crowned by a twisted chimney. The great hall remains with magnificent timbers in its roof, the solar and the room below it are intact, and there are splendid walls of open brickwork round the formal gardens. All this is now only the western range of buildings which once surrounded a square courtyard, and we see it as it has been much refashioned in Stuart times, and again last century.

In this great place all three of Henry the Eighth's children spent much of their early years. Edward the Sixth granted it to Elizabeth and she was here when he died, her sister Mary being 12 miles away at Hunsdon. Here Elizabeth received an invitation to go to court to acknowledge Lady Jane Grey as queen. She refused, saying she was ill, but a few days more and she was well enough to go to town to proclaim her sister Mary, riding side by side with her into the City. Here Elizabeth was when Mary died on a grey November morning in 1558, a brilliant cavalcade riding down to Hatfield to bring the news; it is said that she received it under an oak still growing here. A seat here has a carving of Elizabeth with her courtiers.

It was soon after the death of Elizabeth that Robert Cecil came looking round the grounds of the old palace for a site to build a house in place of Theobalds, which King James had coveted so greatly as to insist on changing it for Hatfield. Robert Cecil built the great house but never lived in it, dying before it was ready. It is built like an E in honour of Elizabeth, involving four years of hard work and costing about £40,000 in the money of that day.

It is one of the most magnificent houses in the land, with towers and domes and a marvellous array of windows. Only pictures can give any adequate conception of its splendour. The south porch rises to a great height with fluted columns one above the other and stone lions at the top, the date 1611, and winged cherubs who appear to be dancing round a coronet. Behind this rises the great clock tower with an octagonal cupola over it. The clock tower rises in three styles from the roof of the great hall and has an arch in the lower stage through which a motor car could drive. There are sculptured figures at the corner of the upper stage, which are repeated at the top round the cupola.

The great hall is every inch superb, the east and west walls most richly screened and panelled, the north and south walls tapestried, and the ceiling arranged in compartments each with a painting set in a sculptured frame. The gallery on the east wall is divided into 12 panels, the top half of it open and the lower half like beautiful fretwork. Everywhere the doorways are stately, and the main staircase has probably never been surpassed. Its newel posts are works of art, carved with formal work and figures in relief and crowned with angry lions, fantastic creatures, and beautiful children with musical instruments. Like the hall, the chapel is two storeys high, with galleries on the upper storey from which we have a close view of the grotesque brackets set in the coved and painted ceiling; they are 16th century and were brought from the old Market House at Hoddesdon. The sanctuary is in the bay of a window crowded with Bible scenes, the work of French, Flemish, and English craftsmen in the 17th century. The front of the galleries is arcaded, and panelling covers the walls of the chapel below, which is entered through a handsome modern screen.

Two beautiful galleries run from end to end of the main building, the lower one known as the Cloisters or Armoury (from the suits of armour which stand as if guarding four splendid pieces of 400-year old tapestry), and the upper one known as the Long Gallery which, with its anterooms, is 150 feet long. The ceiling of this gallery is superb, and the panelling which extends from it to the floor is a magnificent example of the reign of King James, especially the upper arcades, decorated with arabesques. Two of the great chimneypieces which are so striking a feature of Hatfield House are here. In the niche of another marble chimneypiece King James presides in great pomp over the room named after him, the ceiling of which is ingeniously decorated with compartments of various shapes, elaborate pendants hanging down.

It need not be said that the house is filled with great possessions. There is the Rainbow portrait of Queen Elizabeth by Zucchero, the death-warrant of Mary Queen of Scots, a letter in her handwriting which can be compared with one of the eight casket letters that led to her doom, Lord Burghley's diary recording the defeat of the Armada, one of Queen Elizabeth's hats and a pair of her stockings, a letter in the queen's handwriting, a manuscript poem by Ben Jonson, a set of Benvenuto Cellini crystals given by Philip of Spain to encourage his suit with Queen Elizabeth, a missal used by Henry the Sixth (with his signature), and an Elizabethan quilt with mottoes and Tudor roses. As for the cradle in which Anne Boleyn is supposed to have rocked the little Elizabeth, it is believed that it is a little too late for that to have happened.

The wonderful park in which this famous group of buildings stands has the River Lea flowing at its northern end, covers 1300 acres, and is seven miles round. The entrance to its grand drive is off the Great North Road, and has four stone pillars crowned by lions holding shields, with beautiful gates and screenwork in which are satyrs, cherubs, and horns of plenty. In front of the gates, looking throughtfully at the traffic passing by, sits one of the famous men of the last generation, the Conservative leader when Mr Gladstone was leading the Liberals to their triumph. He is the third Marquess of Salisbury, Prime Minister of England longer than any other man who has held the office. His statue was set here by his Hertfordshire friends and neighbours, and shows him wearing a mantle and the Order of the Garter; it is by Sir George Frampton.

His marble monument is in Westminster abbey, near the grave of the Unknown Warrior, but he wished to lie here in the little burial ground by the church, and a simple tomb with a cross marks his grave. Inside the church is Sir William Goscombe John's fine bronze of the marquess, showing him lying on a tomb of black marble, wearing a rich mantle with his Order of the Garter, and holding a Crucifix to his breast. Here also is the figure of the first Earl of Salisbury, who built the great house, sculptured in white marble by Simon Basyll. He is in his robes with a ruff, wearing the Garter and holding his staff, his head resting on embroidered cushions. The black marble slab on which he lies is borne on the shoulders of four white women representing the Virtues, two sitting and two kneeling on a black marble base. Below, under the marble shelf on which the earl lies, is a marble skeleton after the fashion of those days, a reminder that rank and power pass away and all are equal in the tomb. On the floor of the chapel are two memorials in stone, one the 12th century figure of a knight with a great shield, the other believed to be William Curle, Warden of the royal estate at Hatfield. This Salisbury chapel, built by the first earl's spendthrift son, is arresting with its classical arcade dividing it from the chancel, and lovely screens of delicate 18th century ironwork looking like lacework. The 19th century decoration is the work of Italian craftsmen. The walls have marble wainscoting, and both walls and ceiling are painted with the Four Evangelists, the parable of the Wise and Foolish Virgins, and representations of the Virtues. Here lies a second Prime Minister, Lord Melbourne, with his wife Lady Caroline Lamb; their grave is under the modern pulpit. One of the chapel windows is in memory of the mother of another Prime Minister, Lord Balfour.

In the south chapel are monuments of the Brockets and the Reades. The chapel was built at the close of the 13th century, and enlarged in the 15th when the arcade was set up dividing it from the chancel; it has capitals of angels holding shields. In its west wall is a 13th century arch to the transept and a 15th century doorway, and it has modern paintings of roses on its old roof beams. Here is the canopied tomb of Sir John Brocket, a merchant at the time of the Armada; he was a soldier too, and his helmet hangs above his monument. Near him are two ladies lying stiffly one above the other, both with lifelike complexions, both wearing black dresses with white ruffs and cuffs, and one holding her gloves and resting her hand on a skull. One of the two is Sir John's second wife, and the other is her mother, Dame Agnes Sanders. On an 18th century monument are busts of Sir James and Sir John Reades, father and son, with a medallion portrait of Sir James's daughter. They lived at Brocket Hall, which at their death passed to the Lambs and became the home of Lord Melbourne. It is a fine red house in a park three miles away, bounded by the great North Road.

The church, one of the biggest in the county, is striking in its plan, the eastern half with chapels and transepts contrasting with the aisleless nave, which is spanned by a great modern roof with dormers doing duty as clerestory windows. It was built in the 13th century on an older site, but in the restoration of 1871 the nave was rebuilt, the rest of the walls were given new stonework, and the window tracery was renewed. New porches were built with timber from the old roofs, and the transepts, like the south chapel, keep most of their old beams. The massive tower and the arch leading from it to the nave are 500 years old. The south transept has the oldest work to show; coming from early in the 13th century are a blocked lancet and a recess in its east wall, and a beautiful round-headed arch leading to its small west chapel, the mouldings deeply cut and the capitals carved with leaves. The chancel has a modern arch, and a reredos of alabaster and gold mosaic with a white marble Crucifixion scene, showing the three women and St John, and a saint on each side. There are Jacobean altar rails, an ironbound chest of 1692, an old pillar almsbox, a modern font with a 13th

The Stepped Gable

The Great Hall

The Buttressed Walls and the Lofty Porch

HATFIELD'S OLD PALACE

Hatfield   **The Third Lord Salisbury at the Entrance Gates**

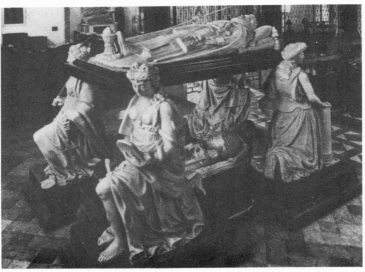

Hatfield   **The First Lord Salisbury's Monument**

century base, and a silver processional cross with the Twelve Disciples round the base. The lovely silver candlesticks and cross in the south chapel were fashioned from plate given to General Lindsay by five other Generals for his service in the House of Commons, and are now a memorial to his wife and daughter. The altar cloth of red plush embroidered with gold, was part of the pall at George the Third's funeral, and the brass candelabra is 1733. A treasure of the church is a piece of beautiful embroidery of roses and fruit in delicate colour and gold, of remarkable interest because it is said to have been worked by Queen Elizabeth when she was at the palace. A curious thing is an old brass box which may be called a forerunner of the automatic machine. In the days of the churchwarden pipe it was at the inn, and when a penny was put in the slot and a knob pressed down the lid opened for the pipe to be filled with the tobacco within it. Now we give a penny to the organ fund to see the lid fly open as of old.

There are shields of old glass. A lovely Whall window in the nave, showing Angels of the Passion, their wings red, blue, and gold, is a tribute to three of the Gascoyne-Cecils (sons of the Bishop of Exeter who was rector here) who fell in the Great War. The ornaments on the chancel altar are in memory of two others who fell. To those who fell in the South African War, the east window of the south chapel has figures of Our Lord holding the Cross, soldiers kneeling, St George and St Alban, Fortitude, and Mercy. A window designed by Burne-Jones has saints and small scenes illustrating the Virtues, in heavy colouring.

The Cecils

THE great family of Cecils comes into fame and history with William Cecil, Lord Burghley, whose father was in high favour with Henry the Eighth, and who himself came into power with the Protector Somerset, whose disgrace he shared, so that he was thrown into the Tower for two months. But he was too clever a man to be behind a lock and key, and was soon made Secretary of State. Wise beyond his years, he saw, even so long ago as the 16th century, that free trade was the secret of a rich and powerful England, and he sought to establish it. When Mary Tudor came to the throne he became a Roman Catholic for convenience, but he settled down under

H   97

Queen Elizabeth, who made him her chief minister in 1558 and left him at the head of affairs for 40 years. For all that time the story of Lord Burghley was the story of England. He was Chancellor of the Cambridge University, was responsible for the execution of Mary Queen of Scots, and all that he did is told in the prolific correspondence preserved in the archives at Hatfield House.

His son Robert Cecil, who became the first earl, was known as the crookback earl. He did two notable things—he built Hatfield House and he secured the accession of James the Sixth of Scotland to the English throne, so launching the Stuarts on their disastrous way. He died deeply in debt.

Lord Burghley's son Thomas became the first Earl of Exeter, and is said to have been a dissolute fellow, but he became a good soldier and fought the Armada, helped to crush the Essex rebellion, and was a benefactor of Clare College, Cambridge.

The great Lord Salisbury of the last generation lived from before the Victorian Era into our own century. He was the third marquess. He went into Parliament at 23, wrote leading articles for a London daily that has now disappeared, and is remembered largely because he was the Conservative leader during Mr Gladstone's triumphant career of Liberalism. He was not to be compared with his great rival. He had little sympathy with democracy or reformers, and it was his own leader Disraeli (with whom he went to Berlin for the peace congress) who called him a great master of jibes, flouts, and jeers. But he was a commanding figure, was much interested in science, and was counted a successful leader of his party.

A Majestic Norman Monument

HEMEL HEMPSTEAD. Very much alive and still growing is this market town, whose houses stretch for a mile and more down to the River Gade, where it had flourishing mills in Saxon times; the Conqueror's Domesday mentions the delicious eels found in the river here.

To this ancient importance it owes its church, a majestic example of Norman architecture, raised on land belonging to Thomas Becket, with Roman bricks among its flint rubble. The only additions to it in 800 years have been two medieval porches and the 19th century vestries, though the exquisite leaded spire, rising to 200 feet on the central tower, may not have been built till the 13th or 14th century. It is this shining spire which draws us from the country round and guides us as we climb the narrowing street, glimpsing weathered roofs through the deep archways breaking the line of shops, and seeing through one archway the wooden balcony from which men have watched for 300 years the comings and goings in the courtyard of the King's Arms.

We come to the church by the town hall, behind which it stands in a churchyard so full of flowerbeds, with a greenhouse here and seats there, that it looks, as a churchyard should, like a public garden. Grouped round the massive central tower are two transepts, a nave with two aisles, and a vaulted chancel with a little chamber opening out of it, one of the earliest sacristies. All this is the work of the Normans, whose four massive tower arches and great arcades, all deeply carved, make a grand and dignified array. On one of the capitals of their beautiful west doorway a quaint Adam struggles with the serpent while Eve stands by with staring eyes. Some of the carving round this doorway was added two or three centuries later, and the font's Norman simplicity has tempted a carver nearer our own day to spoil it with his little figures. The Norman clerestory lights up the plain nave roof, 500 years old like the more handsome transept roofs. The chancel roof should be noted; it is one of the finest examples of Norman ribbed vaulting.

We may climb up the steps of the tower, pulling ourselves up by niches cut to help climbers centuries ago, for it is a steep way, but worth it to see the great cylinder studded with short spikes, like an old barrel organ, which has been playing eight tunes as clock chimes since 1761. Other treasured possessions of the church are an edition of Foxe's Book of Martyrs published in 1610, a 400-year-old chest, a medieval stone coffin, an Elizabethan chalice, and perfect registers back to the opening of Queen Elizabeth's reign. One of the bells first rang out in that reign, and four more were made in Stuart days. The big brass portrait of Margaret Albyn is much older, showing her husband in armour of the end of the 14th century and her inscription written in old French. Another inscription mourns Richard Combe and his son who died in 1692 "the father's first, the family's last"; the ruined porch with a room over it just outside the churchyard is a fragment of their home.

Here is a memorial of Sir Astley Cooper, John Hunter's pupil and the most eminent surgeon of his day, who came to rest at Hemel Hempstead after a strenuous and successful life. He once said that if he laid his head on the pillow at night without having dissected something during the day he would think that day lost. Once he had a fee of a thousand guineas tossed to him in a nightcap by a grateful patient; but it was a small operation on George the Fourth which gained him his baronetcy. He doctored horses as well as kings, bringing many a poor worn-out animal to recover in his grounds at Gadesbridge.

Near the church are two delightful cottages of brick and timber, 300 years old, known for some reason as Henry's Banqueting Hall. Their plaster overmantels are sprinkled with Tudor roses, crowns, and fleurs-de-lys. Lockers, the house on Bury Hill with an Elizabethan wing, has plaster ceilings liberally sprinkled with lions and unicorns, a king's head, and the royal arms.

Two great churchmen have been born in this old country town, one much admired by James the First, the other openly disapproving of Charles the Second. Richard Field was born here in 1561 and was for a long time rector of Burghclere in Hampshire, his sermons drawing crowds and leading King James to remark: "This is indeed a field for God to dwell in." His brass portrait is on his grave in St George's Chapel, Windsor, where he occasionally preached to the king, who exclaimed on hearing of his death: "I should have done more for that man." Nicholas Stratford, a tailor's son born here in 1663, preferred to resign his wardenship of the collegiate church of Manchester rather than approve of Charles the Second's policy, but the Revolution brought him back into favour as Bishop of Chester. He was a notable reformer, and established a school for poor boys at Chester, where he lies in the cathedral.

Domesday Book mentions the mills of Hemel Hempstead, and there is a paper mill at Apsley End which gained a 19th century reputation by supplying the Government with the paper for our early postage stamps. One of the Dickinsons, its owners, discovered how to make paper in a continuous sheet, and so made possible the enormous editions of our daily newspapers; and the mill is also notable because of its association for a whole lifetime with one of the most remarkable men of last century, Sir John Evans. He was one of the partners of the mills, which were founded by his uncle, and it was in his spare time that he did the marvellous work which made him famous as an archaelogist. We come upon him at Abbot's Langley, where he lies.

At the Meeting of Three Rivers

HERTFORD. It is the friendly heart of this delightful county, the capital of its 150 villages and towns, standing at the meeting of three rivers. It has gathered itself about an ancient castle for which it pays Lord Salisbury half a crown a year, and we may think the rent not excessive as we walk about the lovely grounds, bounded on one side by the Lea and on two others by Norman walls.

The castle is in the heart of the town; a step from the street and we are here. It is, of course, the oldest building, having been the home of Saxon kings more than 12 centuries ago, and in 673 there came here a group of men whom we may imagine to have been among the most important people in England in those days, the head of the English Church, called together by Theodore of Tarsus, first Primate of all England. It was the first National Synod held by the Church in this country, and a stone on the wall of the east terrace of the castle has been set up as a memorial of the event. After this peaceful conference came the warlike Danes and burned the castle down, and it was after the tragic visit of the Danes that Alfred's son Edward built his castle on the mound we see. Edward's building disappeared and the castle was raised to the height of its power in the days of the Normans, though nothing remains of their great structure except the walls around, built of flint rubble, brick, and stone. In the centre of the grounds stands the old brick gatehouse of the castle, with an embattled parapet, corner turrets, and an arcaded corbel table of the 15th century, though the whole front has been much altered; it has been a private house and is now used for public purposes.

In the old days a double moat filled by the River Lea encircled the castle for an area of 800 feet by 500 at its farthest points. In Norman days the King of France besieged it, Queen Isabella lived and died here, her son Edward the Third appointing a guard of 14 poor persons at twopence a day to watch over her body for three months. David Bruce, King of Scotland, was a captive here for eleven years, and in 1356 the Black Prince brought home a companion from Poitiers, no less a person than King John of France, whom he had captured there. But the most stirring event of all within these walls was the visit of Henry Bolingbroke, who here drew up his indictment of King Richard the Second:

> *Ah, Richard, with the eyes of heavy mind*
> *I see thy glory like a shooting star*
> *Fall to the base earth from the firmament.*

The charges brought against the king were set down here on paper, the paper Shakespeare tells us Richard refused to read:

> *Mine eyes are full of tears, I cannot see:*
> *And yet salt water blinds them not so much*
> *But they can see a sort of traitors here.*

The town has quaint streets with old houses mixed up with much that spoils it. Some of the houses are 15th century, many of them timbered and whitewashed. Lombard House on the River Lea was built of plaster, timber, and brick early in the 17th century, and the front overlooking the river remains as it was, though the main front has been refaced. It has an overhanging storey, wood mullions at the windows, and five gables, and a tablet tells us that here lived Sir Henry Chauncy, the 17th century judge who wrote the History of Hertfordshire; it was he who declared Jane Wenham to be a witch, sending her for the trial at which she was sentenced to death, though Queen Anne reprieved her and the case led to the abolition of witchcraft from the Statute Book. Near the Shire Hall are 16th century houses with ornamental plaster work on the front, and by the churchyard of All Saints is a delightful little 17th century building of mellowed red brick, with a cupola and original chimneys. It was the old grammar school, whose headmaster lived in the 18th century in a charming house still standing on the other side of the churchyard. The school was founded in 1617 by Richard Hale, and keeps its original doorway, in which hangs an old door with 1667 worked in nails, though the door is believed to be half a century older than that.

The most famous school in the town is Christ's Hospital School for Girls, a delightful irregular block of buildings of varying dates, bought by the governors of Christ's Hospital for younger children in 1683. Much of the 17th century buildings remain, including the gateway and some garden walls. There are quaint Bluecoat scholars set about the walls, five in all, attractive painted figures representing boys and girls, though boys have now been removed to Horsham and Hertford is reserved for girls. Over the main doorway is an oak figure of a bluecoat boy brought here from an old school at Ware, and there are four other figures on the gateposts and in niches on the two wings, fashioned in lead and painted, showing boys and girls in their famous costumes looking down on the street. They have been here since 1697. The school has a fine chapel built in our own century.

The Shire Hall is 18th century and was designed by the Adam brothers, though we should hardly believe it, for it lacks their usual grace. In it hang portraits of our royal Hanoverians and famous men of Hertfordshire, among them being a portrait of Charles James Fox by Sir Joshua Reynolds.

At a meeting of the streets not far from the castle stands the most striking monument in Hertford, the memorial of the men who fell in the war. The architectural scheme was designed by Sir Aston Webb, and the bronze figure of a stag was modelled by Alfred Drury; it is very striking. Not far away, set in a wall outside the library, is a drinking fountain built from fragments of one of the four churches which have disappeared from the town; they are from St Mary the Great, and include a 13th century window with detached shafts. Hertford has lost all its old churches, but has two new ones of much interest.

Across the Lea is St Andrew's, with a timbered Jacobean house beside it, attractive with an overhanging storey and two dormer windows. The church, built last century, has a handsome tower with a graceful spire rising 130 feet. We come in by a medieval doorway decorated with angels holding shields, probably brought from St Mary's. From St Mary's also have come two of the most interesting possessions of the church, an exquisite alabaster carving of the Madonna and Child nine inches high, and an altar stone five inches thick, with five consecration crosses and a recess believed to have been made for holding relics. Both these are in the chapel, where the altar frontal has worked into it a beautiful Mohammedan prayer mat. The east window of the chancel has six fine figures (St Alban in Roman armour, Nicholas with the three golden balls, the Madonna and St John, St Andrew, and St Theodore); and another window has Gabriel in rich red wings bringing the good news to the Madonna.

A tablet on the walls pays tribute to Nathaniel Dimsdale, son of a great friend of the town who was one of the pioneers of inoculation against smallpox, Thomas Dimsdale, who lies at Bishop's Stortford. Thomas was summoned to Russia to inoculate the Empress Catherine and her son, being received with some fear and trembling lest things should go wrong, but as they went right being loaded with riches and honour. The empress gave him thousands of pounds and £500 a year, and made him a Baron of all the Russias.

All Saints stands on the site of a church burned down towards the end of last century. It is built of red stone and has a handsome tower with ten bells. The churchyard has a magnificent avenue of limes and chestnuts, planted in the time of Charles the Second, and unrivalled in this countryside. A tall column among the graves marks the last resting-place of Sir Edward Pearson, a nephew of the first Lord Cowdray; he built the docks and the breakwater at Malta. On one of the gravestones we read of a woman as unrivalled as these chestnuts in whose shade she lies, for we are told that for 38 years she was so kind and loving a wife that she never gave her husband an angry word. Her name was Sarah Young. The east window, in rich colours, represents Our Lord as the Vine, and has fifty figures. The church has four interesting memorials: a peace memorial designed by Sir Reginald Blomfield to the men of the Hertfordshire Regiment; a tablet to Charles Bridgeman who played the organ in the old church for the remarkable period of 81 years, a tablet in memory of Frederick Rainer, founder of the Police Court Mission, and a brass inscription perhaps more interesting than all, for it is dated 1435 and is in memory of the cook to Henry the Fifth's Catherine, who lived at the castle; it is ironic to see that her cook's name was Master John Hunger.

Hertford's Museum is built up from the collections of two brothers named Andrews, who gave their antiquities to the town at the beginning of this century. There are many curious old-fashioned things, among which we remember a primitive mangle, and the 500-year-old market bell of the town, and with these are rubbings of brasses in churches, old Hertfordshire views and portraits, and a portrait of Dickens by his daughter, Kate Perugini. There are some of the original electric telegraph instruments patented by G. E. Dering in 1854, an orrery invented by Jeremiah Cleeve at Welwyn, 17th

Lemsford   **A Scene by the Lea**

Tewin   **The River Maran**

The Peace Memorial in the Heart of the Town

Old Houses in St Andrew's Street
HERTFORD, THE COUNTY CAPITAL

Barnet   Chequered Tower

King's Langley 15th Century Tower

Hertford   **All Saints Church**

Watford   The Morrison Monuments Carved by Nicholas Stone

Hertingfordbury   Sir William and Lady Harrington

THREE OF HERTFORDSHIRE'S OLD MONUMENTS

century altar rails from Little Hormead's church, and panels from a screen 600 years old.

A little way out of the town is a splendid modern house in Tudor style called Goldings, with a long range of gables and mullioned windows, and a handsome chapel added in 1924; it is one of the technical schools of Dr Barnardo's Homes and is equipped for training hundreds of boys to be useful craftsmen and decent citizens.

Like many other proud towns Hertford is gathering to itself the neighbours round about it, and it has brought within the range of its local authorities the six villages of Bengeo, Bramfield, Brickendon, Bayford, Hertingfordbury, and Little Amwell. They are its civic children but they live their own lives and are villages still, and we deal with them under their own names.

In a field not far away, on the road to Ware, occurred one of the critical events in the life of Cromwell.

Cromwell and the Mutineers

ON the day the news reached Parliament that Charles Stuart had arrived at Carisbrooke Castle in flight from Hampton Court Cromwell and Fairfax held a review of their army on a field near Hertford. It was November 15, 1647.

The climax had been reached of a long agitation among the soldiers who had captured the king at Holdenby House and brought him to London. Cromwell was then willing to reinstate Charles if he would submit to the army's demand for religious toleration and would rule constitutionally; but, while the king intrigued and the Commons argued, a mutinous spirit began to show itself in the army. A political sect called the Levellers won vast numbers of the troops to their scheme for a purely democratic government, the abolition of all privileges of rank and birth, and the establishment of perfect equality of all citizens before the law.

About a week before the king's flight to Carisbrooke a deputation of the soldiers handed to Fairfax two papers, *The Case of the Army* and *The Agreement of the People*, demanding a new constitution in the form of a Republic, household suffrage with elections every three years, freedom from forced service in time of war, and complete liberty of conscience. Fairfax placed these papers before Parliament, which denounced them and asked him as Commander-in-Chief to suppress the agitators forthwith. He therefore ordered the greater part of the army to assemble for review in Corkbush Field on the banks of the Lea between Ware and Hertford.

The morning of November 15 found Fairfax and Cromwell, with half the members of both Houses of Parliament, riding to Ware, forgetting the flight of the king in their concern about a more immediate danger, a mutinous army. The regiments summoned were drawn up in the field, but with them were two detachments which had not been invited, a regiment of cavalry under Colonel Harrison, a stern republican, and a brigade of foot commanded by John Lilburne, leader of the Levellers. These two bodies were in a buzz of excitement, and every officer and man had stuck on his helmet a copy of *The Agreement of the People*.

With Cromwell and the Council of Officers beside him, General Fairfax calmly but firmly addressed the troops, pointing out the danger of sedition among those whose highest duty was obedience. Parliament, he concluded, would meet their just demands if the soldiers would sign a promise to return to discipline. All except Lilburne's brigade cheered the speech, Harrison's troopers tearing the Agreement from their helmets. Shouts of angry protest were raised by Lilburne's brigade, and no pleading by Fairfax would move the obstinate soldiers.

Suddenly Cromwell sprang forward, shouting angrily above the swelling tumult "Take that paper from your hats." His order was not obeyed and the men became threatening, whereupon, unable to contain himself any longer, Cromwell dashed into the mutinous ranks ordering the seizure of the ringleaders. Eleven of these were arrested without resistance by their comrades, and a courtmartial was held on the spot, three being condemned to be shot for riot and sedition. Fairfax, however, pleaded for leniency, and the court decided that one man only should die, the three drawing lots. The fatal lot fell to Richard Arnell, a brave soldier but a resolute republican, who was shot in front of the whole assembly. He faced the muskets of his comrades without flinching, and called for the liberty of England with his last breath.

Four days later Oliver rose from his seat in the Commons and reported that the army was sound, whereupon both Houses passed him a vote of thanks.

The Cowpers

HERTINGFORDBURY. With its pleasant 17th century manor house and the school where the village children have learned their lessons for 300 years, it is an arresting picture by the River Maran, whose waters saunter through Panshanger Park, home of the Cowpers for two centuries and of Lord Desborough when we called. The much restored church, with its 15th century tower and its copper spire, overlooks the village from a hill just high enough for us to see the Bayford woods across a wide valley. A line of yews links the porch with a 19th century sedilia removed from the church to make a seat in the churchyard, and six chestnuts rival the height of the tower. Inside the tower are two altar tombs with figures from Stuart days. On one is Anne Calvert, in a ruff and a richly embroidered dress; on the other are Sir William Harrington and his wife, white figures in shrouds, with their little daughter kneeling by them in Jacobean dress.

The Cowper Chapel, entered by gates of delicate hammered iron-work, was added last century, and handsome woodwork and marble tell of rich benefactors in more recent years. Most of the oak seats were carved by Joseph Mayer at Oberammergau. There is no monument to William, first Earl Cowper, who was buried here in 1723, but he lives on in fame as the Lord High Chancellor who made himself unpopular by refusing the customary gifts offered to the new occupant of the Woolsack. Though the Chancellor has no monument, his brother Spencer, the only British judge to stand in the dock on trial for murder, is here in striking relief by Roubiliac, dignified in his judge's robe and wig. It was when he was a barrister that he and three other lawyers were charged with murdering Sarah Stout, a Hertford girl who had lost her heart to him; but the trial proved that she had drowned herself because her love was not returned. He was the grandfather of the poet, whose father is also buried here.

The second earl has for his monument an angel ten feet high pointing to his portrait in relief. In the centre of the chapel is an altar tomb with the stately bearded figure in marble of the last earl, who was Lord Lieutenant of Ireland during the stormy period of Mr Gladstone's Ministry in the early eighties, but was happier as a student of literature, or when beautifying Panshanger Park. Another angel, standing with a tall cross under a yew in the churchyard, mourns the last Countess Cowper.

Sir Frederick Ouseley, the composer, who also made Panshanger his home, laid his father Sir Gore Ouseley to rest in the church in 1844; his tablet tells us that he was Ambassador to Persia, but he was much more than that, for to him we owe much of our knowledge of the literature of Persia and India. It was he who in 1813 arranged a peace between Russia and Persia, and helped Henry Martyn, the missionary from Truro, to produce his Persian translation of the New Testament. When Sir Gore Ouseley brought his son to be baptised in this church the Duke of York and the Duke of Wellington were the godfathers.

Panshanger House is of last century, rather unimpressive in spite of its battlements, but with grounds of rare beauty crossed by avenues and abounding with trees of every kind. There is a giant oak on the lawn. Gilbert White came from Selborne to see it; Arthur Young described it in 1709, when it was reckoned to contain over 300 cubic feet of timber, which had increased to 1000 cubic feet when it was engraved in a book on trees a century ago. Though it now shows signs of wearying from its age, its giant boughs form a circle of over 100 yards round the 20 feet trunk, and its foliage rises in perfect symmetry.

To Hertingfordbury came Jane Wenham of Walkern, the last woman in England sentenced to death for witchcraft, for the kind-hearted Squire Plumer of Gilston supported her in a cottage here after Queen Anne had pardoned the poor woman, and when the squire died Earl Cowper continued to look after her.

A Very Strange Case

IT was one of the strangest murder trials on record in which Spencer Cowper found himself involved, standing in the dock at the assize court at Hertford in 1699 to answer for the death of a young Quaker lady named Sarah Stout. Charged with him were two lawyers and a scrivener, who were alleged to have aided him in the crime.

Cowper had attended the March assizes of the same year as a barrister and went to visit the Stouts, to whom he had to pay the interest on a mortgage he had arranged for them; and he agreed to stay the night. Although he was married, pretty Sarah Stout was in love with him.

That night the two lawyers and the scrivener went from their lodgings to a Hertford inn, and made a night of it, and one was heard to say, "Marson, Sarah Stout was an old friend of yours." "Aye," replied he, "but she has cast me off, but I reckon by this time a friend of mine has done her business. I believe a friend of mine is with her by this time."

Meanwhile Cowper was at the Stout's and after supper sat talking to the young lady till eleven o'clock when, according to the prosecution, orders were given to the maid to warm his bed. The girl went upstairs to do so, but suddenly heard a door slam and on returning to the sitting room found that Cowper and Sarah Stout were gone. Neither returned that night. Next morning Sarah Stout was found dead in the river near the mill, floating on the surface. There was a crease round her neck and she was bruised about her ear. The prosecution said the girl was not drowned, but had been first murdered and then thrown into the water, and they asserted that Cowper and the three men charged with him were the murderers.

Doctor after doctor swore that none but a drowned person would sink; and two sailors fresh from sea battles and wrecks, with experience of hundreds of bodies alive and dead in the water, were called to give similar testimony.

The defence was that the woman was drowned, that her body did not float but was held up by stakes in the river, that a coroner's jury had already found a verdict of suicide. There was no crease round the neck, they said.

But to counterbalance the doctors and sailors Sir Hans Sloane and other famous doctors from London proved that dead bodies, animal or human, do sink in water. Cowper had left the house long before the poor girl went out and drowned herself.

The summing-up of the judge was as strange as anything in Shakespeare or in Dickens. "Truly, gentlemen (he said), these men have given great cause of suspicion by their talking, but whether they or Mr Cowper are guilty or no, that you are to determine. I am sensible that I have omitted many things, but I am a little faint and cannot remember any more of the evidence." All four were acquitted, and it has since appeared that the whole secret was that the Tories of Hertford wished to hang a member of a famous Whig family, while the Quakers, to clear their community of reproach, had done all they could to clear the girl's name. The entire county was stirred by pamphlets, and the excitement was increased when relatives of the demented girl appealed and demanded the right of Ordeal by Battle. The issue was in doubt for a year, when the court held that the whole prosecution was malicious and fined the under-sheriff of Hertfordshire heavily, sending him to prison for a gross irregularity in the proceedings. Cowper attained high honour in his profession, and the poet was his grandson.

In the Shadow of the Hills

HEXTON. We may wonder if any village in the county has a more delightful setting than this. It lies in the shadow of the Barton Hills (a group of the Chilterns) and we came to it by a street paved with gold, for the laburnums on each side had just showered their bloom. Dark yews surround the church, which inherits from the 15th century its tower and a roof supported by gilded wooden angels. There is a handsome 18th century double-decker seat for the priest and the clerk, and a pulpit to match. A king smiles from one of the arcades, and a woman weeps for Josep de Latour, a Guardsman who rebuilt the church nine years after Waterloo. There is a record that the church was dedicated to St Faith early in the 12th century, but it was long before the days of records that men built the earthwork fort of Ravensburgh Castle on a spur of these hills, nearly 500 feet up. Trees now screen the ramparts, which still rise nearly 20 feet high, enclosing more than twenty acres of this steep hillside.

The White Ensign

HIGH CROSS. It is only a hamlet on the Old North Road, but it spans the years from the time when Caesar's fleet patrolled our shores to the days when HMS Achilles sank a German raider in the Great War. The white ensign flown by the Achilles in the war hangs in the church, and on a memorial below the flag are the names of a boat's crew who perished in the fight. It is the most striking possession of this 19th century church.

Making his home here when we called we found the only living man who had won the VC twice, Colonel Arthur Martin-Leake, a surgeon who first won his VC with Baden-Powell in South Africa, and won it again in the Great War for the same devotion to wounded under heavy fire.

At Youngsbury, south of High Cross, is a fine Georgian mansion ringed by trees, with grounds in which the remains of a Roman house were found about two hundred years ago. There are two ancient burial mounds near by.

The Home of Robert Clutterbuck

HINXWORTH. Old Robert Clutterbuck, who devoted years to making a history of his beloved Hertfordshire, lived at Hinxworth Place, a perfect home for an antiquarian, for this stone house was built in the 15th and 16th centuries, with mullioned windows of old glass, pointed doorways, and panelled walls set in a lovely garden—all within a mile of the thatched cottages and the quaint clock tower of the village among the elms. Happily its beauty is safe, for it belongs to the county council, and every passer-by may feel that he shares its freehold. Here Robert Clutterbuck toiled for 18 years on his three volumes of Hertfordshire, published over a period of 12 years, beginning at the time of Waterloo. It has been said that the plates in his work have never been surpassed in such a publication.

Reached by a shady field path, where two Lombardy poplars frame a distant view of the Essex hills and limes form a double guard to the door, is a church of about the time of Agincourt, with a Tudor clerestory and a rebuilt chancel. In the 15th century porch we found a stone coffin lid 600 years old. Four ancient oak angels stand out darkly against the newer roof, and canopied stone niches make beautiful two windowsills. Excelling in beauty is a brass on the chancel floor, a superb portrait of John Lambard, Master of the Mercers Company, buried here in 1497. His wife, their daughter, and three sons, are with him in elegant dress. An earlier unknown couple who would know this church when it was new 500 years ago have their brass portraits on the wall.

At Hinxworth was found a Venus brought here by some art-loving Roman in the days of the Caesars, whose coins have also been found in plenty; and a gravel pit older than the Romans has yielded traces of four distinct British tribes.

Old-World Everywhere

HITCHIN. It is old-world England wherever we turn in this small town, with one of England's smallest rivers flowing by Hertfordshire's biggest church. It is the River Hiz, ten miles long. The streets are attractive with old houses, some so low that we may touch the eaves from the pavements, and there are three groups of attractive almshouses, 16 in the street called Bancroft, glowing in the sunshine behind pretty gardens; the Skynner almshouses of the 17th century; and, most delightful of all, the Biggin almshouses by the church and by the river, a mellow group of tiled and gabled roofs and leaded windows looking out on a courtyard enclosed by a cloister with wooden columns, and with medieval stones from a nunnery built into the walls. The Hermitage is an irregular building linked up with a 16th century timbered barn. In its garden are traces of ancient cultivated terraces.

Church House was at one time a school, and one of its school-masters was Eugene Aram; it is said that the vicar, Pilkington Morgan, once preached before him on divine retribution. A house called Mount Pleasant, standing on the higher ground of the town, was the birthplace in 1559 of the famous George Chapman, and has on it a tablet reminding us of his claim to immortality. It was here during Shakespeare's day that Chapman produced an enormous output of comedies, tragedies, and poems, though he is chiefly remembered now not for the plays with which he collaborated with Ben Jonson, but for the translation of Homer which so stirred Keats, as he tells us in that sonnet beginning:

> *Much have I travelled in the realms of gold,*
> *And many goodly states and kingdoms seen.*

This is the inscription on the tablet on Chapman's birthplace:

> *The learned shepherd of fair Hitchin Hill, as his young contemporary William Browne describes him in his Britannia's Pastorals, himself records in The Teares of Peace that it was while he was "on the Hill next Hitchin's hand" the shade of Homer filled his bosom with a "floode of soule."*

The great medieval church, with a little Garden of Rest beside it is rich in craftsmanship of the 14th and 15th century. Its tower is older still, for it stands on Norman foundations and has Roman

The Massive Tower

The Lovely Medieval Font

South Chapel Screen

The Magnificent Porch

HITCHIN'S IMPRESSIVE CHURCH

Harpenden   **Church with Medieval Tower**

Harpenden   **Rothamsted**

Hitchin   **Hitchin Priory by the River Hiz**

bricks in it. Its doorway is 13th century. Though Hitchin was a home of Nonconformity, it would seem that the congregation at this church was glad to have the Stuarts back, for the sundial on the wall of the tower has a Latin inscription reading, *In the year of security 1660.* The porch is magnificent, with many niches filled with statues 400 years ago. It has two storeys, with pinnacles crowning the walls, and a carving of the Holy Trinity over the doorway. The vaulted roof has carved bosses, and a room above it (now a small museum) has in it a 14th century tile of a man with his right arm across his chest and his left arm pointing upwards, supposed to be the builder of the church. The door opening for us into the church has been swinging on its hinges 500 years. The font is of the same age, and has 12 sides on each of which is the figure of a saint under a beautiful canopy; its cover is like a lovely spire.

It is an impressive interior into which we come. Most of the roofs are 500 years old, with wooden angels looking down from them into the chapels, and among the stone corbels are portraits of Edward the Third and his Queen Philippa, a beggar feeding from a bowl, and an angel and a demon both whispering into the ears of a girl. The roof of the north aisle is partly older still, the elaborate cusping in its panels being the work of a 14th century craftsman. The screens are striking and beautiful, particularly the 15th century screen of the south chapel, which has a central bay with two bays on each side, all with lovely window tracery, a row of quatrefoiled arches and shields above them, and over this a cresting of angels. The work of the medieval craftsman is also in some of the bench-ends of the chancel and in the traceried panels of the pulpit. The unusual length of the chancel is one of the striking features of the church. Hanging on a wall is a painting of the Adoration of the Wise Men which is said to be by Rubens.

The church has a big collection of brasses, most of them worn and of unknown people. On the floor of the chancel are portraits of a 15th century priest, James Hert, an unknown merchant of 1452 with his wife and ten children, and another unknown with his wife in shrouds and their eight children.

In the south aisle Margery Beel is engraved with her eight children and in the nave is a civilian with three wives and another unknown family of ten, all of the 16th century. Against the wall of the north chapel are three 15th century tombs in a row, one having the brass portraits of a man and his wife, the second a man with his wife in shrouds, and a third with the name of John Poulter, a draper.

An unknown 13th century knight in the nave, much worn after 700 years, lies on the windowsill of the aisle leading to the north chapel, and there are two other marble figures here of a knight and his lady in 14th century costume. The first of these figures is believed to represent Bernard Baliol, great-grandfather of the founder of Balliol College, and the knight with his wife is Edward de Kendale, who fought at Crecy and Poitiers and helped to quell the disorders in Hertfordshire which followed the Black Death. In the south chapel are the memorials to the Radcliffe family, who lived in Hitchin for 12 generations; the east window showing Christ stilling the waters is in memory of one of them. Two other windows are notable, one in memory of three brothers, John, Frank, and William Hawkins, benefactors of the town, the other the peace memorial window, showing St George in gold armour, Christ red-robed and crowned, and the Archangel Michael in silver grey. Below these figures are panels of St George slaying the dragon, Satan cast out of Heaven, and St Andrew. There is another peace memorial in the churchyard, a tall cross with the name of 336 heroes on its base, among them F. E. Young, who won the VC. In a heavy barrage he rescued two men who had been captured, and himself silenced a machine gun. He made it possible for his battalion to hold a line of great value, and was last seen fighting hand to hand against a number of the enemy a few weeks before the war ended.

An interesting man lies under the south aisle, Captain Robert Hind, the original of Laurence Sterne's Uncle Toby in Tristram Shandy. Who does not remember Uncle Toby and the corporal at the lieutenant's deathbed, the corporal insisting that he must die, Uncle Toby insisting that he shall live?

"He shall not die, by God," cried my Uncle Toby. *The Accusing Spirit, which flew up to heaven's chancery with the oath, blushed as he gave it in; and the Recording Angel, as he wrote it down, dropped a tear upon the word and blotted it out for ever.*

Hitchin has a modern church founded by the first vicar, George Gainsford, and built in 1865 by the well-known architect William Butterfield. It has much interest, having a small gallery of pictures by well-known artists. One is the head of the Madonna by Carlo Dolce, another is the Good Shepherd by Frederick Shields, a third is a good copy of Raphael's Entombment, and a fourth is the Nativity probably by a Flemish artist. In the sanctuary are two gilded candlesticks which once belonged to John Mason Neale, the famous writer of hymns who founded a religious community at East Grinstead in Sussex.

Hitchin has an interesting possession in a chapel, for in the Baptist Chapel in Tilehurst Street is a chair John Bunyan gave to the minister in his day. Behind the chapel is a graveyard in which lies Agnes Story, who as a girl was Agnes Beaumont, a devoted follower of Bunyan. She figures in a story which must have been a source of much distress to Bunyan. Her father, a farmer at Edworth in Bedfordshire, had been much moved by the tinker's teaching and her own name is entered in Bunyan's handwriting in the register at Gamlingay, of which he was pastor. It happened, however, that the father lost his love for Bunyan, and Agnes, who had become an ardent disciple, found it difficult to obtain permission to attend the meeting-house. She had arranged on one occasion to go with a minister from her brother's house to hear Bunyan, but as the minister did not turn up John Bunyan rode over to take his place. John Beaumont lifted his wife on to his own horse and Bunyan lifted Agnes Beaumont on to his. The father, looking out from the fields and seeing what had happened, was indignant, and barred the door against his daughter, so that she spent the night in a barn and afterwards took refuge at her brother's house. The next Sunday she decided to obey her father and went home again, and in two days, by a dramatic stroke of fate, her father died suddenly. The story was spread abroad that he had been poisoned, and there was scandal and enquiry, but Agnes was acquitted, she having been entirely innocent.

To the South of Hitchin is a lovely park of over a hundred acres in which stands all that is left of Hitchin Priory, now incorporated in the old home of the Radcliffes. Most of it was built in the 18th century, but there is a beautiful arcade and panelling from its 17th century predecessor, with fragments also of the medieval house of the White Friars.

At Hitchin was born (brought up at the 17th century gabled house called The Grange) the famous Sir Henry Hawkins, an unrivalled criminal judge for about 20 years of the last generation. His court was always crowded, though he sat long hours and kept every window shut. He died as Lord Brampton, and is chiefly remembered because he won his spurs in the romantic Tichborne case.

There was born at Charlton hereabouts, in 1813, a man with over a hundred inventions to his credit, the chief of them being the manufacture of steel. He was Sir Henry Bessemer. During the Crimean War it was felt that there was weakness in the metal used for guns, and Bessemer began fusing cast-iron with steel. During his researches he found that fragments of iron which had been exposed to an air-blast remained solid in spite of intense heat, and on touching them with an iron bar he discovered that they were merely shells of decarbonised iron. He instantly realised that by the aid of the air-blast iron could be entirely freed of carbon, the unknown quantity removed and the desired quantity introduced at will. The process created a great sensation, but early experiments failed and iron-masters who had clamoured for licences to use the process abandoned them in scorn. But Bessemer went on, brought his invention to triumphant success, and was soon selling steel £20 a ton cheaper than his rivals. He was on a flowing tide, and added new resources to engineering all over the world.

The Man Who Stirred Keats

WE know from George Chapman's own pen that he was a Hitchin man, born in 1559. It is believed that he was at Oxford, where, according to tradition, although he excelled in Greek and Latin, his weakness in logic and philosophy prevented his gaining a degree.

He was closely associated with Ben Jonson, who "loved him," with Spenser, Marlowe, and others of the immortals, and he attested his friendship for Inigo Jones by dedicating one of his plays to him. As poet and dramatist he filled a high place in Elizabethan England, but his original poems and his 18 dramas are dead beyond revival. In an age whose every breath seemed charged with inspiration, Chapman had his hours of serene inspiration, and left us examples of lofty thought. Snatches of lyric passion, flashes of humour and satire (one exercise in which, supposed to reflect on the needy followers of James the First, landed him in prison). Generally, however, he is arid, ponderous, and dull.

But as a translator he soared supreme, his Homer earned him undying fame. It was here that he translated the last 12 books of the Odyssey in 15 weeks!

The work was begun for Prince Henry, from whom he had expectations of high preferment; and with the death of that bright hope for England Chapman wrought in a sustained ecstasy, as if the spirit of Homer himself animated his faculties. Marred by occasional obscurity, harshness, and mistakes in Greek, the work yet remains the finest metrical translation of Homer we have. It was superseded by Pope's translation with its modern spelling and idiom, for every age requires its new translation of the Father of Poets, but it was Chapman that Keats found "Speak out loud and clear," Chapman's Homer which caused Keats to break faith with his own deathless sonnet:

> *Then felt I like some watcher of the skies*
> *When a new planet swims into his ken.*

Thus at a stroke the names of Keats, Chapman, and Homer are linked in lines that will sing the Elizabethan's glory as long as an Englishman survives to read his mother tongue.

The Plot that Went Astray

HODDESDON. If Izaak Walton could walk once more up its wide old street, his fishing-rod in hand, he would look in vain for his favourite Thatched House, though other inns he would pass by seem to have changed little. The oldest have overhanging storeys, and there is another which caught a poet's eye, Matthew Prior putting the Bull into some doggerel lines, in company with a stone nymph he found standing with her pitcher as a conduit-head for the well in the High Street. The nymph was given to Hoddesdon by Marmaduke Rawdon, the rich merchant for whom St Monica's Priory was built in 1622. A convent now, the red house keeps the old chimneys, the tower with a pierced parapet, the fleur-de-lys and Tudor roses in the hall (where plaster figures flank the wide fireplace); and a magnificent oak staircase rises to the top floor with carvings of heroes and heraldic dragons. Here came the merchant's nephew to live with him, the other Marmaduke Rawdon who, when in the Canary Islands on his uncle's business, achieved fame by climbing the volcanic Peak of Teneriffe. His notes of life in 17th century England are treasured in the British Museum. He died here but lies at Broxbourne.

Stanborough House, which we found transformed into a club, has a wing 300 years old. The clock tower in the main street rose in 1835, but has a 16th century bell dedicated to St Anne; it probably came from the old chapel once on this site, for the church itself, mainly Victorian, goes back only to the 18th century.

The River Lea which Izaak Walton loved (where many anglers still spend long and meditative days) fills the moat of what is left of old Rye House a mile away—just its 16th century gatehouse with an upper room big enough to house the Great Bed of Ware, which it did house for many years, though now we must go to South Kensington to see it. But still there falls on this old gatehouse the shadow of the Rye House Plot, for here, had the plot not been discovered, Charles the Second and his brother James would have been assassinated one spring morning in 1683. It is thrilling to look on this gateway and think of how profound a change might have come over our history if the plans hatched here had not gone astray.

It was at Hoddesdon that Gulielma Penn, wife of the Quaker founder of Pennsylvania, died; she was taken here to Jordans in Buckinghamshire for burial in the little graveyard there. A young smith of Hoddesdon was among 13 people burned alive at Stratford-le-bow in the days of Mary Tudor.

£60 Becomes £1000

HOLWELL. It keeps in its modern church a most curious brass designed for the rector of the old one 400 years ago. His name was Richard Wodehouse, and his crest may have been a wild man of the woods, for two of these weird creatures are drawn on the brass, though below them appears a chalice to show that this was a priest and no wild man. The creatures are known as wood-wodes and are probably a play on his name. We learned here that land in London and other property left as a charity to the village 150 years ago (when it brought in £60) now yields an income of over £1000, so that out of it almshouses and village halls have been raised. Hitchin Grammar School has received grants from it, and £160 a year is spent in helping those who need help.

The Norman Door

HORMEAD. It is Hormead Great and Hormead Little, and they are half a mile apart, both with ancient churches, one of which we found sadly in need of restoration, hoping that the petition on its 500-year-old bell would be answered, *St Margaret, pray for us.*

It is Little Hormead that needs St Margaret's prayers. It has a Norman doorway in which a magnificent door has been hanging for 800 years, splendid with 12th century ironwork, a very rare survival. We found the door itself being kept at Great Hormead, but here at Little Hormead is the fine rounded doorway with scalloped capitals to which it belongs, and the splendid Norman chancel arch; the medieval bell with its silent prayer in Latin was on the floor. Some of the old houses here have fared better than the church, one black and white timbered farm making an arresting picture down the road, and the Old Glebe House having given a new lease of life to its long thatched barn by turning it into a home.

The precious door, so beautiful with its scroll ironwork, has a companion of its own age in Great Hormead's pillared font. The nave and the north aisle are 13th century, the south aisle 14th, while the tower was finished in the 15th, and the whole church was made to look new when the chancel was built last century. There are animal gargoyles on the outside walls showing rows of grinning teeth, and queer stone faces inside staring down from the open timbers of the roof. A rusty helmet hangs over the 17th century memorial of William Brand, and there is a memorial to a soldier of the manor house, Colonel Stables who served under Wellington and Sir John Moore, and sleeps near the battlefield of Waterloo, where he fell. A lovely face looks down from another stone, a relief of Betty Romer, who died in 1916.

Great Hormead has still the sails of its old post-mill stretched to the wind near the stump of a small smock-mill, and two miles down a lane we come upon a queer place called Brick House, which seemed to us to have lost itself in time and place, rising from the middle of an overgrown field, with stepped gables, and forbidding air enhanced by small peepholes in the walls, which command a view of every corner of the house and every point of the compass.

Persuading Mary Tudor

HUNSDON. Away from the village with its row of 300-year-old cottages stand the church and Hunsdon House in a park where Henry the Eighth's children used to canter their horses. Henry bought this house, which Sir John Oldhalle had built when the Tudors were still Welsh gentlemen, and turned it into a palace for his children, and here came Master Ridley to persuade Princess Mary to change her faith. She held her own against him, and when he offered to preach to her in the church she replied that he might preach but that neither she nor any of hers would listen.

Ridley hoped that she would not refuse God's word, but she declared that God's word now was not God's word in her father's days, whereupon the bishop begged her to believe that God's word is all one in all times, but better understood and practised in some ages than in others. "You durst not for your ears have avouched that for God's word in my father's days as you now do, and as for your new books I never read any of them. I never did, nor ever will do." Then in dismissing him she said, "My lord, for your gentleness to come and see me, I thank you, but for your offering to preach before me I thank you never a whit."

It was from Hunsdon that Mary set out on that exciting drive which lasted through 12 summer days and brought her to the throne.

Both house and church have changed since then, but the walls of the house are of Tudor brick, and we can imagine our royal Bluebeard's burly form sheltering under the stout old timbers of the 15th century church porch. Elizabeth gave the palace to her cousin, Sir Henry Carey, first Lord Hunsdon, and the church's most handsome possession is the Jacobean screen in front of his family chapel. On the top of this screen rear horses' heads like the knights of a chessboard, with the Careys' painted shield between them and a swan standing triumphantly at the highest point. On a great monument in the panelled chapel lies Sir Henry Carey's son with his wife, two lovely alabaster figures with their feet on a swan and a poodle. This was that Sir John Carey whom Elizabeth sent to Berwick as Lord Warden of our East Marches, and who returned ten years later with a new king, the first of our Stuarts. Between his monument and the screen is a huge anchor made of timber and metal from HMS Caledonia in memory of Admiral Montgomerie, who died in 1908.

Lying in coloured robes and cap is Sir Thomas Forster, a judge in Sir John's time, under a canopy and behind iron railings. There is an elegant panelled recess to Francis Poyntz of 1528, and brass portraits of two humbler folk, Margaret Shelley in her shroud of 1495, and James Gray, a park-keeper of 1591, whom a skeleton of Death pierces with an arrow as he draws his bow at a stag. His inscription records that he served

> *Yeares thirtie-fyve in good renowne,*
> *Parke and housekeeper in this towne.*

The tower is 15th century, like the porch, but the rest has been rebuilt with only traces left of the Norman origin of the nave. In the east window are fragments of early 16th century glass, enough to show that once it pictured the Annunciation, the Ascension, and the Resurrection. Still on their hinges are two plain medieval doors. A chalice made to celebrate the return of Charles the Second to the throne, a poor-box, an altar table, and three bells are all of the 17th century.

Standing under one of the great beech trees in the churchyard we may read these lines on the chancel wall:

> *They lie at rest, the blessed dead,*
> *The dews drop cool above their head,*
> *They knew not when sweet summer fled.*

And our mind goes back to those lovers who met for the first time in Hunsdon Palace, Henry, the Earl of Surrey executed for treason in 1547, and Lady Elizabeth Fitzgerald, the fair disdainful Geraldine of his sonnets, who ranks with Petrarch's Laura and Sidney's Stella.

The Gipsy King

ICKLEFORD. Passing along an avenue of cedars from where the road widens in the middle of the village, we come to the ancient church entered by a Norman doorway with three arches. When the aisle was added last century Sir Gilbert Scott set up a massive arcade that would have pleased the Normans, and a chancel arch rich with carving, leading to the new sanctuary. Grotesque stone creatures hold up the 16th century roof, and on the floor are the brass portraits of a 14th century couple, Thomas Somer and his wife. The stone steps to the roodloft remain.

A worn stone marks the grave of a gipsy king, who was born on the Six Hills of Stevenage the year after King James fled, lived to see the American War of Independence, lived on through the reigns of three Georges, and travelled nearly every road in England till he died at 90. They carried him at last along the Icknield Way and laid him here, with his name, Henry Boswell, on his stone.

The pleasant new cottages do not spoil the attractiveness of Ickleford, and for company they have an old timbered inn, and a gabled house with 1599 over an oriel window.

The Horse-Doctor Saint

IPPOLLITTS. Everyone must wonder at its curious name, which is said to be explained by the church on the top of the hill, one of only two in England dedicated to St Hippolytus. He was a 3rd century martyr and a doctor of horses, and the story goes that sick horses were led into this village church in the hope of a miraculous cure. Most of the church, with its little lead-covered spire, is 14th century, but part of a Norman window and an arch carved by the earliest English builders are left where the arcades were cut in the old nave walls. It was in the 13th century that this was done, when the stone figure of a priest was laid in a recess. The timbers of the south porch are 15th century, and the central arch of the chancel screen is from the same time. From the 16th century are the brass portraits of Ryce and Alice Hughes, with their three children all kneeling in handsome Elizabethan dress. Some of the old corbels remain with new ones keeping them company, and the old font is in use after 700 years. A lady of our own day, Anne Fletcher, is remembered in a bright window picturing Dorcas with some poor cottagers. A few hundred yards to the south of the village is a little hamlet called Red Coats Green, to which Charles Dickens and 12,000 other people made pilgrimage last century with the morbid desire of seeing a poor madman called Lucas the Hermit. Dickens told his story in "All the Year Round," but it is a pitiful tale of one who in these days is taken care of instead of being made a public curiosity, and it is better forgotten.

The Ancient Doors

KELSHALL. It keeps the basic stones of two old crosses, one at the meeting of the roads, and one in the churchyard marking time as it flies. The 15th century church is light and cheerful, with a flat roof painted in black and red and gold, and four panels of the medieval screen still dimly glowing with the robes of pictured saints. The old door that has been opening for 500 years, with the iron strappings, the great key, and the old lock, still opens for us, and there is another old door strengthened with ironwork opening to the room above the porch—the room in which the village children long ago may have been taught by the rector's son James Janeway, who was Bunyan's only rival in the nursery. We read of him and his queer books in the village of Lilley.

Kneeling at the chancel wall is the small figure of Edward Franklin, a rector before the Janeways, and in front of the chancel step are the brass portraits of Richard Adane and his wife, who have been sleeping here for more than 500 years. There is a very curious wall recess, 12 feet high and under two feet wide, which was made for the storing of the processional banners in ancient days.

The Church Peeping Over the Barns

KIMPTON. We see the tiny lead spire of its church peeping over a group of old barns in a valley by the Bedfordshire border. The church is 13th century, with stiffly ornamented capitals on its 14th century round pillars, but was much transformed in the 15th century, when the tower and the spire were added and the two-storeyed porch was built; it has a stone figure of a child on the doorway. To the same century belongs the roof over the south aisle borne by stone angels, and the beautiful arcade between the chancel and the chapel. The chapel has two medieval oak screens, one with a richly vaulted canopy, and poppyheads 500 years old. There is an angel in a medieval painting on the splay of one of the chancel windows, and a brass portrait of an unknown woman of the middle of the 15th century is let into the chancel floor. The priest's desk is Jacobean, and is carved with symbolism of the fruitfulness of the earth; we noticed on it a bird pecking at a bunch of grapes. The east window has figures of Our Lord and the saints in memory of the 24th Baron Dacre and the second Viscount Hampden. Many of his family lie in the church, having been brought here from their home at Hoo, set in a beautiful park of 250 acres.

King's Friend and Queen's Tears

K ING'S LANGLEY. A king's place indeed, and Shakespeare's. Every King of England from Henry the Third to Richard the Second would know it well, and still on the hill we find a fragment of their royal palace with the garden that comes into Shakespeare. Tragic memories it has of the fall of one king and the death of a king's friend, and of a queen's unhappy hours. From this palace Edward the Second rode to the wedding of Piers Gaveston at Berkhamsted, and when his wild day was over, and the barons had wrought their vengeance on the Gascon knight, the king brought his body to King's Langley and stood by mournfully while his friend was laid here in a grave now levelled and unknown.

It was a grievous hour for the young king, for his favourite, though unworthy of a king's friendship, had been everything to him, and Edward had loaded him with honours, made him Earl of Cornwall, and given him great estates. The barons hated him, for though he was artistic and witty he was insolent and rapacious beyond all precedent, and his influence on the king was wholly bad; it brought the country to the verge of civil war. In May 1312 Edward and Gaveston parted for the last time, Edward to take refuge at York, Gaveston to stand a siege in Scarborough Castle. At the end of three weeks he was driven to surrender and was carried off to Warwick, where he was tried and beheaded. Friars took care of his bones for two years, and in 1314 Edward brought them to King's Langley and gave them a rich burial here.

Edward the Third's fifth son was born at the palace in 1341, and there were great rejoicings in the village over this baby, Edmund of Langley, who grew up to become our first Duke of York, great-grandfather of our first king of the house of York, Edward of the White Rose. Edmund fought in France and Spain with his elder brothers, the Black Prince and John of Gaunt, but he was easy-going and preferred the time spent in the country here. Three times he served as Regent while Richard the Second was abroad, and during the third regency his nephew Bolingbroke put himself on the throne.

Shakespeare gives a good picture of this kindly old man, whose life began and ended here, where his tomb still flaunts the royal arms. The Duke of York's Garden, he wrote at the head of one scene, and then follows one of the most pathetic stories of this place, when the queen overhears the gardeners saying that Richard has been deposed, and says:

> Gardener, for telling me these news of woe,
> Pray God the plants thou graft'st may never grow.

The gardener looks after her sadly as she turns away in tears:

> Poor Queen! so that thy state might be no worse,
> I would my skill were subject to thy curse.
> Here did she fall a tear; here in this place
> I'll set a bank of rue, sour herb of grace:
> Rue, even for ruth, here shortly shall be seen,
> In the remembrance of a weeping queen.

We looked at the broken wall and the rough field in which it stood, and it seemed to us that the poor queen's curse was still upon the land; but we came again and found a crop of little houses growing up with their own gardens, the gaunt broken stones from the king's palace in their midst.

When kings lived in this palace, monks lived close by at the friary, which is now a school. The children have a medieval barn for a playground, and sleep in long dormitories under fine old timber roofs, with coloured tiles from the priory church embedded in the window seats. Below is another long room beautiful with low arched windows, and in the garden are many carved stones from the vanished church.

When this friary was suppressed, the tomb of Edmund, Duke of York, was moved from the church of the monks to the village church of All Saints, where it rests today with the arms of England and France, of princes and nobles, carved on its alabaster sides, a grand array still, though many of the 20 shields are missing. Close by it is the stone which may have covered the tomb before it was moved, and if so the silhouette on it of a missing brass must represent the duke's first wife, Isabel of Castile. Shakespeare sets her in a passionate scene when their son's plot to murder Henry the Fourth is discovered by the old duke, who is revealing the plot to the king when the mother comes thumping on the locked door:

THE KING'S ENGLAND

> *Speak with me, pity me, open the door,*
> *A beggar begs who never begged before.*

But it is of another and more tragic spectacle that we are reminded here, the last sad scene of all. Shakespeare has given it an immortal setting, the closing scene of his Richard the Second at Windsor Castle, when Sir Pierce of Exton, who has foully murdered Richard at Pontefract, brings him in his coffin to Bolingbroke:

> EXTON. *Great king, within this coffin I present*
> *Thy buried fear: herein all breathless lies*
> *The mightiest of thy greatest enemies,*
> *Richard of Bordeaux, by me hither brought.*
> BOLINGBROKE. *Exton, I thank thee not; for thou hast wrought*
> *A deed of slander with thy fatal hand*
> *Upon my head and all this famous land.*
> EXTON. *From your own mouth, my lord, did I this deed.*
> BOLINGBROKE. *They love not poison that do poison need,*
> *Nor do I thee.*
> *The guilt of conscience take thou for thy labour,*
> *But neither my good word nor princely favour:*
> *With Cain go wander through the shades of night,*
> *And never show thy head by day nor light.*
> *Lords, I protest, my soul is full of woe,*
> *That blood should sprinkle me to make me grow:*
> *Come, mourn with me for that I do lament,*
> *And put on sullen black incontinent:*
> *I'll make a voyage to the Holy Land,*
> *To wash this blood off from my guilty hand:*
> *March sadly after; grace my mournings here;*
> *In weeping after this untimely bier.*

It was here, at King's Langley, the place he had known in his happier days, that Bolingbroke laid King Richard, though Henry the Fifth removed him and laid him in the dazzling glory of Westminster Abbey, beside the tomb of Edward the Confessor.

In the Church of this place of royal memory are stone figures of Sir Ralph and Lady Verney, who died at the close of the 15th century when this church was new. Sir William Glascocke, one of Charles the Second's judges, has another tomb, and there are several brasses of the 16th century. One shows John Carter and his two wives, both wearing broad-brimmed hats and ruffs, and with them a crowd of children, four sons and five daughters to one wife, five sons and four daughters to the other. Another brass shows a little lady of the

15th century, very small and simple in contrast with the woman below her, whose elaborate portrait in Elizabethan dress is engraved on the back of an older Flemish brass.

One other memorial holds us, the stone on the floor to little Mary Dixon, who was buried here in 1632, "being then but three years of age, to whose sweet remembrance (we read) I.B. for the love she bore her here dedicates herself and this." Then the mysterious I.B. adds:

Affection only consecrates this stone
That it should melt when I forbear to moan.

The chancel walls, like the piscina, are 700 years old, but most of the church (its aisles, the chapels, and the tower) was made new in the 15th century. It has a fine 16th century chest, and a canopied oak pulpit 300 years old, with many a dragon lurking in its deep carving. There is beautiful modern carving in the marble reredos.

The pleasant village street, with a raised side walk and an ancient cottage among the houses, leads on to Apsley Mills, where paper has been made for over a century; it was one of the first mills in England where paper was made in a continuous sheet, a device which made possible the enormous editions of our newspapers. The high bank of the road by the mills has been made into an attractive rock garden as a memorial to those men who left the mills to go to the war and did not come home again. One of the most remarkable men of last century was associated all his life with these mills, Sir John Evans, who devoted his spare time to research into the antiquity of man, and made a great reputation as an antiquarian, a geologist, and an authority on ancient British coins.

The Delightful Screen

KING'S WALDEN. It has hills rolling round it, and, having a royal name, it has a king and a queen to help to bear up the roof of its ancient church. They represent the unhappy Henry the Sixth and his tragic wife Margaret of Anjou, and are set above the 700-year-old arcades which rest on capitals sculptured by the Normans. The church has a charming 14th century screen, delightfully painted and equally beautiful on both sides, with exquisite tracery and elaborate little ornaments (some of them tiny gilded heads) picked out in reds and greens against a background of black and white. Keeping this lovely screen company is a modern oak figure of St George slaying the dragon, in memory of the men who did not come back. In the Jacobean vestry is a panelled screen in memory of Thomas Harrison, a shipowner who died in 1916, and the beautiful east window of the Crucifixion is in memory of his wife. They rest together in the shadow of the 14th century tower, having been brought here from their beautiful home behind the church. The house stands among great trees with acres of gardens, being on the site of an Elizabethan house in which lived many of the Hales family who are remembered in the church.

About a mile away is the hamlet of Breachwood Green, where the Baptist Chapel has a pulpit made and dated in 1658, the year of Cromwell's death. John Bunyan preached from it.

The Home of the Lyttons

KNEBWORTH. Modern Knebworth on the Great North Road has a church on the hillside, reached by an avenue of limes, designed by Sir Edwin Lutyens, with great eaves overhanging the brick walls, and an unusual interior with many pillars and arches, two huge pillars at the crossing reaching to the roof.

Written in Domesday Book as Cheneepeworde, old Knebworth, a mile to the west, has an old church in the 260-acre park, looking from its lawn to the great house with its medley of towers and domed turrets, famous for its beautiful grounds and as the home of Bulwer-Lytton and his ancestors. There have been Lyttons at Knebworth for over four centuries. Many of them sleep in the church, but the most famous of them earned his resting-place in Westminster Abbey.

Beginning as a simple nave and chancel in the 12th century, the church received its tower in 1420, the Lytton chapel 100 years later, and the porch perhaps in the 17th century; but the chapel was rebuilt about 1700 and the chancel in the 19th century. The roofs are of mellowed tiles. The nave has leaning walls, medieval windows, 15th century oak benches, and a roof with its old traceried trusses over the hammerbeams. In the old oak pulpit are still older Flemish panels carved with scenes in the Life of Our Lord, one on the stairway dated 1567. The font is about 1480, and one of the old rood stair doorways is blocked. The fine iron screen across the tower arch is

The Fine Avenues

The Old Village Church
THE GARDEN CITY OF LETCHWORTH

St Albans
Old Lectern in St Stephen's

St Albans
Francis Bacon in St Michael's Church

St Paul's Walden
The Stapleford Monument

Little Hormead   Norman Door **Ware**   14th Century Font

18th century. Still entered by a simple Norman arch, the chancel has the arch of a Norman window in the north wall, a 15th century piscina, and a 17th century Italian painting of the Last Supper over the altar. The Madonna and Thomas Becket, patron saints of the church, are in the west window of the tower.

Crowded with memorials, the small chapel has all the pomp that 18th century marble monuments can give. Of three which are railed round and nearly reach the roof, one has a lavish canopy on Corinthian columns, under which Sir William Lytton of 1704 lies in his lace cravat and cuffs. In the second monument Lytton Lytton of 1710 stands on a pedestal, under a classical pediment, wearing a long curling wig and a long buttoned coat with a cravat; at the sides cherubs are weeping. He died at 21, having changed his surname of Strode on inheriting the estate, which at his death went to the Robinsons, his mother's family. The third great monument shows his father, Sir George Strode of 1707, in similar dress; he sleeps at Etchingham, Sussex. Sir George's mother was Judith Lytton, who has a memorial with her bust in the chancel; she died at 23 in 1662, and by her floorstone is a small stone to one of her three children, with the words: Judith, the one-year-old little daughter of Nicholas and Judith, lies next to her mother.

The three names were borne by William Robinson Lytton Strode of 1732, who kneels with his wife in a dainty monument with a sarcophagus and three children playing with an hourglass, a skull, and a serpent with its tail in its mouth—symbols of mortality and eternity. A fine brass in the chapel has portraits of Sir Rowland Lytton of 1582, his two wives in gowns with ruffs and brocaded petticoats; we read that he was a gallant leader in war and a worthy magistrate in peace. He was knighted by Elizabeth, and entertained her at Knebworth. In the chancel is a beautiful brass portrait of a priest, Simon Bache of 1414, with rather sour expression; the engraving is deep and rich; his cope is adorned with saints, wonderful in detail, and on the clasp is the head of Our Lord.

All that is left of the tomb and brass portraits of Sir John Hotoft and his wife are three shields and a few strips of the brass inscription. Sir John, who was given the estate by Henry the Fourth and was Treasurer of the Household of Henry the Sixth, is said to have restored the nave and built the tower; his arms are on the west doorway. One of his daughters married Sir Richard Lytton; the other inherited Knebworth.

An inscription tells of Captain Charles Earle, who fought in the Kaffir War and at the Relief of Lucknow, and served the Lyttons for 20 years. We read of Fraser Campbell Buchanan, killed at Arras when he was 23, and see beautiful Whall glass in a window to Leslie Arnott Paterson, who also fell; it shows a knight setting forth to the fight, and unbuckling his armour when it was over.

At the entrance to the chapel is a beautiful iron screen surmounted by a golden cross which bears a winged sword and has 29 stars in its 57 rays of light. Screen and cross are in memory of Viscount Knebworth, who was 29 when he was killed while flying at Hendon in 1933, when his father was 57. Designed by his uncle Sir Edwin Lutyens, the screen was made in Hatfield and the cross in London. On a silver cross on the altar in the chancel are the words, In memory of Anthony, May 1st, 1933; an offering from his mother.

Sir Edwin designed the beautiful memorial marking the airman's grave in a garden of remembrance to the east of the churchyard, shaded with silver birch trees. On a flat stone is carved the winged sword emblem of the Auxiliary Air Force, in which he was a pilot. The headstone is a frame for a lovely figure of a woman with her hair in long plaits and a crown of stars on her head. Holding a sphere on which is a falcon, she represents Our Lady of the Sky, sculptured by Sir William Reid Dick. Seven shields on the back of the stone include those of his parents, Eton, Magdalen College, the City of Westminster, and Hertfordshire. A stone with five cherub heads round a star, marking the grave of Annie Louisa Sleath who was "forty years friend and Nannie of the Lutyens family," was designed by Sir Edwin.

The great Tudor house Sir Robert Lytton began to build was completed during the 16th century. Its original plan was of four sides enclosing a courtyard, and so it stood till the 19th century, when three generations of the family made it the house we see. The great transformation began in 1811 with the pulling down of three wings; then came the lavish enrichment of the remaining west wing with battlements, panelled turrets crowned with copper domes, stringcourses dotted with flowers and grotesques, dragons on pinnacles, and faces and gargoyles peeping out everywhere. The south wing with its tower-gateway was added last century. The wall round the other sides of the court is adorned with quatrefoils, and dragons holding shields are on the gateposts. The grounds are delightful with spacious lawns, formal avenues of pollarded limes, and carpets of primroses, daffodils, and narcissi under trees. A great almond tree is an entrancing sight in spring. There are noble avenues in the park, and near the church is a stone mausoleum decorated with urns and crowned with a sarcophagus.

The three rooms in the house which all may see belong mostly to the old mansion. As we enter we come upon a fine bronze bust of the earl of our time, Viceroy of India. In the staircase hall is a saddle and halter embroidered in solid silver, the gift of the Emir of Afghanistan to the first earl when he, too, was Viceroy. Here is a big array of armour of Queen Elizabeth's day, and some from the time of Cromwell; the Dutch musical clock is about 1700. Bulwer-Lytton converted the next room into the library, and here we see the novelist's writing table with his ink-stand, cigar case, and blotting pad. First editions of his works are on the shelves, and in a case are manuscripts of The Last Days of Pompeii, The Caxtons, and My Novel, a cast of the author's hand, and letters he received from Charles Dickens. In the same case is the manuscript of Lucile, a novel in verse written by his son, the first earl, under the name of Owen Meredith. Treasured in another case are snuff boxes which belonged to Charles Fox and William Pitt, Lord Byron's ruler, a crucifix of gold and pearls which belonged to Mary Queen of Scots, the inkstand used for the signing of the treaty between Charles Stuart and the Commissioners of the Long Parliament, and a ring with a miniature of the king. It was one of three which Charles gave to his friends on the scaffold. Furnishing the library are chairs of the time of William and Mary and Queen Anne, and a 17th century Spanish cabinet made of tortoiseshell, ebony, ivory, and gilt metal; and there is a long wooden pipe shown in a portrait of the novelist over the mantelpiece.

By a door disguised among the shelves of books we come to the charming white drawing room, where nothing was lovelier when we called than the window peep of the laburnum trees flowering in a corner like a shower of gold. Here we see Sir Robert, the first Lytton of Knebworth, and among other family portraits are Peter

Lely's Ruth Barrington and Sir William Robinson Norreys. Hepplewhite and Chippendale are represented among the furniture; there are two tortoiseshell and ivory English cabinets of the time of Charles the Second, and another Spanish one of the same century. By Daniel Maclise's portrait of Bulwer-Lytton as a young man is a door leading to the banqueting hall, a splendid chamber with an oak ceiling, screen, and gallery from the time of James the First, and rich panelling said to have been designed by Inigo Jones. Most of the furniture here is Jacobean, including a valuable set of 12 chairs of applewood, made in the time of Charles the Second. Portraits include one of the Duke of Gloucester, son of Charles and Henrietta Maria. Hanging here is a banner with the Lytton arms which hung above the throne from which Lord Lytton proclaimed Queen Victoria Empress of India at the great Durbar of 1877. One of the bedrooms has a noble four-poster in which Elizabeth is said to have slept, richly carved in oak.

The Man Who Missed Greatness

THE first Lord Lytton was one of the most versatile men of all time in England. He was a novelist, dramatist, and politician, and succeeded in every ambition, though not to the extent of high and lasting eminence.

He was born in London in 1803, and brought up by his mother, his father dying when the son was four years old. From childhood he wrote poetry, and was expected to become a notable man. At Cambridge he took the Chancellor's medal for a poem on Sculpture. He found popularity in prose when he was 25 with his novel Pelham, and he needed it, for he had only inherited £200 a year from his father, and his mother, who was well-to-do, had cut him off for marrying against her wishes. That marriage was a complete failure, except that from it have followed two generations of Lyttons honourably distinguished by public service. Lytton and his clever but hysterical wife could not live together, and they separated.

He soon had an ample income from his writings. Eventually the standard edition of his novels was issued in 48 volumes. The most striking feature of this enormous production, which was spread over nearly 50 years, was its variety in character and in style.

His first series of stories, beginning when Scott was nearing the end of his wonderful career and before Dickens began his, owed something to the craze of Byronism, but soon became deflected into a study of crime, not unlike the crook element in fiction a century later. It began incidentally in Pelham, and continued in Disowned, Paul Clifford, and Eugene Aram, with Paul Clifford the highwayman as its most typical and popular example. Then he turned to history, with an attempt to build up round a central character a picture of a succession of ages past. The Last Days of Pompeii, Rienzi, The Last of the Barons, and Harold illustrate this phase of his progress, for progress it was. He tried drama, not unsuccessfully in The Lady of Lyons, Richelieu, and Money, plays that have attracted the public, in later years. In poetry he essayed the satirical and the romantic, but he failed in both. He made a vicious attack on Tennyson, who was then emerging into fame, and Tennyson retorted, in a poem that is not reproduced in his collected works, and (as Andrew Lang has said) knocked Lytton out in the first round.

Lytton now turned to the staple theme of fiction, the ordinary life of the people, and wrote his best novel The Caxtons, which was followed in the same quiet spirit but not with equal success by My Novel and What Will He Do With It? Later he sought to picture society and art as he saw them towards the end of his life in France and England, in contrast with what he had known in more aristocratic days. From time to time all through his life there was a strain of the eerie and abnormal in him, and in one of his last books, The Coming Race, he experimented in imaginative prophecy. He saw mankind's powers of catastrophic destruction ensuring peace. Such an extraordinary range of interest in so many books could hardly be sustained, and Lytton, especially in his early periods, was often extravagant and melodramatic. He was adept in following popular fashions, and so failed in creating a style of his own. Though unquestionably clever, he never crossed the boundary line of greatness.

He sat in Parliament as a Whig for ten years and was offered a lordship of the Admiralty, but declined it. In 1852 he returned to Parliament as a Conservative, and was decidedly successful as a speaker. He served as Secretary for the Colonies, and was made a peer as Baron Lytton. Thrice he was elected Rector of Glasgow University. He died at Torquay in his 70th year.

A Maker of Beautiful Things

LANGLEYBURY. It is by the canal, between King's Langley and Watford, with its church in the midst of the busy road. The church, which has a graceful shingled spire, is entered by a fine oak lychgate, the churchyard is fringed with trimmed limes which make arches over two other gates; they were planted when the church was built of flint and stone in 1864 by William Jones Loyd, of the big house in the park. A tribute to him is the great cross of Silician marble near the porch, richly carved with the Crucifixion and four panels with groups of the Disciples, the work of a Florentine sculptor. In the south chapel, where he and his family sleep, the founder has a monument with cherubs. Gertrude Loyd's monument of 1898 is an angel with uplifted hand, sitting on a tomb. A tile mosaic showing the Good Shepherd is to Sir John Runtz, and there are two Flanders crosses. Rich stonework is a feature of the church inside; angels are between the arches of the arcade; and the chancel arch resting on angel corbels is adorned with 24 canopies sheltering angels with shields and scrolls and musical instruments.

One of the windows is in memory of a 19th century Lord Mayor of London, William Taylor Copeland,who was for many years head of the Spode pottery firm at Stoke-on-Trent. He sat in Parliament and took great interest in civic affairs, and his wise direction of the pottery works, in cooperation with well-known sculptors, won for it world-wide renown. He died at Russell Farm, Watford, and he is known to collectors everywhere as the maker of beautiful porcelain.

Lovely wooded hills rise gently behind the church, and a charming walk leads by West Wood to Buck's Hill a mile and a half away. At Hunton Bridge, across the canal, is the house called King's Lodge, a low building dating from the 17th century, lengthened in the 19th, and refaced with brick. On its wall outside are old panels with leaves and flowers and 1642, when it is thought to have been built. It is said to have been a hunting lodge of the Stuarts. One of its rooms has a finely decorated plaster ceiling, and a big fireplace with the royal arms and 1642. For a time it was divided into two dwellings.

Here Two Prime Ministers Died

LEMSFORD. It lies in the valley of the Lea between the Great North road and the park of Brocket Hall, the fine 18th century house which witnessed the death of two Prime Ministers, Lord Melbourne and Lord Palmerston.

The famous landscape gardener Capability Brown laid out the grounds and planted beeches, cedars, and cypresses to vie with the glory of the ancient oaks. He formed a lake by widening the River Lea, and across this the architect James Paine built a stone bridge to enhance the beauty of the waterfall.

The hall is richly adorned in the Adam style and has a grand pillared staircase, and ceilings painted by Francis Wheatley and John Mortimer. Among its art treasures is a Reynolds portrait of George the Fourth, given by him to that brilliant woman the first Lady Melbourne. Often the house has echoed with the footsteps of illustrious people, among them Lord Melbourne, the first Prime Minister of the young Queen Victoria, and Lord Palmerston, who married Lord Melbourne's sister, and held office in every government except two between 1807 and 1865. He died here when he was 81, an unfinished despatch by his side, for he would not give up. One of the most pathetic stories told of him is that not long before he died he was seen trying to leap over the railings in front of his London house to show that he was well. Lady Palmerston, who for a quarter of a century had been his unfailing helpmate, lived on here for another four years and was then laid beside him in Westminster Abbey. Lord Palmerston had no children, the property descending to William Cowper, one of the children of Lady Palmerston's first marriage; and it was the Cowpers who gave the village its church.

The church has a handsome tower with two dragon gargoyles, and a lovely chapel with coloured arms on its vaulted roof. Over the altar are five oak panels portraying Adam and Eve, Abraham's Sacrifice, the Annunciation, the Nativity, and the Resurrection. Under an arch leading to the chapel from the chancel is an altar tomb in 14th century style, with a sculptured figure of Lady Florence Brocket, who died in 1927, angels supporting her head and other mourning figures standing under canopies below.

In the churchyard a granite cross marks the last resting-place of Lord Mount Stephen, a Canadian financier who gave a million pounds to charity. George Stephen, as everyone knew him before he became a peer, was born in 1829, the son of a humble Scottish carpenter. He left school to be apprenticed to an Aberdeen draper, and seven years later, after working in Glasgow and London, went to Canada at the invitation of a draper cousin in Montreal. There he prospered, first at his own trade and later as a financier, and in 1878 (like another of his cousins, Lord Strathcona) he became one of a group of six men who, in the face of tremendous difficulties, built the Canadian Pacific Railway and made huge fortunes. He spent his last few years at Brocket Hall and died here in 1921.

But the romantic story of Brocket is the strange, pathetic tale of Lady Caroline Lamb, who here spent her last tragic years.

Lady Caroline Lamb

LADY CAROLINE LAMB survives as a legendary figure of Hertfordshire. Extremely beautiful, petite, and dainty as Ariel, gifted with talents which made her notable as poet and novelist, a clever talker, she was a brilliant figure of gilded Mayfair and the tragic heroine of a career more strange than any which she pictured in her romances. She was in girlhood a kind of Cinderella, for, although she was a daughter of the Earl and Countess of Bessborough, the illness of her mother, with whom for several years she lived in Italy, led to her being brought up by servants; and when she joined her cousins at Devonshire House in London the children were so neglected that they would take their silver plates into the kitchen and beg for titbits.

Tiny, delicate, and romantic, Caroline could never speak without lisping, yet she could tame and ride an unbroken horse, and, despaired of by unsympathetic governesses, she taught herself ancient and modern languages. Tomboy, student, half-fairy, she declared to William Lamb (later, as Lord Melbourne, Queen Victoria's first Prime Minister), that she could not marry him as he desired, but she would dress as a boy and serve him as clerk in the grim chambers where he awaited the coming of his first barrister's brief.

But she did marry him, and as Lady Caroline Lamb she was one of the most famous and most astonishing figures of the age. She became the wayward heroine of volcanic friendships with men who were destined to win immortality in our literature. The most celebrated and unfortunate of these friendships was that with Byron, who was fascinated by her beauty and intellect. She was in love with his poetry and deemed him an Apollo. As both loved praise with equally ardent appetite, they soon quarrelled, and Caroline dramatised her grief and embellished it with the pageantry and ceremonial of high tragedy.

Her country home as Lady Melbourne was at Brocket Hall, and it was here that she collected a company of Young Village Beauties and robed them all in white. She caused a great fire to be kindled in the grounds to resemble a funeral pyre, and on this fire, as her chorus of white-clad maidens danced a tragic measure, she cast a miniature of the poet and a number of his letters, reciting sad Elegies as they burned. Then, with a sigh of satisfaction, she returned to the house to study afresh the originals. It was only copies of the poet's correspondence that she had consigned to the flames.

But there came one day to her at Brocket Hall a real tragedy. As she drove out of the park her progress was arrested by a funeral procession passing the entrance. She enquired the name of the dead, and was answered, "Lord Byron." The poet's body, brought from Greece, had lain in London while his friends sought burial for it in Westminster Abbey, and the dean had sternly refused. Thus the last remains of the author of Don Juan were on their way to the colliery village of Hucknall Torkard in Nottinghamshire, hard by Newstead Abbey, the scene of his turbulent youth.

So passed the man with whom the little Fairy Queen, as she was called, had so bitterly quarrelled, and she fell swooning to the ground with her reason unhinged. She recovered, and reproached with extravagance, wrote a book, about stables and economy, to prove, as she said, that she had been "a good housewife and saved William much." To which William (Lord Melbourne) gently answered that it was useless to save in one place and squander the saving in another.

Lest They Forget

LETCHMORE HEATH. Those who pause here in the shade of the little green on their way between Elstree and Aldenham may wonder at the tablets on the cottage walls. They are a homely memorial of a kind we have not come upon elsewhere, one of the most touching tributes to the men who went out from here and did not come back, for each tablet marks a home saddened by the toll of war, and on each is the name of a soldier with the words, *Lest we forget*.

The Dream of Ebenezer Howard

LETCHWORTH. It is the city built by dreams, the dreams of Ebenezer Howard, who while others talked of garden cities, went out spade in hand and made one. It is worth while to think a little of his story before we come to Letchworth.

He was born in London, tried office life, was private secretary to Dr Parker of the City Temple, went out to Chicago, and then came back to London to find himself disgusted with its slums. He felt as he looked at them like Abraham Lincoln when he looked at slavery, and he decided that if ever an opportunity came he would hit them hard. He saw a city of the future, like a New Jerusalem in a green and pleasant land, where people could live with trees and lawns and flowers about them and feel the wind blowing everywhere.

It was not enough, he said, to think of the town as one magnet and the country as another, pulling different ways; there should be a town-country magnet which would as far as possible combine the advantages of the other two while reducing their disabilities. This Utopia would join beauty of Nature with social opportunity, low rents with high wages, low rates with plenty to do, low prices without sweating, pure air and water with good drainage, bright homes and gardens with no smoke and no slums, and freedom with co-operation. He proceeded to draw plans of such a garden city as he imagined. He set out a site of 5000 acres planned with streets and houses and gardens, with allotments, fruit farms, pastures, woods, water supply, and space for factories and markets as well as for schools and convalescent homes, and all with access to a railway.

Such was the plan, and he handed it over to the critics. They were not silent, nor was he. Having begun the movement on paper he brought it into the public eye by every means within his power. With a dozen friends he formed a Garden City Association. The fruit of his hundreds of public meetings and the clear business-like nature of his propositions so convinced the sceptics that three years after the publication of his practical propositions the Letchworth site was purchased for £150,000. That was in 1903. From that time forward, despite jealousies, ridicule, and afterwards the interruption caused by the war, the scheme advanced and took continually more concrete shape. After Letchworth came Welwyn, and more remarkable than either, Wythenshawe.

These were all his foster-children, but they had many descendants. Out of his scheme sprang the Town Planning Act. Garden suburbs and garden villages all owe their existence to this man who loved the countryside and wished our people to enjoy it.

Letchworth is perfectly delightful, planned on 1500 acres with a green belt of twice as much round it. It has 30 miles of roads with 7000 trees planted along them in about 50 varieties, and it is so spaced out with fine avenues, quiet walks, squares and gardens and cloisters, that 200 factories make no difference to its rural aspect. It has a shopping centre, a civic centre, residential areas, a museum and a grammar school, and, of course, the old church which was here long before it, when all this place was three small villages. The Icknield Way runs through the centre of the town with a mile-long stretch of almond trees, the beauty of which must be seen in spring-time to be believed. It is all hardly more than a generation old, yet it will not be long before 20,000 people have their homes here, among the limes and chestnuts and poplars growing tall and shady. The grass verges and the belt of lovely country, which must never be built on, are an example for all reformers and a rebuke to every slum.

Close to this city of the 20th century is the site of a British settle-ment of 20 centuries ago; we may see some of the finds from it in the museum, together with Roman and medieval objects and a fine photographic survey of the whole neighbourhood.

The museum, admirably arranged by the well-known naturalist Mr Percival Westell, has in its natural history collection skulls of mammals and birds, eggs and nests, insects, shells, and stones and local fossils of the Chalk Age and the Ice Age. The cases of Bygones are of remarkable interest to students of old Hertfordshire life, and the room of Roman and prehistoric antiquities is constantly growing in a county which has so much history beneath its feet.

But there is an old Letchworth still in existence, aloof from the new. First we come to the timber house with dormer windows which is now the post office, an outpost of 300 years ago; then to a house as old which has been turned into a row of cottages; and then to a screen of great chestnut trees with the 17th century Hall on one side and a diminutive church with a queer little 16th century bellcot on the other. A copy of this church has been erected in the garden city, but there is history in these old walls which cannot be repeated.

For 500 years the porch has sheltered a door strengthened with 13th century ironwork. The nave walls were probably laid by Norman masons though the doorway and the windows are later. The chancel arch seems to have been made new in the 16th century, and the chancel is a medley of the centuries going back to the 13th. Fragments of medieval glass are in two windows. The font bowl has served for 600 years and all that time a bell with Ave Maria written on it before the Reformation has continued to call people to church. Some of the benches were made 500 years ago, and medieval beams are glimpsed through the plaster roof. The brass portrait of a 15th century rector, Thomas Wyrley, is near the brass portraits of a couple he knew well, William and Isabelle Overbury; and lying on the sill of a window where glows the shield of the Hertfordshire Montfichets is the small stone figure of a knight in chain mail, much worn after more than 600 years. He holds a heart case to show that only his heart was buried here, and he was probably close of kin to Richard Montfichet, one of the 25 barons appointed to see that the liberties won by Magna Carta were not lost.

The old hall, now a hotel, has a fine oak screen 300 years old, and a plaster of the Judgment of Paris over a fireplace. It was the home of an eccentric rector who would hold services here to which he would summon giant musical boxes and any wandering minstrels who would add to the din, and it was his fancy to ride up and down the hall on his velocipede after the service, now crashing into the screen, now stopping to hand a jar of snuff round the congregation.

The Incredible Book

LILLEY. Rupert Brooke knew it well and brings it into one of his poems; here he would walk when he was at Cambridge University, by

The Roman road to Wendover,
By Tring and Lilley Hoo.

A rampant lion raises its head on cottage wall and gatepost, the crest of the Docwra family who lived in the fine park of Putteridge

Bury generations ago. All that is left of the church they knew is the Norman chancel arch which has been reset in the chancel wall, the linen-fold panels and the old oak of the pulpit, the piscina, and the 15th century font at which were baptised a 17th century curate's two sons, John and James Janeway. John was a mathematical genius; James seemed at one time something like a rival to John Bunyan. They built a chapel for him in Jamaica Row at Rotherhithe, and there he preached while plague and persecution were rife, escaping both to die of consumption in 1674.

Today he is a literary curiosity, and it is almost incredible to read the books he wrote; yet for generations he was Bunyan's only rival as an author for children. The moral blight that spread through England with the Restoration brought its reaction, and for a time there was a fashion in such books as James Janeway's, one of which was called by the terrible title, A Token for Children, Being an Account of the Conversion, Holy and Exemplary Lives, and Joyful Deaths of Several Young Children. It was the book that upright parents gave their little ones in those days. To the parents the author would say, "Your child is never too little to go to hell," and to the children he would warn them to pray and weep by themselves.

His heroes and heroines all die, monuments of piety and virtue, at the tenderest age, and William Godwin (Shelley's father-in-law) who was brought up on the book, declared that he was so fired to emulation by their example that he felt willing to die with them "if I could with equal success engage the admiration of my friends and mankind." A six-year-old Janeway hero whose brothers had not said grace before the meal asks them, "Dare you do this? God be merciful to us, this bit of bread might choke us." He and others make a perfect end, and the author asks his little readers, "Are you like these children? Are you willing to go to hell to be burned with the devil and his angels?" A little girl in the book, surveying herself in a mirror, cries:

What a pity such a pretty maid
As I should go to hell.

It is terrible, but it is English, and the children who read this Janeway book created our Augustan age of literature and played their parts in building up the British Empire.

Tom Ken's Village

LITTLE BERKHAMSTED. Trees close in the appealing sound of the three old bells in the church's wooden belfry, the oldest bell having Ave Maria moulded on it 600 years ago. It would be the first peal heard by Bishop Ken, for in this village he was born, and we like to think that the ancient bell may have stirred in him the message of the hymn he was to write as the years rolled on, Awake, my soul, and with the sun. . . .

The altar table in the church is a memorial to this saintly Bishop of Bath and Wells. The church was made new in his day, and has been rebuilt since, but a name from the 17th century stops us at a stone in the chancel floor, the name of Cromwell. Here lies Cromwell Fleetwood, Oliver's grandson, whose mother Bridget married two leaders of the Parliamentary Army, first Ireton, then General Fleetwood. This grandson was married in the chancel here in 1679, but he died childless nine years later; his sister was that Bridget Ireton who, of all Oliver's descendants, is said to have been in some ways most like him, though she was one of the most extraordinarily wild and unbalanced women ever known.

Facing the church is a charming row of wooden cottages under red roofs, and from the churchyard we see the red tower John Stratton built 300 years ago, so that from its battlements he might see his ships anchored in the Thames. It was later made into an observatory. His house, the Gage, has been much altered since it was built of Elizabethan brick and timber. Manor House Farm has also seen many changes in its three centuries, but is remarkable still for its open timber porch.

It was in the summer of 1637 that life began here for Tom Ken. After his father and mother died he lived for a time under Izaak Walton's roof before going on to Winchester, where his name may still be seen in the cloisters. In 1663 he was living in an Essex rectory, and four years later, when he was only 30, he was a rector in the Isle of Wight, and was becoming famous as a brilliant preacher who often stirred London congregations. Living in the unsettled times of Charles and James the Second, he stood for decency and right, and did not hesitate to tell kings what he thought of them; but he never lost his humility. He sailed for Tangier with Samuel Pepys, was made a bishop in 1684, attended Charles the Second in his last hours, and was present at the execution of Monmouth.

But he was most loved for the little things he did. He helped all who were in trouble. He gave away nearly every penny. He worked as few bishops had ever been known to work, and had 12 poor folk to dinner every Sunday. When other bishops drove in fine coaches Bishop Ken walked on foot in London's streets.

One of the Seven Bishops sent to the Tower in 1688 for petitioning James against his Declaration of Indulgence, he soon afterwards found himself deprived of his See; and as he had never saved money and had no private income he became a poor man. Happily there were friends ready to go to his aid, and in his old age Queen Anne gave him £200 a year.

He was a little man with dark eyes, a familiar figure in London and Winchester, his hair hanging loose about his clean-shaven face. He had a winning smile, and was always courteous and kind, always eager to help. Unaffected, generous in his thoughts if sometimes quick in temper, he was as true as steel in all his dealings with others.

He is remembered best of all today for one or two hymns still sung in chapel and cathedral. He died in 1711, having been taken ill in Dorset, and setting out for Bath, found himself unable to go beyond Longleat, the great house of his friend Lord Weymouth. There in a few days his long life ended and he was buried on the first day of spring at the east end of Frome Church. His funeral took place, at his own request, at sunrise, and those who followed him to his last resting-place must have been thinking of the famous hymn he wrote for the scholars of Winchester:

> *Awake, my soul, and with the sun*
> *Thy daily stage of duty run.*

Everyone knows Bishop Ken's evening hymn, beginning:

> *Glory to Thee, my God, this night,*
> *For all the blessings of the light:*
> *Keep me, O keep me, King of kings,*
> *Beneath Thine own almighty wings.*

In both hymns is the famous verse known as the Doxology:

> *Praise God from Whom all blessings flow,*
> *Praise Him all creatures here below;*

Praise Him above, ye heavenly host,
Praise Father, Son, and Holy Ghost.

No verse has been sung more often than this throughout the world; it may be said that these four lines of Tom Ken have been on everybody's lips at some time or other.

The Romantic Story of a Great House

LITTLE GADDESDEN. He who takes his car or his bus or his legs and comes to Little Gaddesden will go back satisfied, and should he come in rhododendron time he can be guaranteed a perfect day. For here is Ashridge Park, with the stately tower of a house like a little walled city rising from the loveliest garden in Hertfordshire, a superb piece of England with the rhododendrons in their glory. The house has become a political college for training in citizenship in memory of Mr Bonar Law (Prime Minister in 1922), and we can imagine nothing more calculated to stir in youth a great love of our country than a little schooling in this noble place.

The great house, with the park stretched in front of it for miles, full of marvellous oaks and beeches, with the terraces and the gardens and the impressive avenues, stands where stood in ages past a monastery of 20 Bonhommes who came from France in Norman days. Their monastery became a royal home for the children of Henry the Eighth; where we walk in gardens unsurpassed for beauty came Edward the Sixth, Mary Tudor, and the great Elizabeth. In these wonderful gardens played these three sovereigns of England. It was here that the Princess Elizabeth, a girl of 19, sought refuge from her dread sister Mary Tudor, and from this place they led Elizabeth captive to the Tower. Her wit was to save her and to preserve her for that wonderful reign which raised her country to the summit of its greatness; but it was here that she faced her darkest hour. It is said that she fainted three times as the procession passed through the park. Such memories has this gracious place, and these three children of our Bluebeard King would find no place more worthy of a king could they come back today.

Early in the 17th century Ashridge became the home of the Egertons, the Earls and Dukes of Bridgewater, famous in history as one of our great families, but chiefly because the last duke, eccentric man, had one wise idea—that of developing the resources

Little Gaddesden   The Lovely Chapel of Ashridge

Little Gaddesden   The Stately Walls of Ashridge

of his coal mines by building a canal, thus becoming known to history as the founder of inland navigation in this country. He lived at Worsley in Lancashire and let his house here fall to ruins; but in the family vault of the village church he lies, this man with whom a dukedom died but whose work lives on.

The house was built up again on the eve of Waterloo by his cousin the seventh earl, and it is not unworthy of its great foundation, though it is the work of the restorer-destroyer Wyatt, at whose door lie so many architectural sins in our churches. It has a magnificent front of about 1000 feet from tower to tower, and one of the noblest halls built in its century, nearly 100 feet high, with a great stone staircase, splendid windows, and nine statues looking down from its walls, most of them benefactors of the monks, all sculptured by Richard Westmacott, the fashionable sculptor of the day. They stand in niches round the walls, an impressive company with five royalties among them: Edward Earl of Cornwall, founder of the monastery, his father and his mother; the Black Prince who came over here from his Berkhamsted manor and remembered the monks as he lay dying; and Edward the Sixth who lived here with his sisters. The other four statues are of St Benedict, the first rector of Ashridge (Richard Watford), Bishop Cantelupe of Hereford, and one of the monks.

The house that Wyatt built has been transformed into a college, but it has all been finely done, and the stateliness of this place, the charm of its beautiful little chapel, is still unspoiled. The chapel is a rare delight, with elegant panelled benches, stained windows, and a delicately carved roof borne on wall-piers crowned with noble fan-vaulting. Down below we walk in the vaults that have been here all the time, under the stone roof where the old monks walked, where the wines were kept in the days of the Tudors and the Dukes. The chapel adds a spire to the great towers and turrets which make the house look like a small walled city.

And all about it is one of the loveliest gardens in the loveliest garden country in the world. Was ever such a terrace, such living walls of box, such trimmed yews in living urns, such laburnum canopies, such cedars, oaks, and firs, such masses of oldfashioned flowers? We walk down a grass lane with rhododendrons piled like houses on either side, red and mauve, yellow and white. Was ever such a dazzling mass of colour? And beyond it all stretch three avenues lined with Wellingtonias; we have not seen so many of these great pines in any garden; we feel that Kipling must have seen them when he wrote:

Our England is a garden that is full of stately views
Of borders, beds, and shrubberies, and lawns and avenues.

These three avenues run, we imagine, for a half mile, and at the bottom of one of them we came to a ring of trees. In the centre of this ring we found a kind of altar with an open book carved on it, on which we read that *God is a spirit* and that *Blessed are the pure in heart*. We walk on and on and come to another ring, the old monks' garden with arches cut through its circular hedge, leading us back to the lawns again.

One of the great avenues in the park, lined with beeches and nearly a mile long, frames at one end the tower of Ashridge House and at the other a slender column to the canal-making duke. Facing the village entrance to the park is a marble fountain with a tall cross on top of it, and behind it a round stone seat inscribed to the memory of Lady Marian Alford, who died in 1888 at Ashridge, her son, the second Earl Brownlow, having inherited it from his grandfather after the House of Lords had been called in to settle his claim. No mean artist herself, Lady Marian was a patron of art, and our Royal School of Art Needlework grew up at Kensington under her influence. One who knew her said that she was a perfect grand dame, not able to harbour an ignoble thought, incapable of a small action. It was she who, when somebody protested to her about burning the candle at both ends, said that surely that was the way to make both ends meet. Here she was much beloved, and she built the home for 11 poor widows still known as the Bede Houses.

Not far off is an interesting 16th century manor house in which are two painted panels of Queen Elizabeth, one showing her as a child walking in Ashridge Park with her attendants, the other showing her at the moment of her summons to ride from Ashridge to the Tower at the command of her sister Mary. The same little house which in her day stood opposite the north-east entrance to the park is there still, a black and white medieval home with an overhanging storey behind a row of apple trees. It keeps its 15th century hall roof of open timbers, and is still called John of Gaddesden's House, after the first Englishman to become Court Physician.

A pathway leads us by Lady Marian's Bede Houses, through the fields, to the medieval church. It stands among cedars, flowers, and trimmed yews. The tower and the nave arcades are 15th century. Here in this small place we found ourselves back among the people of the great house long ago. There is a girl kneeling at prayer between stone pillars, a little widow of 16 who died in Shakespeare's day, granddaughter of Thomas Egerton, trusted minister of Queen Elizabeth and devoted friend of Essex. Here lies her father with many other Egertons, including John, the second earl, who played the elder brother in Milton's Comus when it was first acted under his father's patronage at Ludlow Castle; and on down to the last Duke of Bridgewater who gave us our first canal. Among their memorials is a beautiful relief of a shepherd family with their little sleeping child. The timbers of the nave roof are 500 years old, and there is a fine old chest with great strappings of iron.

Little in name but great in achievement and interest is this village, and all round it are magnificent beech woods and commons high with bracken, great oaks, walnuts, and wild cherries, now part of our National Trust. It is a veritable sanctuary of wild life and wild beauty.

The Duke Who Went On

FRANCIS EGERTON, last Duke of Bridgewater, was the ugly duckling of his family. Born in 1736, he was so puny and slow of mental development that, as his brothers died, it was proposed to secure the succession to a distant heir, but nothing was done and he became duke at 12, lived neglected for the next five years, and then was led through Europe by a tutor who stirred his mind and made a man of him.

Returning to England, he owned and rode racehorses and became engaged to one of the beautiful Miss Gunnings, then the widowed Duchess of Hamilton. As she would not consent to hold aloof from her sister Lady Coventry, whose life the duke considered scandalous, he broke off the match, and from that time forth would not even have a woman as a servant in his house.

Driven in upon himself, he turned his thoughts to the improvement of communications with his rich coalfield at Worsley. The idea of a canal was his own, but his plan was to build a succession of locks down to the Irwell, and another flight of locks up the opposite bank, and so across country.

Fortunately he was introduced to James Brindley, who persuaded him to amend his scheme, to build an aqueduct across the river and make the canal at one level throughout. Experts ridiculed the project as a madman's illusion. To send heavy barges and even ships across a bridge spanning a river with craft already upon it, certainly seemed a startling proposition in an age that knew nothing of inland navigation by artificial methods; such a thing as a canal independent of river supply had not yet been contemplated.

But Bridgewater went on. It was a strange combination, the rich and eccentric nobleman and the engineer who had to do his calculations in his head and was never sure whether navigation should be spelled navacion or novogation. But they blended perfectly, and, thanks to Brindley's unflagging fertility of resource, they built their canal with its aqueduct and its miles of waterway in the heart of the coalfield itself. Worsley and Manchester were linked by water for a distance of nearly ten miles and in July 1761 the first barge-load of coal made its way along the canal at half the former cost. A more ambitious enterprise followed, the making of a canal from Longton Bridge to connect Manchester and Liverpool. Fierce opposition had to be met, and immense difficulties overcome. There were times when the duke's steward had to borrow £5 from tenants for wages, and when nobody would discount a £500 bill bearing his signature. But he went on undaunted, brought the work to a successful conclusion, and, having laid out £220,000 on his two canals, found himself master of an income of £80,000, a fitting reward of his courage and enterprise.

Lancashire owed him much for its industrial prosperity, but he felt that he owed still more to his country, and at a moment of national danger he gave £100,000 to a patriotic fund. He left a splendid collection of pictures and some ancient sculptures. The marbles he had bought in Italy during his youth, and they were found at his death unopened in the packing-cases in which they had been brought to England more than fifty years before. We must presume that in his energetic life he had no time for such enjoyments.

He died in London in March 1803 and the dukedom died with him. Bridgewater House is a neighbour of St James's Palace, and one of the most magnificent houses in London.

The Heart in the Silver Casket

LITTLE HADHAM. A silver casket with a story links the noble-fronted Elizabethan hall with the modest church of St Cecilia over which eight centuries have passed. In the hall and the church centres the historic interest of Little Hadham, but on the rising ground outside is a delightful windmill, and round Bury Green's three-cornered plot of grass are three farmhouses, one from the 17th century, one with an Elizabethan brick wing (where a double-headed eagle presides in the elaborate plaster ceilings), and one (Clinton's) with a wing nearly 500 years old, where a great roof beam stretches from wall to wall enriched with Tudor tracery.

Hadham Hall, though fire has destroyed half of it, remains a triumph of the Elizabethan architect who built it for the Capel family, a grand sight with its entrance turrets, its octagonal chimneys, its gallery 135 feet long, and its ancient gatehouse and barn. The church has no such outward grandeur, but its nave owes something to Norman masons, its 14th century tower has a splendid arch, and outside the 15th century timber porch, near an ancient yew is the grave of William Harvey, who sailed as a midshipman three times with Captain Cook. He was with him on the last tragic voyage to the Sandwich Islands, and gained promotion as lieutenant when the officers all moved up one to replace their murdered captain.

Inside the church is a rich pulpit carved in 1633, with sounding board and standard; an early 16th century screen of elaborate tracery; a fine array of panelling from the doors of the 17th century pews; and two figures and a shield in glass 500 years old, St Lawrence with his gridiron, Isaiah, and the arms of Bishop Braybrooke who built Much Hadham's great tower. There are brass portraits of a 15th century family of father, mother, and four girls (probably the Bauds), and a priest of their time, Richard Warren. Up in the tower hang one bell about 500 years old and another dated 1595. Down below is the family vault of the Capels, which brings us to the story of the silver casket.

For years this casket lay in the Tudor hall, and was then carried to this vault, its contents reverently buried, for it contained as loyal a heart as ever served a king, the heart of one of Charles Stuart's noblest followers. He was Arthur, Lord Capel, a man in whom even his enemies could find little fault; but after unsuccessfully defending Colchester for ten weeks he was one of the first to be sentenced to death when the king himself had walked out on to the scaffold in Whitehall. While he lay in the Tower a cord was smuggled to him with a message that his friends were waiting on the other side of the moat. He let himself down from his window, and waded chin-deep through the mud and water, which, but for the fact that he was a head taller than most men, would have drowned him. For two or three days he lay hidden by the Temple, and then went by boat to a house in Lambeth Marsh; but the waterman who rowed him was suspicious, followed him, and betrayed his hiding-place for ten pieces of gold.

Back in the Tower, with death on the scaffold now inevitable, Capel asked that if it should not be thought a vain ostentation his heart should be put in a silver casket and laid at the feet of his dead king. It was not to be. Charles was buried at Windsor, and his faithful follower's heart was turned to dust at Little Hadham, where on Lord Capel's stone we read that he was "Murdered for his loyalty to King Charles the First." It was put in a silver casket as he desired, the keys of the two locks being kept by his friends, Lord Beauchamp and Sir Thomas Corbet. When Sir Thomas lay dying he passed the casket to Lord Capel's son, and for years it was kept at the hall, and then forgotten. Not till 1703, when the family had moved to Cassiobury, was it found again, and then the heart was carried to the family vault in this church; but lest the silver casket should tempt a thief an iron box was substituted, and the silver casket was sold to help the poor.

The Two Knights

LITTLE MUNDEN. Set in a network of narrow winding lanes, with a church crowning one of the rolling hills of this country-side, it has many old associations. At Dane End, nestling in a hollow at the foot of the hill, the cottages face the grounds of the great house. To the south-west is the modern Rowney Abbey, reminding us of Rowena Priory, a house for Benedictine nuns founded in the 12th century. Libury Hall, between the two Mundens, has a name old enough to be in Domesday Book, and is now a home for old and poor foreigners.

The flint church, with a sturdy 15th century tower, stands in a churchyard glorious in spring with daffodils, and with a magnificent old yew among its trees. Most of the old work is 14th and 15th century, but the priest's doorway is Norman, and the modern arch of the western bay of the nave arcade rests on Norman uprights with three rows of cable carved on the capitals. The rest of the arcade is 14th century, and in one of three dainty niches is part of a figure. The chancel arch is 15th century, the south doorway 14th. The roof of the nave has fine old kingposts and trussed rafters; there are kingposts in the old chapel, old benches in the chapel and chancel, and a 15th century traceried screen between the chapel and the aisle, with the rood stairs and two doorways close by. Two of the bells have been here since the middle of the 15th century.

Under the arches of the chancel arcade are two tombs on which lie two 14th century knights and their ladies, the men thought to be John Thornbury and his son Philip. Round the older tomb are shields in quatrefoils, and figures of sons and daughters. The pigeon-chested knight has armour with a rich belt, and he peeps from his fine ornamented helmet through a curtain of mail. A lion is at his feet, and two dogs are huddled at the feet of his wife who wears a netted headdress. The shaft of the 14th century arch above them has been cut to form a canopy for the knight's head. The other tomb is adorned with arcading, and is set under an arch carved with quatrefoils in lattice pattern, and angels holding shields. The two figures have extraordinarily big heads. The knight has armour with a rich belt and a collar with a pendant; round his head with long curling hair is a band beautifully carved with leaves and flowers and a jewelled ornament. His head rests on a helmet with a lion plume, and a lion is at his feet. His wife has a striking and elaborate headdress, beaded and draped, a mantle held by a rose clasp, and a triple necklace with a pendant.

Neighbours

LITTLE WYMONDLEY. It has two old neighbours of the centuries, the big barn and the little church. The church, set on a knoll, has an Elizabethan bell still ringing in the 15th century tower. The barn is a grand sight, 100 feet long and 40 wide, divided into nave and aisles by rows of posts, while an elaborate framework of medieval timbers supports the tiled roof. The barn, with some 13th century arches left in the moated farmhouse beside it, comes from the great priory Cardinal Wolsey used to visit from Delamere House at Great Wymondley. Close by is the conduit head of the monks' water supply, its medieval rubble patched with 16th century brick. The monks were driven out and James Needham, the Clerk and Surveyor of Works, whose name is on a brass in the church, took possession and put in a few doorways that are still here, his successors adding good panelling. To the south of the church is 16th century Wymondley Bury, with a gabled brick dovecot in its grounds. The rest of the village gathers round a 17th century inn.

A Village Takes Leave of its Senses

LONG MARSTON. It lies in a corner of the county almost ringed round by Buckinghamshire, with a new church which has preserved many features brought from the old one. It has medieval clustered columns built into its new arcade and the south doorway has stones marked with pilgrim's crosses 600 years old. In the chapel is a recess with a Norman arch on Norman pillars, and the chancel has a 13th century recess and a 14th century piscina. Some of the aisle windows have their old stonework, and the screen has some 15th century tracery and panels with a little of their ancient colour. Up in the roof between the nave and chancel is a fine beam 500 years old, with carved spandrels, and in the nave is the plain 600-year-old font. The 15th century tower of the old church with two scratch dials on its walls, stands solitary not far away.

It was this village which witnessed the last witch tragedy in England, a terrible event involving three deaths. The law against witchcraft had been repealed years before as the result of a jury's decision in this county, but in 1751, a mob at Long Marston went out of its senses and dragged from their homes two harmless old people over 70, Ruth Osborne and her husband John. It was said that a farmer's misfortunes had been caused by Ruth, and notice was given by the town crier that these old people were to be tried by ducking. The old folk hid in the vestry of the church, but were dragged out and stripped, their hands tied to their toes, and so thrown into the pool naked. The old woman died choked with mud, and she was tied to her husband, who died soon after. The authorities resolved that stern notice must be taken of this outrage, and a chimney-sweep who had been a ring-leader of the mob was charged with wilful murder. He was Thomas Colley, and was tried at Hertford assizes and sentenced to death, being executed next morning at Gubblecote Cross, Tring, where he was afterwards hung in chains.

It is odd that two Hertfordshire villages (this and Walkern) should be so dramatically associated with the ending of the witch-craft craze.

The Poet at School

MARKYATE. Roman soldiers marched down its street, and long after them black-robed nuns here found a retreat until Henry the Eighth gave their house to one of his favourites. Traces of this history are before us. The houses line the Roman Watling Street as it passes into Bedfordshire, and in the park surrounding Markyate Cell, the red house beyond the village, are magnificent trees which would be saplings when Humphrey Bourchier pulled down the nunnery and set up his Tudor house. It has been much rebuilt since then, but in the 16th century kitchen walls are stone mouldings from the church of the nuns.

A row of giant limes leads us to an 18th century church, with a handsome gallery, a carved pulpit, and two elegant chairs. It has a stone cut with a flowery cross which came from the nunnery, and a tabernacle with painted saints from Italy. It was to this church that the poet Cowper came as a boy when at Dr Pitman's school in the village; he was here for two years, unhappy and ill-treated, and long afterwards he hated schools and wrote a long tirade against them in a poem called Tyrocinium, in which come these lines:

> *Lascivious, headstrong, or all these at once;*
> *That in good time the stripling's finished taste*
> *For loose expense and fashionable waste*
> *Should prove your ruin, and his own at last;*
> *Train him in public with a mob of boys,*
> *Childish in mischief only and in noise.*

The east window is in memory of one of the VCs of the Great War, Colonel John Collings-Wells. He had won the DSO early in the war, and the VC came during the last desperate thrust of the Germans. When the English rearguard was surrounded by the enemy he called on volunteers to stand with him, and they held up the German advance for nearly two hours, till their ammunition was spent. A few days later he led a counter attack, and though twice wounded continued to lead it till he died at the very moment the position was won.

The Church in the Wood

MEESDEN. Leaving the long green with the houses scattered about it, we find a wood with a path climbing to a church with a simple Norman door, masked by a high Jacobean porch. The elaborate porch was added in the days of Robert Younge, whose bust presides over the chancel, a saintly man with texts over his head, in his hand, and written across his open book. The font and the chalice are also of his day, but the tiles arranged in a handsome mosaic before the altar are 300 years older, laid down in the 14th century when the chancel was new. They are yellow and dark green, and two of them have shields. It was a friendly thing the Victorians did for this small church in the wood, opening up the blocked 13th century arcades and rebuilding the miniature transepts to which they led 700 years ago and now lead again.

A Farmhouse and the Tudor Dynasty

MUCH HADHAM. Just where the River Ash bends round Bush Hill is a farmhouse of such dignity that we should guess it had a history; and so it has. It is the Palace, the country home of the Bishops of London for 800 years, and here began our Tudor dynasty, for Henry the Fifth's widow (Shakespeare's Katharine) gave birth in this farmhouse to Edmund Tudor, whose son Harry won the throne on Bosworth Field. The building has changed since then. Today it is mainly 16th century, with an outer casing of 17th century brick and later wings. A floor cuts in half the fine old hall with its gabled windows and mighty oak girders, but there is an elegant staircase, and 17th century panelling.

Giant survivors from the bishop's avenue of trees lead to the road, and another avenue of mighty limes leads to the ancient yew, sturdy sentinel by the spacious church, which has been growing since the 12th century. Nothing is here of the Normans, and it is 13th century masons who have left their mark; we see it on almost every chalk stone at the end of the south arcade as clearly as if it had been scratched yesterday. The north aisle with its grand arcade was added about 1340, and at the end of that century Bishop Braybrooke built the massive tower and set his arms over the door.

Bearing up the 500-year-old roof of the nave are stone carvings of a sceptred king, a recumbent knight, a lady with a distaff, and the four Evangelists. The capitals and arches of the superb north arcade are rich in carvings of flowers and heads of lions and of men. The 15th century added carvings in wood to that in stone. The lions in the roof, the rood screen of elaborate tracery, the choir stalls with their misereres, the chancel panelling and some panels in the pulpit, two high-backed chairs, and some of the nave seats, are all of that time. The altar table is Elizabethan. Round the 15th century Easter Sepulchre are patterned tiles 600 years old, and the old vestry door has ornamental ironwork a century older. Some glass in the east window has wonderfully survived 500 years; it shows Peter and Andrew with a row of saintly women.

A wife of one of the bishops, Judith Aylmer of 1618, is here in stone, but without her head. Among the portraits in brass are a serjeant-at-law who died about 1420, an Elizabethan mercer called Clement Newce with his wife and 17 children, and William Newce (who died in 1612) with his two wives and 13 children. One brass tells us of Simon Flambard who heard the news of Bannockburn when he was parson here, and another asks us in French to pray for the soul of a later 14th century parson. A more famous rector was Alexander Nowell, the Dean of St Pauls who wrote the Catechism. Elizabeth thought highly of his learning, but that did not prevent her rating him soundly for presenting to her a prayer book with pictures of saints and martyrs, and once when he was preaching she called out "To your text, Mr Dean. Leave that; we have heard enough of that," so disconcerting the poor man that he was unable to finish his sermon.

The rectory is a little later than his day, a Jacobean house of brick and plastered timber. Several other old houses with over-hanging storeys give great charm to the village, and there is an inn with a secret passage behind its panelling.

The Little Rhyming Priest

NETTLEDEN. The grand avenue of beeches shading the road from Little Gaddesden opens on this sweet place, where two old buildings look at each other breathing a common friendliness, one the church, the other a 17th century house. We found the timbered house in a setting of flowers so brilliant that even motorists slowed down to look. The church is long and low and narrow, with battlemented walls and a 15th century tower left standing when the rest was rebuilt last century. Here, as we open the church door, is a feast of colour to match the garden. The aisleless nave has patterned walls with painted panels, and the chancel and the ceiling are completely covered with a rich design. Two Elizabethans, Edmund Bressey and his wife, kneel in stone wearing the stiff ruffs of 1600, their only daughter kneeling below with four brothers. Before the altar lies another who lived in a colourful age, Sir John Cotton, Vice-Chamberlain to Edward the Sixth; he is pictured on a big brass wearing his armour and with his shields about him. In the sanctuary is a carved 17th century chair.

On the pulpit is carved a verse found among the papers of one who preached here not so very long ago and now lies under the giant yew. It is not difficult to guess his trouble from these brave lines:

> Beneath the shelter of this yew tree's shade
> A little harmless rhyming priest is laid.
> He loved his life, though not of death afraid,
> And loved his Maker, though so strangely made.

The names of six other brave men are cut on the stone gateway at the end of the trimmed yews, all torn by war from this small place with barely a dozen homes.

Family Groups

NEWNHAM. Its medieval church has facing it a row of cottages fashioned from the 17th century malting house of the old manor. The church itself has kept its 14th century porch, with the old roof and carved angels, and the three medieval centuries are still represented by the chancel of the 13th, the arcade and aisle of the 14th, and the clerestory of the 15th. The 14th century gave the church a tower by cutting off a bit of the nave and building two side arches within the original walls to support the weight. The font is 500 years old. There are fragments of medieval glass, an Elizabethan chalice, a bell of Shakespeare's time with an inscription no one can understand, and two family groups in brass. One group pictures a 15th century man with his two wives and four children, the other is of a Jacobean lady, Joane Dowman, with six or seven daughters.

The News that Stirred All England

NORTHAW. Charles Lamb, who loved this countryside, would climb up here from the deep wooded valley where the rivulets flow to the Lea on the east and the Colne on the west. Centuries before Lamb came this way to spend his holidays this pleasant country attracted someone else, for James the First took part of Northaw Common to complete his Cheshunt estate of Theobald's Park. The money he paid for it still brings the village a few hundred pounds a year as the interest of what is called King James's Fund. Theobald's Park is no more, and the old church by the green has given way to a handsome new church, which has kept from the old the 15th century font with crosses and Tudor roses, and a Stuart chalice. On the green is the striking memorial to the men who fell in the Great War, a cross rising 25 feet high with the figure of Our Lord.

For a long time many folk in this quiet countryside will remember the dramatic event of the war for which an obelisk stands at Cuffley near by; it was the fall of the first Zeppelin, and only those who were living in those dark days are able to understand the emotion that vibrated through the land when the news was told. Night after night people waited in fear for the coming of these ships of death. Night after night they came and went away. William Leefe Robinson became famous one Sunday morning in 1916 by breaking up the plans of the biggest raid during the war. He had been two hours in the air, and had attacked one of 14 Zeppelins unsuccessfully when he met another at Cuffley, and emptied into it three drums of ammunition from his Lewis gun. It crashed to the ground and burned for two hours, its fall being witnessed by thousands of Londoners and by the crews of other raiding airships. Robinson was given the VC. He lived through the war, but by a cruel stroke of fate died on the last day of 1918, just after the Armistice, from influenza.

Poor Peter

NORTHCHURCH. There are stones in its church walls which were laid before the Conqueror set foot in England, and near by is a fragment of the mysterious Grim's Ditch, a rampart and boundary line of unknown origin.

In its nine centuries the church has seen many changes, but the south and west walls of the nave are as the Saxons built them, the walls having been thickened at the end to support the Saxon tower, which is no more. The central tower which has replaced it was built in the 15th century, and there are medieval stones in the two transepts and the chancel. Most of the rest is modern. The chief possession of the church is a grand Flemish chest deeply carved 500 years ago, a beauty. Some of the new windows are attractive. Four bells hanging in a frame of 1615 were made in Cromwell's England, and we found a stone set up by the ringers in memory of one of their company who had rung these bells for over 70 years.

A gravestone outside the church porch marks the last resting-place of a piteous waif of circumstance, Peter the Wild Boy, whose picture is on a brass. He was found wandering in the forest near Hanover as a boy of 13, walking on his hands and feet, climbing trees like a squirrel, and eating grass. King George the First took an interest in him and placed him in a home, but Peter escaped and took refuge in a tree, from which he could not be rescued save by cutting the tree down. The king had him brought to England, where he was at first shown as an object of interest to the nobility; but it was found impossible to teach or train him, and he never spoke more than a few syllables. It was clear that poor Peter was an imbecile, but he remained a sort of popular craze in those days, and Dean Swift, on a visit to London, wrote home that little else was talked about. He wrote that Peter was a Christian, and had been taken to court all in green to the great astonishment of the quality and gentry, and he followed this with a pamphlet, by himself and Dr Arbuthnot, called The Most Wonderful Wonder that ever appeared to the Wonder of the British Nation. Many absurd things were said about this poor wild boy, such as that he neighed like a horse in his joy. Queen Caroline tried to educate him, but the brass in the church tells us that "after ablest masters had failed to make him speak he was sent to a farm, where he ended his inoffensive life in 1785, aged about 72 years." For years poor Peter had wandered about these fields and woods with a collar round his neck requesting all who found him straying to return him to Mr Fenn of Berkhamsted, and in the end they laid him in this churchyard, the saddest human mite known to this countryside.

From the 16th century comes a timbered church house with an overhanging storey, now turned into cottages, a delightful break in the houses closing in on the overcrowded motor road from London to Aylesbury, and another pleasant reminder of days that are gone is the 300-year-old dovecot, of brick and timber, in the grounds of Norcott Court a mile away.

Arrival of a Cat

NORTH MIMMS. It luxuriates in the rich possession of three parks: Brookman's, with the spidery masts of the BBC piercing the sky; Gobion's, the site of Sir Thomas More's ancestral home; and the thousand acres of North Mimms Park, with its noble house and church. In Gobion's Park stood the old home of the family of Sir Thomas, and when Sir Thomas More's son John died, 12 years after his father's execution, Mary Tudor gave the confiscated property to his widow, who gave it to their son Thomas. Thomas, an ardent but secret Roman Catholic, died in 1626, and his two sons (Thomas and Cresacre) succeeded. It is interesting to note that Cresacre wrote the life of his great-grandfather, printing it at Louvain and dedicating it to Queen Henrietta Maria. His grandson sold Gobion's in 1702. Brookman's Park is the station from which London wireless programmes are sent out. Its 200-feet aerial masts are seen for miles round Hatfield. The station is on the main road a mile or two south of Hatfield, and in the low buildings which nestle at the foot of the great aerial system are housed two complete transmitters, one for the Regional programme and one for the National, the electric power being supplied by the BBC's own generating plant operated by oil engines. Transmissions from Broadcasting House come here by post office landlines to be sent out far and wide through the ether.

It was about the year 1600 that the future architect of Hatfield designed the dignified house, North Mimms Park, with its three brick storeys and its fine chimney stacks, its projecting wings and pinnacled gables, and its great mass of transomed windows. The church, reached by a long elm avenue, is older. Begun in the 13th century, the nave, aisles, and chapel were made new in the 14th, and red brick patches mark other changes since. The beautiful west doorway was removed from its old wall and built up again when the 15th century west tower, with its copper spire, was added.

The pulpit, the altar table, and some panelling in the vestry are Jacobean, and the church possesses such a fine 17th century German tankard of amber and silver that it has been shown at the British Museum. In the chapel built for a chantry about 1328 the light shines through fragments of 15th and 17th century glass in the fine old tracery, and falls on the tomb of a 15th century lady, Elizabeth Coningsby. A Tudor lady, one of the Barfords, is sketched on the flat stone of her alabaster tomb in the aisle, her outline filled in with black.

Above the nave pillars solemn stone faces of medieval folk look down on us, and grotesque heads hold up the roof. A gallery of brass portraits decorates the chancel wall, chief among them the magnificent brass of Thomas de Horton, vicar nearly 600 years ago. Arrayed in his vestments, he stands under a canopy, with Christ and the angels above him and saints at each side, a Flemish masterpiece. The others show an Elizabethan couple (Richard Butler and his wife), Elizabeth Knowles in her fashionable dress of 1458, and an armoured knight and a civilian and his family from the troubled days of the Wars of the Roses. A marble figure of Justice honours a man worthy of honour, for he did more than any other man to establish a constitutional monarchy in England. He was John Somers, who played so great a part in our constitutional history.

On a buttress of the nave is a sundial put up in 1584, eight years after Henry Peacham was born at the rectory. In the British Museum we may see his illustrated translation of King James's Basilicon Doron, which he did as a present for Prince Henry; it ends with the music and words of the madrigal, Wake softly with singing Oriana sleeping. But his best work was a book entitled The Complete Gentleman, dedicated to a boy of eight and written to urge young men to devote themselves to the arts. Sad to say, his own devotion brought him little profit, and in his old age this painter and engineer was writing books for children and selling them for a penny apiece.

An odd little memory has North Mimms. One September afternoon in 1784 a country woman here was astonished to see a great
spherical monster descending from the sky, coming low down near
the ground, so near that a man in the car of the balloon was able to
hand to her a cat to take care of. He rose again and went on to
Standon, where he arrived with a dog; it was Lunardi completing the
first successful balloon flight ever known, bringing the first English
aerial travellers (a man, a dog, and a cat) down in Hertfordshire.

A Pillar of the State

JOHN SOMERS, who lies at North Mimms, died Baron Somers of
Evesham. He was born near Worcester in 1651, son of a Puritan
lawyer. He was a brilliant scholar and linguist, and so distinguished
himself at the Bar that the leading counsel for the Seven Bishops
insisted on having him at his side.

A man of broad and liberal views, Somers on entering Parliament
at once became a force. By convincing the House that James had
abdicated and was no longer king, he made smooth the path of
William the Third to the throne; but he safeguarded the future by
framing the masterly Declaration of Rights, a second Magna Carta.

He advocated religious tolerance, and moderation and mercy in
State prosecutions; and proved a just judge and a model Lord
Chancellor.

With the decline of Whig ascendancy, Somers suffered the common
disfavour of his party, and was singled out for vindictive persecution.
Two attempts were made to impeach him, one of the counts being
that he had promoted and profited by piracy on the high seas. The
fact was that Somers had patriotically subscribed towards fitting out
a ship to suppress piracy, and that Captain Kidd, appointed to the
command, had turned traitor and developed into an arch-pirate
himself. A more serious charge was that Somers had been privy to
an unconstitutional secret treaty between Dutch William and Louis
the Fourteenth, proposing the partition of the Spanish dominions by
France. Nothing came of the matter, but William was constrained to
take the great seal from his Chancellor.

Somers threw the weight of his wisdom and authority on the side
of the Union of England and Scotland, and, triumphing over bigotry

and interested opposition, secured liberal provisions for the safety of Scottish religion and government.

In April 1716 he died here after a paralytic seizure, honoured and mourned by both parties in the State. He was a great upright counsellor, a fearless champion of public rights, a scholar and a warm friend of learning, the patron of Addison, and the man to whom Swift dedicated his Tale of a Tub. His own writings are contained in the famous Somers Tracts, 13 volumes of scholarship, wise philosophy, and good English.

Two Gipsies

NORTON. The Garden City of Letchworth has linked itself with Norman days by appropriating this bit of Old England, adding Norton's common to its own more prim avenues and gardens. Yet it has left the village its integrity and its charming church, which has that delightful quality of age which we call homely.

It is simplicity itself. Worn red tiles pave the floor, the rough uneven walls are whitewashed, the roof is like a barn, and some of the benches are a little weary after 400 years and more. The plain chancel arch is of soft chalk, yet it has survived from Norman days; it has a mysterious opening over it looking into the new chancel. Part of the nave walls are also Norman. The tower is 15th century and has two ancient bells. The canopied pulpit is Jacobean. There is a chalice made in 1570, and a service book which has been busy changing the names of the royal family since 1793. Stupid nobodies from Stuart times to our own day have scrawled their initials on the 700-year-old font, which has a quaintly panelled stem. On one wall is a tablet to three little sisters called Cole, one of whom was born in September 1752 and died in February of the same year, a curious effect of the change in the calendar.

One of the vicars here (G. H. Pierson) has the astonishing record of 68 years. He would know two gipsies who lie in the churchyard, Cornelius and Polly Smith, who died here from smallpox. All the world knows their famous son Gipsy Smith, one of the most remarkable evangelists of our time.

Offa's Village

OFFLEY. It may be that the village owes its name to Offa, King of Mercia. Matthew Paris says he died in his palace here, but tradition probably goes too far when it tells us that his bones were laid in the stone coffin now lying in the church. Here are thatched cottages and an inn 300 years old, and more than twice that age is the church among the trees of Offley Place, where Dr Johnson's Mrs Thrale stayed as a child with her uncle, Sir Thomas Salusbury. Sir Thomas rebuilt both his house and the chancel of the church, where his huge marble monument by Nollekens matches the black sarcophagus (with a statue of Truth) of another 18th century judge, Sir Henry Penrice. The two monuments are too heavy for the old church, as the old roof was, for its weight tilted the 13th century pillars with their beautiful capitals. The nave and both the aisles are 13th century, with later windows and doorways, the north aisle retaining fragments of 14th century glass, and a record of the consecration of its altar a year or two after the Battle of Agincourt. The judge's chancel, though square outside, is apsed inside. The tower was made new last century.

There are 16th century brass portraits of John Samwell, with his two wives and a son, and one of a nameless man with three wives and nine sons. There are some good 15th century benches, and a grand tomb of 1699 on which Sir John Spencer reclines stiffly in stone in Roman dress, a lady kneeling at his feet. But the treasure of the church is the font, one of the most beautiful in Hertfordshire. Within rose-tipped arches round the bowl a 14th century mason carved the favourite patterns of window tracery of his day, and a Jacobean craftsman gave the font its cover.

The Judge in the Chapel

OXHEY. Here a group of early Christians settled 100 years before King Alfred, when much of England was still heathen, and here in 1612 Justice James Altham built a red chapel on the site of their house of prayer. Two copper beeches overhang the chapel, a green grass carpet bordered with flowers leads to its door, and inside we find Judge Altham in his red robes saying endless prayers in stone, his wife with him. When his house was rebuilt in 1688 its old oak was used for the handsome reredos, with massive twisted columns and a pediment. More old woodwork and finely carved modern teak fills the rest of the chapel. Framed on the wall is a fascimile of a Latin charter of 1007 now in the Bodleian Library, with a translation telling

THE KING'S ENGLAND

that King Ethelred grants once again to St Albans Abbey Offa's stolen gift of Oaxanehaeg, or, as we call it today, Oxhey.

Old Doors

PIRTON. Its houses, now scattered on the Chilterns, are the descendants of a fortified village of the Conqueror's day, which clustered round Toot Hill, on the top of which a Norman knight built his castle. We can trace the encircling ramparts. The castle has gone, but to the south-west of Toot Hill's clump of trees is a church with something from the Normans left—two of the old patterned arches of their massive tower, one opening into the nave and one into the chancel. The tower itself has been rebuilt. The rest of the church is a patchwork of medieval and Victorian masonry, with a few fragments of 14th century glass, an old chest, a bell of 1634, and two doors which have lasted 600 years.

Several of the farms about were the homes of Elizabethans. Hammond's Farm they would find scarcely altered if they could see it now, and they would recognise the huge barn, 135 feet long, of the moated Rectory Farm. The Grange also has a moat from the days when fortifications were still thought necessary. Away on a wooded hill is High Down, an interesting Stuart house bearing the arms of Thomas Docwra and his wife Jane, who lived and died here, and has a stone to her memory in the church. The oak door which closed on her for the last time in 1645 still opens to her successors.

The General

PRESTON. It has a delightful green with fine elms and a church-yard with four avenues of cypresses, but its church belongs to our own time. In it is an interesting witness to the days when a house of the Knights Templars stood here, founded in the reign of King Stephen by Bernard de Baliol, ancestor of the founder of Oxford's famous college. The Knights Hospitallers succeeded to the Knights Templars, and held the house until the break-up of the monasteries by Henry the Eighth, who gave it to his secretary of state, Sir Ralph Sadler. His family held the house till Queen Anne's day, when the present manor house of Temple Dinsley was set up on the site.

The witness of those days which we find in the church is the lid of a stone coffin with a long-stemmed cross carved in relief upon it.

It was dug up with other coffin lids and with human fragments, and there is no doubt that it covered one of the ancient knights. His name is unknown, but all the world knows the name of a humbler soldier of Christ who came this way, for John Bunyan would often come to preach in a dell in Wain Wood, half a mile north of the village. Not far away are the ruins of Minsden Chapel over which ivy has been creeping for three centuries.

Castle Farm is interesting because it is said to be the site of a home of Lawrence Sterne's Uncle Toby. It is declared that this famous character in Tristram Shandy was drawn from Captain Robert Hind, whom Preston folk knew as the General. Here he would disturb his neighbours by firing a battery of guns rigged up on the terrace of his castle, which he fitted with portholes, turrets, and a portcullis, and he would parade the terrace with friends and children dressed in scarlet uniforms with blue sashes.

The Old Inns

PUCKERIDGE. Some of the timbered inns at which the old coaches stopped on their way to Cambridge have remained to greet the motor-car. The wide timbered gateway and the old doors of the Crown and Falcon first opened to the traveller 400 years ago, when Henry the Eighth was disputing with Rome. The George saw the Hanoverians in, and the 17th century Thorpe House, which also began life as an inn, may have welcomed Samuel Pepys, who had a liking for Puckeridge. The Old Hall at Old Hall Green, has seen many changes since those days and is now a Roman Catholic College. Founded at Twyford in 1685, the College was moved here about 80 years later, and the flight of English Roman Catholics from the French Revolution added so greatly to its numbers that the Old Hall was rebuilt. Two generations later Pugin added several buildings to it, including the chapel and the library, which has now 15,000 books and some rare manuscripts.

All the Men Came Back

PUTTENHAM. Hertfordshire's Farthest West, it has a small gathering of houses and farms in peaceful meadows where the county points a finger into Buckinghamshire, with the Chiltern chalk hills not far away. The old work in the attractive little church of flint and stone comes from the 14th to the 16th century, but the chancel, the porch of stone and timber, and the top of the chequered medieval tower were made new last century. The tower has a turret rising above the battlements, and the porch shelters a Tudor doorway with a medieval door on its old hinges. The arcades and the chancel arch are 600 years old; the clerestory is 500. There are medieval oak benches, a few 15th century tiles in the chancel floor, and an old priest's desk. From the 17th century come the altar table, a plain cover to a font looking old enough to be Norman, and the quaint six-sided pulpit, its wide border carved with curious dragons or sea-serpents with curled tails. The chalice is Elizabethan.

The glory of the church is the almost flat 15th century roof of the nave, its mass of moulded beams enriched with bosses of flowers and shields; one plays on the name Hutton, spelling the first syllable and picturing the last with a tun or cask. Angels are on the ends of the beams, and the roof rests on eight saints standing on the shoulders of quaint birds. The south aisle has a simpler roof with old beams.

Puttenham is one of England's Thankful Villages. On a marble tablet in the church we read that out of 71 souls 15 went forth to serve in the Great War and were welcomed home again. Their names are here, with the words, *Thanks be to God*. This is the only village in the county where all the men came back from the war, and one of only thirty such villages in all England.

RADLETT. It lies on the old Watling Street, by a brook that feeds the River Colne; a Roman kiln has been discovered in a sandpit here. Watling Street today divides the old churchyard from the new church, built on a hillside terrace from which is a fine view of a well-wooded green valley. Finely carved heads of kings and queens from the ancient church peep out from the walls of the new, and jutting from the wall near the doorway is an exquisite figure of an angel bearing a crown to Our Lord. In the windows are figures of St Michael, St George, and St Alban, and below a window of Christ blessing the children is a children's corner with books and paintings and Della Robbia plaques.

Dear Lady

RADWELL. Here the River Ivel becomes a placid lake, with many a brood of waterfowl sheltering in its reeds. The mill has ceased to work, and trout are hatched in the quiet waters. The old folk of Radwell are here for us to see in the small medieval church above the river. It has a pillared font of the 15th century, a Tudor chalice, two ancient bells, a Jacobean chest, and Jacobean altar rails; but its best possessions are three interesting sculptures and brass portraits of three centuries.

The brass portraits show us William Wheteaker and his wife, their son between them in his priest's robes, holding a chalice; he was vicar here in 1492. Small brass figures by the pulpit are of John Bele and his two wives in 16th century dress; one wife has two little sons with her, the other has lost the portraits of two daughters. A fine big brass shows John Parker's wife in the rich dress and cap of Queen Elizabeth's days. There is another Tudor John Parker, "lord of the manor and of all this little town," sculptured with his wife and son kneeling one behind the other. Facing them is a lady sitting in a chair, a stiff little statue of Mary Plomer, "vertue's jewel, bewtie's flower." She must have been a neighbour of the Parkers, and her death (in 1605) must have been a village tragedy, for she was only 30 and she was bringing her eleventh child into the world. She wears a ruff, and over her head is a mantle; her baby lies in swaddling clothes beside the hourglass in her hand, and at her feet kneel the other ten children. She was a dear lady, we gather from her epitaph:

So that the stone itself doth weep
To think of her which it doth keep.
Weep, then, whoe'er this stone doth see,
Unless more hard than stone thou be.

Kneeling close by is Will Plomer, dressed in his armour, who, left alone with these ten little ones, took another wife to mother them; her monument is with the rest, decorated with three quaint animals.

Norman Tower and Medieval Screen

REDBOURN. The new Redbourn watches the traffic pass along Watling Street in the ghostly wake of Roman legionaries; the old Redbourn clusters beyond the pond and the common and lines a narrow street to the church.

It is an imposing church with a square Norman tower and an arcade of Norman arches, part of the church consecrated by Herbert Losinga, Bishop of Norwich, early in the 12th century. Two centuries later the chancel was rebuilt with its steep gable, and the south aisle was added. The 15th century rebuilt the north aisle, lengthened the south to make a chapel, added the porch and the clerestory, and framed a pointed arch inside the Norman tower arch. Then, about 1500, the richly ornamented corbel table of red brick was put round the outside by the Abbot of St Albans, who received the tithes of Redbourn for clothing his monks.

The church has one of the most beautiful of 15th century screens, its tracery and its double canopy (with pierced vaulting) carved shortly before the Reformation which destroyed its roodloft. Portrayed together in brass is an Elizabethan family, Sir Richard Rede with his wife and their six children. The Pecok family has been broken up, the brass of the father (who died in 1512) being left with four of the children, and even their punning crest of a peacock has lost its head. Eight little girls in brass of about 1470 must have been earlier members of the same family, for they also had a peacock, but have lost it, as they have lost the portraits of their parents. A plough and a crude coat-of-arms marks a farmer's grave to the east of the church, where Jonathan Rose of 1813 has his rake, hand-mill, sieve, and sheaf quartered in heraldic fashion, with his hoe, pick, shovel, and flail as supporters.

A sundial scratched on a nave buttress takes us back to the days before clocks; and a plateau fort above the valley takes us back to the ancient Britons who dug its double ramparts, the inner one still over ten feet high. The fort encloses over 17 acres, and unknown centuries have not obliterated its two entrances.

The Saxon Shrine

REED. It is one of those small places which send us dreaming down the corridors of time, for it has traces of six moats, some now little more than ponds, from the days when men sought security by surrounding their houses with water. Even today there is no friendly village street, but the houses are scattered with only winding lanes to link them together.

The church is apart in the fields, its nearest neighbour an old farmhouse with an overhanging storey. It is a miniature shrine to which about 30 generations of village folk have come, for the nave was built by the Saxons, and their long-and-short work is at all the four corners. They or the Normans made the small but perfect doorway

Sandridge   Church and Inn and Village Pump

Radlett   Modern Church **Stevenage**   Ancient Church

Stevenage   **The High Street**

Sarratt   **Church of Red-Roofed Gables**

Sawbridgeworth   **Overhanging Storeys**

Rickmansworth   **A Picture of Rural Charm**

now blocked up in the north wall, a sturdy and well preserved structure. We enter by a 14th century doorway, pushing open an ancient door four inches thick. The tower is 15th century, the three bells are all from Shakespeare's day, and the altar table is Jacobean, with massive legs.

The House and Tombs of the Monmouths

RICKMANSWORTH. Three rivers meet here, the Colne, the Chess, and the Gade, and as if they were not enough the Grand Union Canal passes the town on its way north. It has lovely riverside walks, fine open spaces, and a noble avenue of great trees. In the High Street are still a few of the old houses, among them Basing House, where William Penn brought his bride Gulielma Springett soon after their marriage. Here they lived four years. The charming timbered house called the Priory is much as they would see it, and so is the manor house, with its old chimneys, staircases, and panelling. The vicarage they would know has changed much, and has on it the date 1737, but it is one of the oldest in Hertfordshire, for it has Tudor ornament in a gable and timbers older still. The most famous house at Rickmansworth has been surrendered to the golfers, so that we may hope that this magnificent domain is safe from spoiling.

It is Moor Park which was given to the Earl of Oxford as a reward for his services on Bosworth Field, where the end of the blood-stained march of Richard the Third gave Shakespeare the chance to say, "The day is done, the dog is dead." After that Moor Park passed to Cardinal Wolsey, and after Wolsey's fall it passed to the Earls of Monmouth, and finally to the Duke of Monmouth, who began building the house we see. He was, of course, the son of Charles the Second, and he dreamed of a great house and a throne. Both dreams were broken, for all the world knows how this most wretched man was dragged from a ditch after the Battle of Sedgemoor and beheaded on Tower Hill. As for his house, it was taken over in course of time by Benjamin Styles, who had grown rich in the South Sea Boom. He lavished a king's ransom on Moor Park, spending £130,000 on it, engaging Sir James Thornhill, who had painted the dome of St Paul's, to do the painting for him. After his day came Admiral Anson, who spent another £80,000, which he could well afford to do as he went round the world in 1744 and came home with £500,000 in Spanish treasure, and three years later seized £300,000 more from the French. The house has had its adventures since, but it has kept its grand portico with columns 50 feet high, the enormous hall with five marble doorways, and the original panels on the walls. And, whatever else it may lose, it must forever keep the noble view from the highest point of the park, marked by a clump of noble trees. It is an unforgettable panorama.

The great tomb of the Monmouths is the chief monument in the church. In the tomb sleep the two earls, Robert Carey, and his son Henry. They were strangely different characters, Robert, the son of a cousin of Queen Elizabeth, soldier and courtier, who was present in the last dramatic days of Queen Elizabeth when she lay refusing to die; it was he who rode in haste to Holyrood to tell King James of Scotland that he was now King of England, so launching the Stuart dynasty on its tragic way. James promised him much and gave him little, and at last he became chamberlain to Prince Charles, who made him an earl when he came to the throne. Henry Carey, though brought up in the gilded atmosphere of the court, loved most the quiet of the study, spending life translating histories of foreign lands while the history of his own was being written in blood.

Above the Monmouth tomb is a tablet to Sir Thomas Fotherley, who was active in the service of Charles Stuart. There is a brass from those days showing Thomas Day with his two wives.

The church itself is mostly modern, but there remains the handsome 14th century tower that William Penn would know, with its medieval wooden window tracery and its evil-looking gargoyles, and it has still the little spire the 17th century gave it.

We found at Rickmansworth the most remarkable example of long service we came upon in this county, a family record on the Grand Union Canal. The lockkeeper here had been at his post for 31 years, his father served at it for 41, his grandfather for 58, and his great-grandfather for 62, so that four generations seem likely to complete two centuries.

The memorial to the men of Rickmansworth who never came back is set at a meeting of the roads with a background of trees; it has an upraised lion on a high pedestal, with a seated figure of Victory holding up a laurel wreath. Another memorial of much interest has been set up in the forecourt of Joan of Arc Convent School, where a statue of Joan was unveiled by the French ambassador in 1939.

Father and Son

RIDGE. True to its name, it stands on a wooded ridge with a view stretching to distant Barnet. Its narrow church was made new by 15th century builders who left only the piscina to show that there was a church here 700 years ago. Much has been altered since, but there are fragments of 15th century glass in a window, fragments of a painted St Christopher on a wall, and fragments of three medieval sun clocks cut in stone on the outside. In the tower (less than nine feet square) hang two bells from Stuart England.

Those were the days when Sir Henry Pope Blount, whose memorial is on the wall, lived at Tittenhanger Park, the fine Stuart house he built near London Colney on the site of a house where Wolsey and the king took refuge from the plague. Sir Henry was born at Tittenhanger in 1602, and at 32 he made the famous journey described in his Voyage to the Levant, a book which ran into eight editions while the Stuart throne was lost and won again. This journey took him through the Balkans to Constantinople, with the Turkish fleet to Egypt, through the dark passages of the Great Pyramid at Gizeh, and home by way of Florence, which he reached after travelling 6000 miles in 11 months. He died here at 80 and was buried in the church, and his son Thomas proceeded to make the family name still better known by publishing a vast compendium of what 600 great writers of all ages had written about each other. Thomas, who lies here with his father, was a scholar who believed heartily that scholars were not of much use to the State. It is clear that Thomas must have been a man of great modesty, for he himself was of wide learning, and in addition to the great book he produced in 1690, with the opinions of famous writers about one another, he published a Natural History extracted from the best authors, and a great book of poetry surveying the poets of all time.

The Cave and the Palace

ROYSTON. A town of narrow streets lined with old inns and houses, it has three notable things to bring a traveller here: a cave unique in Europe, the remnants of a palace famous for a poignant event in the history of the Empire, and a church with something in it from every century since our English builders first built churches.

The cave, an extraordinary place like no other we have seen, is deep down below the road at the meeting of the Icknield Way and Ermine Street. It is cut out of the solid chalk, bell-shaped, 25 feet high and 17 across, and its walls are covered with crude carvings. A winding passage brings us down to it, leading us till we are 30 feet below the road, with a candle to light up the queer crude figures of saints and crusaders, kings and martyrs, a curious medley of scenes from legend and history. It would seem that the carvings were once coloured, and that most of them are of Bible scenes; they are described to us as Mary and Joseph lifting the Child on to St Christopher's shoulder, St Catherine resting on the Everlasting Arm, John the Baptist, Thomas Becket, the Holy Family, the Vision of Paul. The history of this strange cave is mysterious, but it is thought the Romans may have found it here and used it for a tomb, that the early Christians may have used it for an oratory, and that the carvings were made about the time of the crusades. The cave was found by chance in 1742, when men were driving a post into the ground as the foundation of a bench for the market workmen, and 200 loads of earth had to be moved before the cave could be reached.

The palace of King James the First has almost entirely vanished, but a fragment remains in Kneesworth Street, with a front of about 50 feet looking on to the garden, the back facing the street. It is part of the palace to which the king often came for hunting on this heath which still stretches over 400 acres, a beautiful windswept hill with here and there a hump of a great burial mound, and from the top a wide view of fields and distant hills—blue and green with those shades which seem inseparable from the chalk range of the Chilterns. The people of Royston found the king's presence expensive for them, and seem to have presented a petition that his majesty might be pleased to leave the town as they were unable to entertain him any longer. One good effect the palace had, however, for it preserved the great stretch of country round from poachers, "persons of base condition, and the scholars of Cambridge." One thing to his eternal shame Macaulay's "ricketty-legged king" did here—it was in this palace that he signed the document betraying the founder of the British Empire to his enemies, the document which sent Sir

Walter Raleigh to the block to please the Spanish ambassador. The wheel of time brought its revenge, for the king's son was to come back to Royston in due time, not as a king but as a captive, to spend two nights here as a prisoner of the army.

The church is interesting for its possessions. The nave and aisles were built in the middle of the 13th century, but the north aisle was rebuilt a few hundred years ago except for the middle pillar, which is 700 years old. There has been much 19th century restoration, but the west tower is much as it was re-made from the old stones in the 16th century. The south aisle roof is 15th century, and the north aisle roof has medieval timbers in it. There is 14th century oak panelling, a 13th century font bowl on a 15th century base, a 13th century piscina, and a pulpit with part of the medieval rood screen worked into it. There is a curious 15th century brass showing the Five Wounds, brass portraits of an unknown man and his wife of 1500, and the canopied figure in brass of Thomas Tabran, a rector of 1462. There are ancient sculptures of the Madonna showing the Child with a bird in his hand, and of a bishop who has lost his head; but the most impressive monument in the church is of a knight of the 14th century, carved in alabaster.

In the graveyard lies Henry Andrews who, born in the 18th century, gave more than 40 years of his life to making astronomical calculations, being also an astrologer in the days when astrology was not the quackery Fleet Street has made it today.

Carrying On

RUSHDEN. We found it far away from the strife of the world, with as lovely a group of thatched cottages as ever stood round a garden of flowers. We found men here carrying on the tradition of their ancestors, climbing up to the roof of the church away in the fields, fixing new beams and carving them as they were carved 500 years before. The beams rest on the 15th century corbels, some of which are carved into angels and some into queer heads. There is a niche probably carved by the medieval craftsman who carved the corbels, and the font is from the same time. Almost as old must be the great ladder that curves like a snake up into the tower. On the walls are tablets to the Meetkerkes, who lived at the 16th century house in the park; Sir Adolphus was ambassador from Flanders to Queen Elizabeth.

A Tragic Day

SACOMBE. It was once called Suavecamp because of its quiet charm among the hilltops north of Ware. The charm remains, with a noble park and a lake to add to it, and a church which, though greatly changed, has a handsome piscina to witness that it is 600 years old. The windows and doorways are new, and the tower curiously placed on the south-west side was rebuilt last century; but in the new vestry are a few things from the past; the iron stand of an hourglass, a chalice of 1688, a flagon of 1715, and a memorial to Sir Thomas Rolt, who must have been high in the service of the East India Company, for his tablet speaks of him as Agent of Persia and President of India. A monument by Rysbrack to another Thomas Rolt recalls a tragic day for Britain. He was a captain of the guards who fell in that disastrous engagement in 1758 when our troops, having failed to capture St Malo from the French, were embarking at St Cast and the Duke of Aiguillon's forces fell on them and left a thousand dead.

Here Was a City Before the Christian Era

ST ALBANS. It is of towns like this that the history of the world is made; there is no more thrilling town within an hour of London unless it is Windsor. It was here that our long roll of martyrs began, and the town is named after the first man in our island to die for his faith. It was here that the Wars of the Roses began in the tragic days of Henry the Sixth and Margaret of Anjou. It was here that King Offa of Mercia built a little Saxon church which has grown into a vast cathedral with the handiwork of the Romans in it, collected from the ruins of the city of Verulamium. Farther back than Rome it goes, for the story of Verulamium, the only Roman town in Britain made into a municipality, begins before the Christian Era as a prehistoric settlement in Prae Wood, a plateau richly clothed with trees today and marvellously beautiful with bluebells in due season.

The city crowns a hill washed by the little River Ver flowing on its way to the Colne. As a bishopric it is not a century old, but its story is linked with the tale of cities which stood across the valley before and after the Romans came, and ended as a city of the Romans on the other bank of the river. The walls enclosed an area of 200 acres, roughly oval in shape, and crossed by Watling Street as well as by the road from Silchester to Colchester.

Though it is the third in a line of cities claiming descent from prehistoric Verulamium, the story of modern St Albans begins with the death of Alban, the first martyr in Britain. Born and educated here as a pagan, he was converted by a Christian priest who had sought refuge in his house from the persecution of Diocletian. For helping him to escape, Alban was condemned to death, led across the ford to the brow of the opposite hill, beaten with rods, and beheaded. That was early in the 4th century. In the 5th, after the decline of Verulamium, the Saxons built a new town on this eastern slope of the valley, which became known as St Albans after Offa founded in 793 a great Benedictine abbey in honour of the martyr, building it on the spot where he is said to have died, and founding it in atonement for his murder of Ethelbert. Offa found Alban's bones and placed them in the abbey church.

Offa's abbey was rebuilt soon after the Normans came. The 38th of its 40 abbots was Cardinal Wolsey. Matthew Paris and Roger Wendover were among its famous monks and chroniclers. Lawn and field have taken the place of most of its buildings, for, except for slight traces here and there, only the splendid church and the fine 14th century gatehouse are left today. Built largely with material from the ruins of the Roman city, the church was bought by the people of St Albans for their own after the Dissolution, and carries on as the cathedral; second to Winchester in length, it stands at a greater height above the sea than any other English cathedral, and is a landmark for miles with its tower rising 144 feet. Imposing with three storeys and a vaulted roof with carved bosses, the gatehouse was built about 1363 by Abbot de la Mare as the entrance to the abbey court. It served as a prison for French soldiers in the Napoleonic wars; the dungeons are still below. Since 1870 it has helped to accommodate the flourishing school which is said to have had its origin in the 11th century, or even earlier, and Matthew Paris recorded that in his day it had more scholars than any other school in England. After Edward the Sixth's charter had given it a new lease of life the school was housed for three centuries in the lady chapel. Among its famous men were Nicholas Breakspear, the only Englishman to become Pope; Sir John Mandeville, the 14th century man of travel and mystery, who was born in the town and has an inscription in the cathedral; Francis Bacon, and his father Sir Nicholas, Lord Keeper of the Great Seal, who obtained from Elizabeth a charter for the town to grant licences for the sale of wines, the proceeds of which were to go to the school. St Albans still has this privilege, which is possessed in England by only two other towns, Oxford and Cambridge. During the peasant revolt of 1381 the gatehouse was besieged in a riot led by John Ball, who was executed in the town. A proud memory of St Albans is that the third printing press in England, following those at Westminster and Oxford, was set up here about 1479, and that on it the Chronicle of the monastery and the famous writings on heraldry and hawking by Dame Juliana Berners were printed. She lived here at Sopwell Priory in the 15th century. Another press was set up here in 1534, and in the Old Library of the school are books from these early presses.

Printing has become one of the chief industries of this city in which old and new are intermingled, as is to be expected in a place which has more than doubled its population since the beginning of our century. Its 35,000 people live on 5000 acres, traversed by four old highways which meet almost at right angles near the Clock Tower, where traffic is for ever streaming by. As we travel these roads and the network of narrow ways between them, old houses and inns come constantly into view, though many have had their ground floors converted into shops. Some have Georgian dignity; others have Tudor timbering, plasterwork, mellowed brick, old roof tiles, gables and dormers, and overhanging storeys. The fourstoreyed Clock Tower facing the High Street is one of our few medieval belfries; it was built early in the 15th century and restored in the 19th, and the city clock now strikes the hour on a bell which is older than the tower itself, a curfew bell cast 600 years ago. It weighs a ton, and on it is the Latin inscription, I have the name of Gabriel sent from Heaven. It used to ring at four in the morning to summon apprentices to work, and at eight in the evening to close the market and the shops. Till 1702 an Eleanor's Cross stood in front of the tower, for Edward's queen passed this way on her last journey to Westminster, resting for a night in the abbey church.

The spirit of the old country town is vividly alive in the neighbourhood of the Clock Tower, for about it is a conglomeration

St Albans Cathedral

The Abbey Gatehouse, now part of the Grammar School

The Fighting Cocks, one of England's oldest Inns

FAMOUS OLD BUILDINGS OF ST ALBANS

of old buildings of all styles and at all angles. The tower is at one end of an island of them; at the other end is a charming gabled storey of 1637. To the west of the tower is the quaint narrow street called French Row, reminding us that the French troops occupied it in 1216. Next to a tilting gable-fronted storey projecting over shops is the Fleur-de-Lys inn with a roof of old tiles and overhanging eaves. Though it is much restored, the inn has its old timber frame, and is part of a larger house built in the 14th century, in which King John of France was imprisoned after the battle of Poitiers in 1356.

French Row brings us from High Street to the little marketplace and the 19th century town hall, its pillared front facing the spacious St Peter's Street. Ending the fine vista along this busy street is the memorial to over 600 men who fell in the Great War, standing in a Garden of Remembrance, with the church of St Peter rising behind it. Shaded by limes, and bustling with the business life of the city, St Peter's Street was the setting for two of the three most important battles in the Wars of the Roses. The Clock Tower was young when the alarm for the first battle rang out from it in 1455, a battle in which the king's forces were crushed with great slaughter. Three noblemen who fell lie in nameless graves in the lady chapel of the cathedral: Henry Percy, Earl of Northumberland, Edmund Beaufort, Duke of Somerset, and John, Lord Clifford. Henry the Sixth was found sheltering in a cottage, and was imprisoned in the abbey. The second battle of St Albans, in 1461, was a victory for the Lancastrians, the army of Queen Margaret defeating the forces of the Earl of Warwick with great loss. It is said to have been fought for the most part on Bernard's Heath, to the north of St Peter's Church, and many of the slain were buried here. The day after their victory the king and queen gave thanks at the abbey.

Facing the town hall is a fine old house which keeps its own balcony, dormers in its old tiled roof, an old lion knocker on the door, and massive beams within. Near by, at the corner of the marketplace and Dagnal Street, is the old Moot Hall with its timbered storey overhanging one of W. H. Smith's fine shops. Leading from St Peter's Street, Catherine Street brings us to the Daltons, known locally as Bleak House because it claims to be the original of Dickens's book. Modern building has encroached on its grounds, but it is still a very pleasant place with a beautiful copper beech among its embowering trees, and a drive round its circular lawn. The passage by which it was approached (Gombards) is still here, but the avenue of trees is gone. Charles Dickens was often at St Albans, and Dickens Close, north of Bleak House, keeps his memory green.

By the Clock Tower, a narrow passage leading from High Street to the east end of the cathedral marks the site of an old gate of the monastery. Continuing from High Street, George Street (on the north side of the cathedral) is rich in old houses and inns, serving chiefly as shops but keeping their rambling old rooms upstairs. At the top is a 15th century block with a projecting storey; part of it was once a tallow factory, and now accommodates the wares of an antique dealer, but the rest was till our time the George Inn which gave the street its name, famous in days gone by as a resting place for the pilgrims to St Alban's shrine. After the Reformation its private chapel was turned into stables. Turning from George Street into Spicer Street we come to the Congregational chapel of 1797, facing the Tudor almshouses. At the opposite corner, in College Street, a boot factory has taken the place of the house where the poet Cowper stayed with Dr Cotton during the worst of his periods of insanity; the doctor sleeps in St Peter's churchyard.

From George Street we drop down Romeland Hill and the narrow Fishpool Street to the mill by the Ver, which is here crossed by a bridge as well as by the ford which was so important centuries ago. Among the old houses we pass is a charming one with a gabled tilting storey and plaster decoration. Farther down is St Michael's Manor House, with little in the street front to remind us of its 16th century origin; the site was given by an abbot of St Albans, and on a fine plaster ceiling is the date 1586. Across the river the road continues as St Michael's Street, quaint with gables and dormers in the low-roofed old dwellings, entering the site of the Roman city on its way to St Michael's church. This is one of the three churches of St Albans founded in the 10th century.

The public spirit of St Albans has been vigorous enough to buy over half of the site of ancient Verulamium, which it has made into a charming addition to its parks and open spaces, turning the fishpond into a lake. We come to it down Abbey Mill Lane, at the foot of which silk is made in the 18th century mill now standing on the site of the old abbey mill. Here, too, is one of the smallest inns and one of the oldest houses in St Albans. A pointed roof crowns its eight sides of 16th century timber and plaster, on a medieval stone base which is said to have belonged to a fishing lodge of the abbey. It has been an inn only since the Dissolution, and was for a time a centre for the cruel sport which gave it its name of Fighting Cocks. On the other side of the city are the 25 acres of Clarence Park. Batchwood Hall, the home of Lord Grimthorpe, has become the club house of a municipal golf course. What is known as the ruin of Sopwell Nunnery, a mass of walls buried in ivy, is really the remains of the house built by Sir Richard Lee after the Dissolution of the Monasteries on or near the site of a nunnery.

St Albans has no more delightful scenes than those about its remarkable cathedral, and few cathedrals look out on a fairer aspect than this green valley. High on one slope stands the great pile raised by the Normans and those who came after them; on the other side of the shining river the site of the Roman city climbs gently to Verulam Woods by King Harry Lane, and green fields carry the eye to Prae Wood on the western horizon.

We come to the cathedral from George Street along a road fragrant with lilac and wallflowers in spring, bounding one side of a burial ground known as Romeland, where George Tankerville, a baker, was burnt at the stake in 1556. Old and new are about us here. Looking on to the plot is Abbot de la Mare's gatehouse, charmingly grouped with the modern buildings of the school, and only the space of a lawn away rises the cathedral's stately front with flanking turrets, arcaded walls, and a great west window with rose and wheel tracery, and three gabled porches with vaulted roofs and splendid doorways with clustered shafts. Except for some of the vaulting and other traces of medieval work seen inside, this west front is entirely the work of Lord Grimthorpe's restoration; he is said to have spent over £140,000 on the cathedral last century.

For the rest, the exterior is impressive rather for its size than its beauty. It is gigantic, a cross 550 feet long and 177 feet from north to south of the transepts, covering an area of about 40,000 square feet. The walls are largely of flint and brick and stone taken from the Roman city, so that those great walls might have in them the oldest materials in any cathedral in the land. Many windows have been renewed, two of Lord Grimthorpe's spectacular alterations being the great round window in the north wall of the north transept (with 37 roundels filled with leaded glass looking like spider's webs), and the five lancets (called the Five Sisters) in the south transept, so tall that the middle one is said to be the longest in the country, 60 feet.

The cathedral is an arresting spectacle outside, with its nave 285 feet long, the longest in the world; the pinnacled transepts still looking much as the 11th century Normans built them with the Roman material; and the enormous central tower. Except for the later parapet, and the fact that Sir Gilbert Scott stripped off the plaster to expose the Roman brick, this unique tower, higher than any other Norman tower in England, stands as it stood when the Normans built it after the Conquest. Two of its four stages are open inside, and the arches on which it rests are 55 feet from the floor. In the triforium arcading of both transepts (seen inside) are some of the Saxon baluster shafts from King Offa's church; they were used by the Normans, and are said to have been turned on a lathe. There are no other remains of the Saxon church. Some of the plaster has been removed from the triforium wall in the south transept to show the construction of Roman brick. In the outside wall of the south aisle are remains of the handsome 14th century traceried bays of the vanished cloister, of which the site is laid out on the grass.

It was Paul de Caen, the first Norman abbot, who rebuilt Offa's monastery. It took him 11 years, and when completed in 1088 it was one of the finest in the land, unique with its Roman material and destined to become in the 13th century the wealthiest English shrine. It had the simple plan we see today, except that the nave was only about three-quarters of its present length, and the vestibule and lady chapel at the east end did not exist. St Albans is rich in its early Norman work, for, in addition to the tower and transepts, Abbot Paul's church still exists in the western portion of the presbytery and its aisles, and in 12 bays of the nave—nine on the north side and three on the south. The western end of the nave (four bays on the north and five on the south) was begun about 1195, and completed in about 30 years.

Mounting the five steps from the west end we enter the nave, striking, lofty, and long, though the handsome but rather battered

14th century stone rood screen (enriched with canopies, arcading, and doorways) breaks into the vista. The three periods of the nave's architecture are plain. The richly moulded arches of the main arcading in 13th and 14th century work rest on piers with four attached shafts. The lovely arcading of the 13th and 14th century triforium has ornament in the arches, between the clusters of shafts. Crude in comparison with this medieval work is that of the Normans. Their plain round-headed arches are on massive piers, and their bays are divided by flat buttresses; the simple severity of the style relieved by some of the old wall-painting for which the cathedral is notable. On the underside of the arches is a gay medley of the brick, zigzag, and lattice pattern dear to the Normans, but the figure-work on the piers and elsewhere is chiefly 13th and 14th century, including Crucifixions, scenes in the life of the Madonna, St Christopher, Thomas Becket, and other saints. Remains of three 15th century figures are high up in the choir, and the 15th century ceiling of this part of the nave has its original painting of the Coronation of the Virgin. The rest of the nave is modern, except for the old brackets, on which are some figures holding shields and some at prayer. The north aisle is plain and much changed; the south aisle keeps some of its old vaulting. The beautiful 14th century cloister doorway remains at the eastern end with a cornice of trailing leaves and rich cresting, and spandrels with painted shields. In it hangs an old door with exceedingly fine tracery. It is one of several old doors the cathedral has preserved, two of them 500 years old being in the north transept. Near the cloister doorway is a handsome tomb recess which is said to be the resting-place of two hermits.

Passing to the choir we have one of the most impressive views of the cathedral, dominated by the magnificent stone screen behind the altar. It comes from the time of Abbot Wallingford, about 1484, and ranks with Winchester's great screen as one of the finest in England. For three centuries after the Reformation this beautiful thing stood battered and broken, but thousands of pounds were spent on it by Lord Aldenham last century, and the exquisite canopies of its three tiers of niches are restored to their original beauty, and all the statues (about 70) are new. Under a fine Crucifixion in the centre of the screen is Our Lord with the Disciples in a dainty row of alabaster figures, and below this row we see Him rising from the tomb in a panel sculptured by our famous Alfred Gilbert, whose Eros in Piccadilly Circus the whole world knows. On each side stand three saints, the six being St Alban and the priest he died for defending (St Amphibalus), the venerable Bede, Hugh of Lincoln, St Edmund, and Pope Adrian the Fourth (the Englishman Nicholas Breakspear). On the eastern side of the screen is a lovely Madonna and Child, and over the two doorways are figures of John the Baptist and St Stephen.

All about us as we stand in the choir is Norman work of the Conqueror's own century—the choir itself, the transepts right and left, the mighty tower in front of us with its fine lantern, and the west end of the presbytery. The ceiling of the tower, 100 feet from the floor, has 16th century painting of red and white roses, with shields of the arms of England and St George, St Alban and the Confessor. The roof of the presbytery, carrying our eye eastward from the choir, has a 13th century timber vault with floral bosses; the painting on the moulded ribs, and the leafy roundels with the lamb and eagle, are 15th century. There is much of this old colour still left in the cathedral. In the south transept is an angel with outspread wings still with its 13th century colour, and in the north transept is vine pattern enriching window splays and a picture of St Thomas touching the wound to satisfy his incredulity; it is all 15th century. From the same time comes the picture of King Offa crowned on the west wall of the presbytery aisle. The red and blue figure of William of York in St Alban's Chapel is 14th century, and shows him in his archbishop's robes giving blessing. A big painting on wood in the south aisle here has come down from the transept roof; it shows the martyrdom of St Alban, the head of the saint (just struck off with the sword) having wide open eyes. It is said that the roof from which it came in the north transept covers the spot where the saint was killed.

Two chantry tombs face each other in the presbytery, one built for himself by John of Wheathampstead in the 15th century, the other the tomb of Robert Ramryge. The Wheathampstead tomb has stout iron grilles, a traceried stone roof, and a cornice of shields, ears of wheat, and vines growing from heads of lions. The Ramryge tomb is rich enough in decoration to look like a wing of the screen; it has charming window tracery on its two storeys, shields borne by rams, and a fine oak door with linenfold opening to reveal a lovely stone roof with a pendant boss.

Facing the eastern side of the great screen is the Saint's Chapel, drawing us to it as it drew pilgrims long ago. Here they came in great numbers to kneel at St Alban's shrine, and here by a miracle of restoration still stands the pedestal on which the shrine rested. Set on a base of quatrefoil panels is a series of ten niches with leafy gables under a rich cornice of foliage, and carved in relief is King Offa holding his church, St Alban being martyred, and a company of angels and saints. There are touches of the original red and blue paint in the tracery still clear after 600 years. It is surprising that this rich piece of work is here for us to see, for it was found last century in more than 2000 fragments which have been marvellously pieced together again.

Filling a bay of the north side of the Saint's Chapel is a captivating Watching Chamber, like a little wooden house with an upper storey overhanging an elaborate vaulted canopy. It has been here since 1400, and in its upper room, enriched with traceried panels and reached by a tiny staircase with steps of solid oak, a monk was always on guard to see that no harm befell the shrine. In the cupboards below relics and treasures were kept; now their carved doors open to show us fragments of wood, stone, and tiles, and a wreath of holly leaves and yew which is said to have hung in the church for over 200 years in memory of a bride who died on her wedding day. In the cornice over the vaulting is a gallery of quaint carvings of huntsmen with hounds, a chained bear, a pig and its litter, the shepherd playing pipes to his sheep, a dog, and a boar, a wolf with a lamb in its mouth, and a milkmaid milking a cow. (We noticed that she is sitting on the wrong side.) Near the back of the watching chamber, in the north aisle of the presbytery, are the battered remains of the 14th century pedestal of the shrine of St Amphibalus, the teacher who converted St Alban; the cathedral is fortunate in its possession of fragments of these ancient shrines.

A rare treasure is the beautiful grille of hammered iron on the south side of the Saint's Chapel, made in Sussex about 1275. Fashioned in a charmingly simple design and painted blue and gold, it has 42 panels of square and diamond lattice with studs, and served as a protection for the shrine. Now we see it only from the aisle, for in the bay across which it extends is the 15th century two-storeyed monument of Humphrey, Duke of Gloucester, magnificent with its triple arch, the traceried roof with pendant bosses, the traceried panels with fine canopies, and the shields. The Good Duke Humphrey (called so for his patronage of learning) sleeps beneath his monument. A son of Henry the Fourth, he lives in Shakespeare, and is remembered for having given the first books for a library at Oxford. At the east end of the Saint's Chapel, is a fine group of 13th century arches on clustered shafts, with fragments of tracery above the capitals.

Beyond the chapel is the vestibule leading to the lady chapel, both much changed since they were built 600 years ago. The modern stone vault of the chapel has fine bosses of vines, fruit, and flowers, and springs from exquisite cone-shaped corbels carved with passion flowers, hazel nuts, and leaves of the vine, sycamore, and oak. Also modern is the rich arcading on the walls, and here again are foliage, flowers, and fruit enriching capitals and spandrels. But the windows are original, and arresting for their beautiful tracery, the strings of trailing ballflowers edging their splays, and the dainty niches with statuettes in the splays and on the mullions. Among these figures are kings, queens, bishops, evangelists, prophets, martyrs, the Madonna, and St Anne. In the tracery of the east window is a crescent of five leafy arches.

It is a memorable view that is presented to us as we stand in the lady chapel and look across the vestibule to the Saint's Chapel, seeing the three pointed arches as frames for three fine pictures— the shrine (with the lovely Madonna for a background), the Duke of Gloucester's chantry tomb, and the Watching Chamber. In the vestibule hangs a beautiful bronze candelabra copied from one of Cromwellian days, now lit by electric candles; and on each side is a modern oak screen with linenfold base, dainty shields in tracery, a cornice of vine and lace-like cresting. Beyond the screens are the eastern chapels of the aisles of the vestibule, the south chapel restored by the Mothers' Union for their own, the north chapel of St Michael restored in memory of men and women who have worshipped here or been associated with the cathedral. In it stands a delightful figure of the Archangel on a serpent; he has silver armour, a green mantle, and purple wings, and he holds a sword with his hands on his breast. On an oak lectern in the vestibule,

A Splendid Norman Doorway in St Albans Cathedral

The Choir of St Albans Cathedral

The Stone Screen of St Albans Cathedral

The Shrine of St Alban

The Vaulting of the Presbytery

The Lady Chapel

Saxon Columns

IN ST ALBANS CATHEDRAL

surmounted by a golden St George with the dragon, are the illuminated Books of Remembrance with the names of more than 12,000 men in the Diocese who fell in the Great War.

Under the great lancets in the south transept is Norman arcading from the 12th century; below it is an elaborately carved doorway of the same time. In the blocked arches in the east wall are two 14th century doorways. The west wall has two 13th century lancets, and a blocked 11th century doorway which opened to the cloister. In it are three beautiful little cupboards with baluster fronts (two Elizabethan and one Jacobean) from which bread is given on Sundays to 20 poor women from a 17th century bequest. In one cupboard are three old wooden bosses, the biggest carved with foliage coming from the face of a grotesque. On the same wall hangs Frank Salisbury's impressive painting (15 feet long and 5 feet high) of the Passing of Queen Eleanor. King Edward in his crown (his hands at prayer) sits astride his horse, which is draped in black; behind the abbot in his white robes trimmed with gold are the red-robed monks; figures in black robes and hoods are bearing torches, and Eleanor, lovely with auburn hair, lies on her bier. We read that the panel represents the honour paid at St Albans to Queen Eleanor by the king, and links his efforts as the last great Crusader of 1272 with the deliverance of Jerusalem by British arms in 1917. It was given to the cathedral as a thankoffering for the men of Hertfordshire who offered their lives in the Great War, but years before the war broke out the picture had been in the Royal Academy. It was this picture, we believe, which resolved Mr Salisbury's career as a historical painter, for at the end of the Academy Exhibition the Committee of the House of Lords desired the artist to paint one of the frescoes in the Peers' Corridor. He painted the Trial of Catherine of Aragon, and since then Mr Salisbury has been for most of a generation the accepted master of colour and pageantry among our English painters.

From the 17th century come several chairs, a settle, and a chest in the south presbytery aisle—the chest having locks and a slot for alms, for which a little wooden man with a stick is holding out his wide-brimmed hat on the wall above. The capitals of the stone arcading in this aisle are exquisitely carved with hawthorn, nuts, primroses, and vine. In the north transept are some medieval tiles, and four fine old shields in a window, with arms of Edward the Third and three of his sons. Rich glass in the lady chapel has the Nativity, Simeon with Jesus, the Flight into Egypt, and saints. Two beautiful windows in the north aisle of the nave have the Annunciation and scenes from Our Lord's life. Glowing red and blue, Mr Comper's glass in the great west window is a memorial to the 12,778 men and three women of the diocese who fell in the Great War. In the crowd at the foot of the Cross are the holy women, soldiers, sailors, nurses, warrior saints, Joan of Arc, and shields of the dominions, the allies, and the towns of the diocese.

There is fine modern craftsmanship in the oak stalls and the bishop's throne. The stalls are vaulted, and the tracery of the panels is tipped with angels playing instruments. Those across the west end form a screen and have rich canopies; the entrance arch has pelicans and leaves; and the finial is a pedestal for a statue of St Alban. Minstrel angels stand in niches at each side. The bishop's throne is exceedingly rich. Built in our own century, it is a mass of carving from the floor to the tip of its soaring spire. On the finial in front of its canopy St Alban stands with a sword and a cross, and at the back of the throne is the Crucifixion. There are angels on pillars, and on the cusping, the desk has poppyheads of roses and pomegranates, and at each side of the seat are panels of pierced carving of birds among vines and berries. The Freemasons of England gave the stone pulpit (one of the biggest we have seen), carved with diaper of flowers and a border of ivy, oak, and acorns. The font has a white marble bowl set on a stem of black marble, and its striking cover is like a coloured spire with three tiers of Corinthian columns, adorned with figures of Matthew, Mark, Luke, and John in golden robes.

In the presbytery and its aisles are many stones which have lost their brasses of abbots and monks, knights and ladies, civilians, priests, and family groups. One has remains of a border engraved with quaint animals and grotesques, and one has three canopies left. The brass of Master Robert Fairfax, doctor of music, was renewed in 1921, 400 years after his death; the dainty portraits are of Robert in his fur-edged gown and his wife in a headdress embroidered with roses, a dog at her feet; with them are two sons and two daughters. Ralph Rowlatt of 1543, a merchant of Calais, is a civilian with six little daughters in kennel headdress, but he has lost his wife and sons. Another wool merchant, Thomas Faryman of 1411, is with his wife. Brother Robert Beauner, who served the abbey for over 40 years before he died in 1460, is a tall monk holding a heart. Near him in the floor of the presbytery is a charming brass of a Yorkist knight, Sir Anthony de Grey, of 1480; his armour has curious elbow guards like leaves; he has a sword, a tiny waist, long hair, and a crown at one side of his head. He was Elizabeth Woodville's brother-in-law.

Mounted on a board in the Wheathampstead chantry are four complete brass portraits, a headless figure, half of a figure with hands at prayer, and halves of a man and a woman. On the floor of this chantry lies one of the finest brasses in existence, brought here for safe preservation from its stone in the presbytery. It is of Abbot Thomas de la Mare who died in 1396, and was the work of a Flemish craftsman about 1375, made under the supervision of the abbot himself. His vestments are exceedingly rich. His hands are crossed, and he has his crook. The background is diapered with leaves and heraldic beasts, and at each side and above his figure are a score of saints, angels, and prophets in canopied niches.

On an unknown tomb in the south presbytery aisle is an altar stone with five crosses. High on the wall we see Radulf Maynard of 1613 kneeling in cloak and ruff. In the north transept the first Bishop of St Albans, Thomas Legh Claughton, lies on his tomb, and Bishop Blomfield, the first suffragan bishop, has a slab of black marble on a tomb with rich open tracery and canopied figures of the Evangelists.

A charming picture to keep in our memory of a visit to the cathedral is seen as we stand outside its eastern arm. Here a fine cedar reaches out to the cathedral wall and the garden of the deanery, which hides in its lofty trees, and ending the vista along the quiet little retreat called Sumpter Yard (where packhorses with supplies for the abbey were unloaded) is the timbered White Hart Inn on Holywell Hill and near it the Saracen's Head, both 17th century. As we stood by the cedar the fine ring of bells were playing Home, Sweet Home.

The cedar was one of two brought from Lebanon; the other is on the lawn of the almshouses founded by Sarah Jennings, Duchess of Marlborough. Facing these is the County Museum, a small place rich in its collection of local antiquities from prehistoric, Roman, and medieval days. Stone Age implements and tools are here in fine array, and of the Bronze Age there are celts, palstaves, daggers, and spear blades. There are necklaces, bangles, and brooches of the Iron Age, Roman pottery, urns, lamps, tear-vases, plates, and a fine glass bowl; a good collection of English silver and copper coins and Hertfordshire tokens, coins from Verulamium, old books and illuminated manuscripts, and a collection of swords and daggers and helmets from the 15th century. We see an old loom that was making bonnet trimmings 80 years ago, a quaint fire engine with leather buckets, an exquisite piece of coral, beautiful chalices, an ivory sceptre with four rows of cherubs, ivory plaques with Bible scenes, and the Yard of Ale glass, a yard high. Among the old domestic objects typical of the county are toys, utensils, dress, and straw hats in the process of making. The foot of the stairway is set out as a period room, with a settle, cradle, and spinning-wheel.

From the museum we are soon at St Peter's Church, which, like those of St Michael and St Stephen, was founded in the 10th century by the sixth abbot. Standing in a green churchyard, it is a fine picture outside with its massive tower rising between the nave and chancel, the transepts having been destroyed last century. Except for the nave arcade and the south aisle (which are medieval), the church was largely rebuilt by Lord Grimthorpe. The striking feature of the bright interior are the lofty arcades of seven bays, with arches on clustered shafts reaching the low wide windows of the clerestory. The coloured angel corbels of the roof may be 15th century. The north aisle has medleys of old glass with figures and faces. Capronnier's bright glass in the south aisle illustrates the parables and the Ascension, and the rose window at the west end has the Annunciation and Bible scenes. A beautiful window with knights and angels is in memory of Frederick Mead who died the month the Great War broke out, and of his two sons who fell in France. A chest is Jacobean, and the modern pulpit (with the Evangelists in panels) has a richly carved stairway.

Part of Roger Pemberton's brass of 1627 was used in 1515 as a memorial to John Ball. Roger in fur-trimmed gown is with his wife in draped headdress, three sons and two daughters and a babe in swaddling clothes. Roger was Sheriff of Hertfordshire, and founded the simple row of almshouses almost facing the church. The iron arrow pointing upward on the archway in front of them reminds us of the story that Roger founded the hospital because he accidentally killed a widow when he was shooting in the woods.

A small monument has the bust of Edward Strong of 1723 in a long curling wig. He was Wren's master-mason in the building of St Paul's, and in his epitaph we read:

In erecting the edifice of St Paul's several years of his life were spent, even from the foundation to the laying of the last stone. He shared the felicity equally with the ingenious architect Christopher Wren and pious Bishop Compton, of seeing, beginning, and finishing that stupendous work.

He sleeps in the church, and lived in the house facing it. One of the houses he built is now the electricity show rooms, and has its original staircase.

Nearly a mile from the city centre, St Stephen's Church stands at the top of St Stephen's Hill, at its meeting with King Harry Lane and Watling Street, which continued north-west through Verulamium. It is on the site of a Roman cemetery, and things brought to light in recent digging are in the Verulamium museum. In the church-yard of fine trees and hawthorn avenues is a Roman milestone, and there are Roman bricks in the oldest parts of the church. This is a charming picture, with its porch of stone and timber, and its quaint shingled tower and spire. The Saxon church almost vanished with rebuilding and alterations in Norman and medieval days, and most of the old work is 15th century, but some Norman masonry remains, and a blocked arch in the north wall of the nave is part of a 12th century arcade which led to a lost aisle. Two small Norman lights are in the west wall. The south arcade is 13th and 14th century. On the pillars are old inscriptions and drawings and mason's marks. One inscription tells of Edward Pearse, who was crushed under one of the stones, and another is said to have been cut by a Royalist soldier imprisoned here; there are men fighting, and a Crusader's head. There are 13th century lancets in the south chapel, whose interior, with leaning walls and a roof of old timbering, reminds us of a ship. It has a tiny peephole.

A rare feature is the oak chancel arch with traceried spandrels; it is chiefly modern, with some remains of the 15th century. The battered 500-year-old font has angels and shields on the bowl and the Madonna and saints on the stem. The brass eagle lectern, with three lions at the foot and an inscription to a Bishop of Dunkeld 500 years ago, is believed to have belonged to Holyrood Chapel. It was buried for safety under the chancel during the Civil War, and found a hundred years later. William Robins of 1482 is here with his family in brass, William in armour with a dog at his feet, his wife in her butterfly headdress. In beautiful modern glass we see a boy (with a dog at his feet) touching one of the wounds of St Julian, and the Saxon Abbot Ulsinus holding a little church, with the abbey for a background.

A mile as the crow flies from St Stephen's is St Michael's church, reached from St Stephen's by King Harry Lane and Bluehouse Hill, and from the city by the oldfashioned streets on each side of the river. St Michael's is within the boundary of the Roman city. Together with the churchyard and the vicarage, it is on the site of the Roman Forum, the centre of the municipal life of the ancient city, where, in the Roman law courts, Alban was sent to his martyrdom. Roman brick and flint from the ruins are still in the church walls. There is Saxon walling in the nave and chancel. The Normans gave the nave its first aisles, shaping their arcades in the Saxon walls, and three massive Norman bays still stand on the north side, while four Norman bays of the south arcade are still to be seen—one open to the chapel, the others having doorways built under them. Two of these doorways are 13th century, and one has a 500-year-old door with studs and strap hinges. Above the arcades are remains of Saxon windows made with Roman bricks.

The 13th century clerestory has original lancets, except for three windows of about 1500. Above it is the 15th century roof resting on old angel corbels. The chancel has a blocked doorway of Roman brick probably built by the Saxons, and windows of all three medieval centuries; one lancet has an oak lintel. The altar table is Elizabethan, and two chairs and the fine canopied pulpit were richly carved in Jacobean days. The old hourglass stand is still here. There are three shields in old glass, a 15th century font, a 14th century tomb recess in an outside wall (sheltering a coffin lid), and traces of wall painting which include remains of a Doom. A Roman coffin and part of a Roman pillar are under the tower. One of three fine old brasses is a cross with the small figure of a man in the head; he wears a long gown buttoned at the throat, and a sword hangs from his girdle. A knight in armour and helmet, with a dog at his feet, is about 600 years old and another brass of the same age is of John Peacock and his wife; John has a scrubby beard and a long robe with a cape, and Maud has a fine draped headdress. Three peacocks are on the shield.

No visit to St Albans is complete without a visit to St Michael's, for here in the chancel sleeps Francis Bacon, and here, sculptured in marble by someone unknown, he sits in a chair, resting his head on his hand, wearing the elaborate dress of his time—puffed breeches, fur-lined mantle, and a big ruff, a wide hat on his head and rosettes on his shoes. From the lodge gates near the church, the fine tree-lined Gorhambury Drive brings us to what is left of his old home, a sad ruin now, with roofless walls of brick and flint. The present house, a few hundred yards away, is the seat of Lord Verulam, and was built in 1778 by the third Viscount Grimston. An imposing house with a balustraded parapet, it has been much altered, but keeps its grand 18th century entrance at the head of a flight of steps, with ten Corinthian columns.

Christ Church, on the Verulam Road, has a spreading cedar in front of it. Built in classical style, with a campanile tower, it was begun last century by the Roman Catholics and completed by the Protestants. With the names on its memorial of those who fell in the Great War is that of Edward Warner, who won the VC. He entered a trench alone to keep it from the enemy, and as reinforcements could not reach him owing to the gas he came back and brought up more men, who held the trench till the attack ceased. "This very gallant soldier," as the London Gazette called him, died soon afterwards from gas poisoning.

It would take a volume to tell the story of Verulamium, the rich legacy of our past bequeathed to St Albans. The result of the excavation of its three ancient sites (one prehistoric and two Roman) have made St Albans a Mecca for student and layman alike. Though the great importance of the neighbourhood has long been known, the systematic digging with spade and trowel was not begun till our own time, the work being started in 1930 under the guidance of Dr Mortimer Wheeler with the help of students and volunteers from near and far.

What it has gained by recent research into its past more than compensates St Albans for an old belief which now appears to have been unfounded. For long it was supposed that the old settlement in Prae Wood was the stronghold of Cassivelaunus, whose heroic defence against Julius Caesar was defeated in 54 BC. Dr Wheeler's discoveries have led him to believe that the headquarters of Cassivelaunus were at Wheathampstead, and that Prae Wood was a daughter-city, capital of south-Eastern Britain till the capital moved to Colchester.

About two years after their submission to the Roman invasion of 43 AD, the people moved from their plateau to the shelter of the lower slope of the valley, and thus was established the first Roman city of Verulamium, covering about 150 acres. For a time all was well with this diamond-shaped city of wooden buildings, for it was the only British town to which the Romans gave the high rank of Municipium, and its people had all the rights of Roman citizenship; but in 61 the Queen of the Iceni, Boadicea, indignant with the people for having submitted to the Romans, descended upon it in the absence of the Governor and destroyed it with great slaughter.

Out of the ruins rose the second Roman city. Built early in the second century, it included part of the earlier site, and extended southward along the Watling Street. It was the third and final Verulamium, the city in the shape of a rough oval, its 200 acres enclosed by two miles of massive walls of flint with courses of the bricks we see in the cathedral tower. There were half-round towers at intervals in the walls, and four gateways north, south, east, and west. Its buildings were of stone, including temples, arches, houses, and public buildings with mosaic floors; the Forum was almost in the middle of the city, and the theatre fronted Watling Street.

The third century saw the city fall into decay, and though there was an attempt at restoration at the end of the century (with the subjection of Britain once more to the Roman emperor), the glory of Verulamium had departed never to return.

Not only has the story of Verulamium been unfolded so that we may read, but there is much of intense interest actually to be seen—

The Great Norman Arches of the Cathedral

The Excavated Roman City of Verulamium
THE ANCIENT SIGHTS OF ST ALBANS

St Michael's, on the Site of the Roman Forum
AN OLD CHURCH OF ST ALBANS

The site is one of the green and pleasant places of our land, sloping up to fields and deep woods. It has some of the most impressive Roman walling to be seen in Britain, the only Roman theatre (as distinct from the ampitheatre) yet discovered in England, some of the finest mosaic pavements in existence, and a fine museum in which are housed the wonderful array of relics which lay hidden in the ground from the time of the Romans till our day.

Nearly a quarter of a mile of the massive walls (from two to about six feet high) and two of the bastions are now cared for by the Office of Works. Crossing the river by the silk mill and the lake we come to St German's Block, a great length of wall so called from a vanished chapel of that name. Following the Lane to Verulam Woods, the wall of the southern boundary of the city rises on one hand, and on the other is the old rampart, now a shady glade of trees. There are patches of walling on the right of King Harry Lane as we travel to Bluehouse Hill, down which a charming ride brings us across the old city to St Michael's Church. North-west of the site is the great mass known as the Gorhambury Block. The little that was left of the Chester gate has been filled in; so has the smaller Silchester gate, with its single roadway and square towers. The unexcavated gate on the north-east lies under the road and houses of St Michael's Street, but the foundations of the London Gate have been laid out, showing its two roadways for wheeled traffic and two for pedestrians, flanked by boldly projecting round-fronted towers. A hundred feet broad, it was one of the finest of the gateways built by the Romans, and must have resembled a triumphal arch.

Carrying on the illustrated story of Verulamium are foundations of houses whose walls have helped to build the great pile on the other hill, the cellar of a wine shop, Roman streets, and a mosaic pavement lying as the Romans laid it. It is like a great carpet in colours of black, grey, green, red, pink, white, and ochre, and its 16 square panels have individual designs set in circles. It was the floor of the warm room of a private bathing establishment, and at one side of it is the entrance to the hypocaust by which it was heated. Of the Forum, which is said to have been 400 feet long, there is the foundation of a corner where the two ancient roads bisected the city.

Apart from its unique interest to the antiquarian, the site of the Roman theatre is charming for us all, with banks of smooth lawn and the grey outlines of its plan. As we stand here with the open green spaces about us, we see across the river a fine picture of the modern city clustering about its cathedral, while behind us are the trees of Prae Wood, where the first chapter of this long story began. Though the site of the theatre was discovered in 1847 by a local antiquary, Mr Grove Lowe (who cleared the walls and laid out the plan), its complete excavation was not undertaken till our time, being made possible by the generosity of Lord Verulam, under the direction of Miss Kathleen Kenyon.

Thought to have been built between 140 and 150 AD, the theatre fell into decay with the rest of the city during the third century, and shared in its temporary revival about 300. After being for long a ruin, this fine building had fallen from its high estate to suffer the indignity of being a rubbish-tip before the end of the fourth century.

The Roman ampitheatre familiar to us all was devoted to sport and had seats all round the arena; the theatre at Verulamium is thought to have been used for plays, as well as for cock-fighting and animal-baiting, and herein is the reason for its unusual plan. It consisted originally of a circular central space, with a sloping auditorium round two-thirds of it, and a small stage joining its remaining portion. In a few years the size of the stage was increased by the building of a straight wall in front of the original curve, and before the end of the century a second wall was built four feet still farther forward. The purpose of this may have been either to increase the stage again, or to provide a slot into which the curtain could be dropped.

The town has spent £8000 to house the discoveries of Verulamium, and the museum is a sensible building for its purpose, an attractive place in dark brick with flint panels. The museum hall is 75 feet long, and the showcases and fittings are made from Nigerian walnut. As we enter the eye is drawn to three arresting and almost perfect pavements hung like tapestry on the wall. One of these is divided into panels by plaiting and has a great circle round a central flower. Another has a striking head, representing perhaps Neptune or Ocean, with lobster claws protruding from the hair, set in a handsome border of key pattern with roses and vessels, two of which have ladles in them. The third pavement is semi-circular, and has a charming design like a fan. Hardly less interesting than the mosaics themselves is the method by which these floors were lifted from their site and set up here without the disturbance of any of the tesserae. The work was done by Italians, who covered the mosaics first with a sticky substance and then with canvas, then dried them for weeks with stoves, and after chipping away the original cement, rolled them up like carpets, and unrolled them in new cement.

There are coins of gold, silver, and bronze; glass and pottery including rich Samian ware, vessels from the temples, an ox skull which may have been a dedication sacrifice, and a quaint lamp chimney from the triangular temple; a fine amphora for storing wine or oil; tools, spear-heads, daggers, iron axe-heads, spindles, rings, brooches, jet beads, seals, pins and needles of bone and bronze, iron pens which scratched on wax tablets, an oyster shell with pigment from the rouge a painted lady kept in it, and beakers adorned with stags and hounds. From the cemetery on the site of St Stephen's Church are 12 bronze bracelets and many jet beads, rings and spoons, and many burial urns containing bones. A pathetic fragment is the skeleton of a child, lying on the bit of earth which cradled it so long ago ; and a relic of remarkable interest is among the tiles with footmarks of men and animals. From the marks on one of these it would appear that a dog was standing on the tile as it was drying in the sun, when someone threw a stone (which still adheres to the tile) and the deeper paw-marks near by suggest that the startled dog jumped to avoid the stone. A fine thing of today is a scale model of the London Gate of the Roman city, with small figures to give it a touch of reality. A Roman soldier, mounted on his white horse, is on guard : oxen are drawing the water barrel, panniered mules are taking wood and produce into the city, two men are taking in the body of a sheep, and a Roman is doing business with a farmer.

Wisest, Brightest, Meanest of Mankind

FRANCIS BACON, lying here at St Albans, was one of the most extraordinary men who have risen to power and fame in England. On her visits to his father's house at Gorhambury Queen Elizabeth would speak of the boy as her young Lord Keeper, but when, after his brief career at Cambridge, he was left poor and fatherless, she steadily declined to help him. Thrown on his own resources, he took up law, entered Parliament, and attached himself to the Earl of Essex.

Essex in vain sought a wealthy wife for him, vainly begged the queen to help him, and finally gave him a Twickenham estate. But Bacon continued poor; he was once imprisoned for debt. As a Queen's Counsel he absented himself from the Star Chamber proceedings against Essex, and was blamed by the queen for his remissness. He risked no second reproval when the earl was tried for rebellion. It was nothing to him that Essex had been his friend. The blustering Coke, who led the prosecution, so bungled the case that Essex might have escaped had not Bacon, by magnifying the enormity of his patron's offence, made the death penalty inevitable.

After Elizabeth's death Bacon, by flattering King James, steadily advanced his position, declaring the king's right divine and above the law. He held that the law could be altered by the sovereign at will regardless of judges. When he was 41 he married, for money, succeeded to the Gorhambury estate, and after 25 years of striving became Solicitor-General.

His power in the Courts was now unrivalled; his oratory and knowledge of the law were without parallel. Ben Jonson, who heard him argue a case, recorded that "the fear of every man who heard him was that he should make an end." At 56 he followed his father as Lord Keeper, and was next made Lord Chancellor. On the bench his conduct seemed perfect. He disposed of acute legal problems with ease. While he would witness unmoved the torture of a prisoner he planned wise reforms of the criminal laws. All the time he was busy in his scanty leisure with his scientific and philosophic writings.

He kept his 60th birthday in almost regal state, the occasion celebrated by Ben Jonson in a poem, but within a few months of this proud day his fortunes were in ruins and he himself a prisoner in the Tower under a fine of £40,000, banished for ever from Court and Parliament for having accepted bribes. He admitted the crime, but denied having sold justice; it actually seems true that, with incredible cynicism, he took the bribes but decided *against the givers*. It should be remembered that England was rank with corruption in those days, and Bacon was only a guilty scapegoat, but he knew the depth of his sin.

His fine was remitted and, his imprisonment ended, he returned to the writings which ensure his fame. Distrusting the permanence of the English language, though he wrote it magnificently, he produced most of his chief works in Latin. In addition to important legal works, and his history of Henry the Seventh, he formulated a philosophy in Novum Organum. With the confidence of true genius he took "all knowledge for his provence," but was prevented by the multiplicity of his labours from fully exploring his domain.

While fertilising the mind of the world, Bacon was himself singularly fallible. He could believe that the heart of an ape, on being applied to the head, "helped wit" and is good for epilepsy, that a red stone prevents bleeding, and that certain bracelets have magical powers; but he could not accept the teachings of Copernicus, Kepler, and Galileo. He declared that the revelations of the telescope were due to flaws in the lens, and he pooh-poohed the microscope. So limited was the wisest man of his time in those pre-scientific days.

Yet in other ways he was boundless in his outlook. He it was who first hinted at currents in the air, at heat as a form of motion, at the fact that light takes time to travel, at the possibility of transmitting sound to a distance, and at the likelihood that species might not be fixed, but were capable of change, as Darwin was later to discover. From his theory in the New Atlantis, of society governed by men of wisdom, sprang our own Royal Society, and kindred bodies in Europe. Himself achieving nothing in science, he pointed a way which, with all its errors, has led to worlds of wonder undreamed of by him or by his age.

For posterity he lives by his incomparable Essays, which he kept in their native English; he was shrewd enough to see that thus "they come home to men's business and bosoms." The essays teem with treasures of wisdom, and with phrases which have become part of our daily speech and writing.

It is probably true that Bacon, with all his marvellous powers, lacked certain simple qualities. He probably never loved anybody but his mother, with whom he is buried. In some astounding notes which have been found, written for his private guidance, we see the spirit of the man who could betray Essex and send Raleigh to death,

In these notes Bacon prescribes for himself a course of flattery for the king and the great. Alexander Pope did not greatly exaggerate in describing him as the wisest, brightest, meanest of mankind. He died by catching a chill in making a simple scientific experiment, and in his will he declared that he left his name and memory to the judgment of charitable men, to foreign nations and future ages. He made various bequests, but none became effective, for, having sacrificed pride, honour, and reputation in the vain pursuit of riches, he died penniless, owing £80 even to his butterwoman, and sixpence to some poor man in St Albans.

The Queen's Village

ST PAUL'S WALDEN. It is a proud little place, with a distinction never dreamed of when our century began. As long as we live we must remember the 4th of August as a tragic day, the day of the beginning of the Great War, but it was on the last 4th of August in the 19th century that the church bells here were ringing for a happy event with a significance that none could have imagined then.

A little daughter was born at the great house of Walden Bury to the Earl and Countess of Strathmore. One daughter had been born to them 18 years before, Violet Hyacinth Bowes-Lyon. She lived here through her happy childhood, a girl as beautiful as the hyacinths and violets that inspired her name, and when she was eleven years old, in 1893, they laid her in this churchyard. There is a tablet on the wall within showing two small figures holding a wreath.

Seven years passed, and there was born in this same house another daughter, Elizabeth Angela Marguerite. She too grew up here through her happy childhood, baptised at the same font as her sister, kneeling in this little church to say her childish prayers, riding her pony through the long avenue that leads to the church from her father's house. "Lord bless you, I can see her now," said one of the old villagers, "galloping across with the groom behind all out of breath, and her laughing."

There was a sad day in her life in 1930 when she stood by the grave of the sister she had never known and saw her brother John laid there to rest. But seven years before that there had been a happy day when she married the Duke of York, and in seven years to come there was to be a day of dazzling glory, for Elizabeth Angela Marguerite Bowes-Lyon was crowned Queen of England in Westminster Abbey. One brother and sister from the great house at the end of the avenue lie in this churchyard, one brother and sister remain, the Honourable David Bowes-Lyon, friend of this village, and Queen Elizabeth, who has unveiled a tablet recording the fact that in this parish she was born, and in this church was baptised and worshipped.

The church stands with the cottages about it on high ground, approached by a long avenue of great trees from the hamlet of Whitwell on the borders of the River Maran. (We should see the village hall at Whitwell, for it has a timbered storey with 17th century dormer windows.) The village has two fine parks, Stagenhoe, with 130 acres crossed by avenues of limes and chestnuts and adorned with a great lake, and Walden Bury, with the avenue running to the church where the Queen used to ride her pony. The church is 600 years old, with a bold square tower and a lofty nave; there is an old stone coffin in the shadow of the tower; the gravestone of John Bowes-Lyon in a corner of the churchyard; a gravestone with an aeroplane carved on it in memory of Rodney Clarkson; and a cross with a Calvary in memory of Tristram Valentine, a vicar here, the cross being the last work designed by the famous architect G. F. Bodley.

Though the church is 14th century, the chancel has been rebuilt, and is believed to have been designed by Christopher Wren. It has a barrel roof, and a round arch which is nearly filled by a striking classical screen of the 18th century. Between the aisle and the chapel is a more modest screen with delightful Tudor ornament. The fine pulpit matches the 18th century screen. The font is 15th century, and near it is a 14th century coffin lid. In a big table tomb lies Peter Nicol, a clerk in the household of George the Third, and on the wall of the nave is a monument decorated with war trophies to Captain Fothergill, who fought with Wellington in the Peninsular Campaign, "the first in danger, in retreat the last." High on the wall of the chapel is a quaint 17th century monument of Henry Stapleford and his wife, facing each other as they kneel at a prayer desk, with a little daughter holding a skull behind her mother. Henry was an official of the households of Queen Elizabeth and the first two Stuart kings. The east window of the chapel has the Annunciation, but the most interesting glass in the church is a fragment in rich yellow and crimson; it is 600 years old, and is in a little window of the tower. There are six bells in the tower, one the Coronation bell subscribed for by the villagers.

Beams from Our Oldest Windmill

SANDON. We can turn our backs on the new world of the distant masts of the wireless station near Baldock, and look instead at the old—at the church with the overhanging house like a long beehive beside it, some of its windows like photograph frames; or at the 17th century farmhouse of Sandon Bury next door, with its gabled barns and its square pigeon house, still with hundreds of nesting-places. Beyond Sandon's wide common and scattered cottages is Hyde Hall, another old farm, with a 17th century wing tacked on to the new and a 16th century barn roofed with splendid oak beams.

The 600-year-old church is much restored, and its tower propped up with great brick buttresses. It has a fine brass of 1480 showing the young squire, John FitzGeffrey, with his wife and six daughters, a bull at his feet and a pet dog at hers. Nicholas Miller, an only son aged 18, has his bust in an elaborate memorial of 1747. A man sticks out his tongue among the faces on the poppyheads of some 500-year-old seats. The simple screen is 15th century; the carved pulpit is Jacobean; and there is dainty 14th century stonework over an arched recess and behind the sedilia. The heavy kingposts of the chancel roof have also survived 600 years.

Something of the 14th century was found in a great mound behind the church. It was thought to be a prehistoric tumulus, but when the headmaster of Sandon led his pupils in as excavators, so much broken pottery was found that it seemed to have been a kind of rubbish heap of the Middle Ages. Then they came on two oak beams, 16 feet long, which proved to be the foundations of a 14th century post windmill—England's earliest known windmill, 200 years older than the oldest located up till then (at Bourn in Cambridgeshire).

The Roman Arch

SANDRIDGE. We may feel here as we come past the mighty copper beech and the red chestnuts into the old church something of the thrill of a discoverer, for we stand where Roman,

Saxon, Norman, and Tudor stood, and across the River Lea is the Jacobean house called Water End, believed to have been the home of Sarah Jennings whose parents were Sandridge folk.

The passing ages have stamped their mark on the church, but through all these dynasties, from the Caesars to the Stuarts, few things more beautiful can have happened than the devotion of Sarah Jennings of Sandridge to John Churchill, Duke of Marlborough. He chose the title of Lord Churchill of Sandridge when he was made a peer, so marking his devotion to his wonderful wife. A vixen or a shrew she may have been, her life as full of quarrels as an egg is full of meat, but these two little letters of hers will surely never pass into oblivion.

This was to him when she was away in 1689:

Wherever you are, while I have life, my soul shall follow you, my ever dear Lord Marl; and wherever I am I should only kill the time wishing for night that I may sleep and hope the next day to hear from you.

And this was after he had passed out of her life, when the Duke of Somerset wrote asking for her hand in marriage.

If I were young and handsome as I was, instead of old and faded as I am, and you could lay the empire of the world at my feet, you should never share the heart and hand that once belonged to John, Duke of Marlborough.

The church that she would know, and which the Duke of Marlborough must have seen, must go back to the Saxons in its unseen foundations, for Sandridge was a village in 976, when it was given to St Albans Abbey by the son of Offa of Mercia, and long before that were thrown up the mysterious lines of entrenchments known as the Devil's Dyke and the Slad. We know the Saxons must have been building here, for in the walls are Roman bricks they preserved from some ruined Roman building hereabouts. There is, moreover, a remarkable arch of Roman bricks set above the stone chancel screen, a screen rare in itself, with a grave simplicity, erected when the abbot of St Albans rebuilt the chancel in the 14th century.

We have seen no other chancel screen like this, which runs from wall to wall with a beautiful pointed arch in the centre, and on each side three cinquefoil lights. The central arch rises on each side from a rough stone base like a bench-end, with a figure carved in relief on the sloping arm—one of an old bearded man with a rosary and a hand raised to his ear, the other an old woman in a slightly more comfortable position. The space above the screen has been filled in to the roof with a wooden framework divided into dozens of cinquefoil window-like openings, but this is broken in the centre by a remarkable arch resting on the top of the screen. The arch was probably put together in the 14th century when the abbot rebuilt the chancel, but its materials, rough and rather crudely laid, are as old as any materials in any church in England, for they are Roman. The arch was probably here in Saxon days and may be Saxon work. In the midst of it is a tympanum with two lights to match those in the screen below.

The tower of the church fell in 1688, and with the clerestory, was rebuilt last century. The nave itself was built early in the 12th century, 200 years before the Abbot of St Albans gave the church the shape we see.

Roman Bricks in a Tower

SARRATT. We remember it for its long village green, running between an odd assortment of houses for about a quarter of a mile, with 17th century farmhouses in the background, Rose Hall Farm having a Tudor rose in the plaster of its kitchen ceiling. And then, a little way off, is another picture—the church's cheerful cluster of red-roofed gables seen against the red-roofed barns. Even the tower, rebuilt in the 15th century with Roman bricks in it, ends in a gable, and the short nave, cross-shaped with its transepts, has a gabled saddleback roof, the only one in the county.

The Normans planned the nave and transepts, and though their walls are patched with later work the chancel is much as it was when it was lengthened in the 13th century; it has a flower-carved piscina, a double sedilia, deep sunken windows, and old roof beams. The chancel arch was made at the end of the 12th century, and similar arches open into the transepts. The arches opening into new aisles are modern, but the tower arch has stood 500 years and is littered with the names of louts of long ago. A mighty old roof beam crosses over it.

The tiny heads of a man and a woman, not three inches long, are among fragments of old brasses, their hands still raised in prayer.

Another medieval head is in the glass of a window close by. Over the sedilia a Jacobean couple kneel in their sculptured memorial, William Kingsley and his wife, she in a flat hat, with five sons and a daughter all wearing ruffs, and below them a winged hourglass. Some of this family may have heard Richard Baxter preach from the carved Jacobean pulpit, which has a fine sounding board; it is said that Baxter once preached here. One of the bells was ringing at that time, and the chalice has been in use 300 years. Here is the font bowl to which the Normans brought their babies, and the stone lid of a coffin in which someone was laid to rest seven centuries ago.

On the walls the red outlines of frescoes are fading almost beyond recognition after 700 years; but Professor Tristram has interpreted them for us and his reconstructions are in the tower. We see a dramatic Ascension, with Christ's feet showing below his robes and the hands of watchers raised towards them. There is an Annunciation picture, a high priest giving his blessing, and a curious kind of Pan playing the pipes while a shepherdess offers him a sheep from her flock. Modern artists have put their pictures in the windows, where we see little St John going with his mother to greet Mary and her Child, a charming scene; St Helena with her cross, and Barnabas laying money at the feet of the Apostles. By the church stand the Baldwin almshouses, founded 400 years ago, but rebuilt last century; and in Church Field, near Sarratt Bottom Farm, are the foundations of a Roman building, now covered over. It may be that the bricks in the church tower came from this buried Roman house.

In Brass and Stone

SAWBRIDGEWORTH. We turn from the Cambridge road into Bell Street, and it is like going back 300 years. The old cottages of timbered and plastered brick overhang the street on either side, and at the end is a church where the great folk of this small town live on in stone and brass.

They are nobly housed in this spacious medieval church, standing boldly on a wide expanse of lawn among pines and yews, with a view across the River Stort through a row of chestnuts. The nave and the chancel are 700 years old, the aisles and arcades 600, the spire and the upper part of the stalwart tower were added 500 years ago, and on the bell outside the tower the hours have struck since Charles the Second got back his throne.

We enter by the massive iron-strapped door which has been opening and shutting for 500 years. Here is the traceried chancel screen and the aisle roofs with carved bosses all new in those days, the railed pews with linenfold ends, the poor-box into which the Elizabethans dropped their alms, the pulpit and the great chest with five locks, and the font to which rich and poor brought their babies 600 years ago to be baptised by Thomas de Aungervil, whose stone is in the floor of the nave. On another stone is cut the outline of a 14th century nun, nameless, as is the grand 15th century canopied tomb from which the brass portraits have been torn.

The chief families portrayed in brass and stone are the Leventhorps, who were here for centuries, and the Joscelyns, who lived across the river at Hyde Hall, now replaced by a Georgian house. At Hyde Hall was born John Joscelyn, one of our first Anglo-Saxon scholars, who as Latin secretary to Archbishop Parker contributed the Lives of the Archbishops for his employer's History of the British Church, published in 1572. John lies at High Roding in Essex, but here are buried his relatives: Ralph, twice Lord Mayor of London during the 15th century; John, who is sculptured with his wife on a tomb of 1525; and Geoffrey, pictured on a brass of 1470 with his two wives and 18 children. Then come the Leventhorps: Sir John, an executor of Henry the Fifth's will, with a fine brass portrait of himself and his wife; Joan, probably the brass lady of about 1500 who has lost her name and her husband but retains the Leventhorp arms; Mary of 1566, whose portrait is under the tower near those of a nameless 15th century couple in shrouds; Edward and his wife, with brass portraits made in 1600; and last of all Sir John Leventhorp, whose stone figure in Jacobean armour reclines by his wife's, while their eight daughters and six sons (one the jolliest little fellow) appear in relief. There are also figures of their neighbours, Sir William Hewett and his wife, and a small monument of 1606 where Sir Walter Myldemaye kneels with his wife and their bearded son. It was to this Sir Walter that Elizabeth granted Pishiobury, the 250-acre park to the south of the town, but the noble mansion Sir Walter built there was burned down, and only some panelling and a few fittings were rescued for the house raised in its place beside the lake, a battlemented brick house reached by an avenue of oak trees nearly a mile long.

Wren's Right-Hand Man

SHENLEY. Christopher Wren's friend Nicholas Hawksmoor, when he lay dying by the Thames in London (where he had put his handiwork in the dome of St Paul's and on the towers of Westminster Abbey), thought of this Hertfordshire hilltop village and asked that he might be buried here. He lies under one of the churchyard yews, having ended a long life of work in 1736. He was with Wren as his assistant all the time on St Paul's, and finished the western towers of the Abbey which Wren had designed but could not finish. He was a prime mover in the building of fifty Queen Anne churches in London, helped Sir John Vanbrugh with Blenheim, built colleges at Oxford and Cambridge, and restored Beverley Minster. He was a modest man with an infinite grasp of detail, and had a great influence on the architecture of his time. His 200th anniversary was marked by an act of homage from the Royal Institute of British Architects, who were represented at the laying of a wreath on his tomb by the Dean and Chapter of St Paul's.

The church where they laid him lost the tower and chancel soon after his burial here, and they have never been rebuilt. Only the nave and the aisle are left, and a homeless bell hangs from a low beam out in the open, where anyone may reach up to it, the other bells having been hung in the timber framework by the chapel in the centre of the village. A sundial tilted on the wall warns us that Time Flies, and a board tells of one whom Time carried off long since:

> *A parish clerk of voice most clear;*
> *None Joseph Rogers could excel*
> *In laying bricks or singing well.*
> *Though snapped his line, laid by his rod,*
> *We build for him our hopes in God.*

By the pond on the green is a small round hut under a bee-hive roof, its windows barred with stones inscribed, "Do well and fear not; Be sober and vigilant," timely warnings to the villagers of old that they would be behind these bars if they did not behave themselves, for this was the lock-up.

Within a mile is Salisbury Hall, a fine country house built by Sir Jeremiah Snow in Stuart days, within a moat. He spared no pains to adorn it within and without, bringing from the walls of Sopwell Nunnery at St Albans a number of plaster medallions of Roman emperors, thought to be 15th century. Here they still are, above the panelling in the hall, looking like copies of old coins magnified to nine feet round. Charles the Second must have admired them, for he was a frequent visitor here.

The Wooden Chancel Arch

SHEPHALL. An avenue of giant elms guards the vivid green which widens in front of the church and surrounds the village well; and shading the lychgate are the quivering leaves of two tall aspen trees, rare in England now, but prized as the best arrow wood by our ancestors. They are old, but not nearly so old as the timbers which for 600 years have served as chancel arch in this church, one of the few wooden chancel arches in England. More venerable beams support the nave roof; there is a medieval chest scooped out of a huge log; and the top part of the chancel screen is 15th century work of great beauty. All the rest of the church has changed and much is modern.

One of several brass inscriptions to the Nodes family records that George Nodes was master of the buckhounds to Henry the Eighth and his three reigning children. A century after this huntsman was laid here, John Rudd the rector was laid to rest, with a memorial painting of him as a shepherd standing above the alabaster record of his life and service. We found the font at which he must have baptised the Nodes children crumbling away beside the stately yew.

The First Traveller from the Sky

STANDON. Every day the flying man flies over it, but never again will its people look at him with such amaze as came to them one autumn day in 1784, when there arrived at Standon the first human traveller from the English skies. A stone has been set up at Standon Green End, and on it we read of an event recorded as a "wondrous enterprise successfully achieved by the powers of chemistry and the fortitude of man."

It must have seemed a fearful thing to these villagers who were looking up on that September afternoon at a great spherical object floating through the sky, slowly descending until it touched the ground in a field near by, and a voice cried out calling on the people to secure the monster. Out of it, from the car suspended beneath the great silk ball, stepped a man and a dog. The man was Vincenza Lunardi, a young Italian who had made a balloon fitted with racket-shaped wings and oars which he declared would help to control it. He had started at Moorfields, 30 miles away, on the grounds of the Honourable Artillery Company, and had been just over two hours in the air. Three living creatures had entered the car at Moorfields, Lunardi, his dog, and a cat, but, falling very low as he came to North Mimms, Lunardi had astonished a country woman walking there, and had handed her his cat for safe keeping before he rose again and came on to Standon, so completing the first successful balloon flight ever known.

This was the village's great event; its great man lies in his tomb in the medieval church, close by the timbered school which has stood for centuries. The plan of the church is unusual, for in the 15th century a porch was added at the west end and a detached tower built beside the chancel, to which it has since been linked by an organ chamber. By this porch we come into a scene of singular beauty.

The lofty nave, with aisles, doorways, and windows 600 years old, slopes a little upwards, and eight steps mount to the 13th century chancel, five more reaching the altar. The 700-year-old chancel arch is rich with carving, and has on each side of it a peephole through which the altar can be seen. Through the arch as we come in we see three lancets shining over the altar. The tomb we see high up in the chancel is that of as honourable a man as ever served our Tudor kings and queens, Sir Ralph Sadler. Here he is in stone, his seven children carved round his tomb and his armour hanging over it, with his stirrups and spurs. Resting at the tomb is a pole more thrilling than it looks, for from it waved the Royal Standard of Scotland at the Battle of Pinkie. It is over and forgotten, but in 1547 there was a plan to unite the English and the Scots by marrying Edward the Sixth and Mary Queen of Scots. The scheme came to nothing, for the Scots were hostile and war resulted, when 16,000 Englishmen met 23,000 Scots at Pinkie, killing 6000 and routing the rest. Sir Ralph Sadler, who had spent an unhappy time in Edinburgh watching over Mary, brought back with him from the battlefield this mast of Scotland's flag. Facing his tomb is that of his son Thomas, here in stone with his wife and their two children. We may see part of their old home (Lordship Manor) half a mile away by the river, incorporated into a house of a later day. The date 1546 on one of the stones, with Sir Ralph's initials, show that he built it a year before the Battle of Pinkie, and it would be to this house that he brought back the standard pole.

Though the outside of the church has received a new stone face, inside everything is much as it was when the Calais merchant John Field was laid here in 1474. His brass portrait is on the top of his altar tomb with that of his son John, each with his children pictured below. There is a merchant's mark on one of the four shields at the corners. Below the chancel steps are other brass portraits of a man of the 15th century and a soldier named Wade of the 16th, but someone has stolen the portrait of William Coffyn, Master of the Horse to Henry the Eighth's third queen.

The village was the home of one of the soldier poets who gave his life for us in the Great War, Robert Ernest Vernede. He was a scholar at St Paul's School and St John's at Oxford, and became a writer of novels and sketches and poems. He went out to France in the first few months of the war, when he was 40, was wounded soon after, and went back again. He had a fervent love of England. In one of his poems he asks the sleepers in France who will bring them fame in the coming years, and one of the last of all the poems he wrote was this noble prayer for his country:

> *All that a man might ask thou has given me, England,*
> *Birthright and happy childhood's long heartsease,*
> *And love whose range is deep beyond all sounding,*
> *And wider than all seas:*
> *A heart to front the world and find God in it,*
> *Eyes blind enow but not too blind to see*
> *The lovely things behind the dross and darkness,*
> *And lovelier things to be;*
> *And friends whose loyalty time nor death shall weaken,*
> *And quenchless hope and laughter's golden store*
> *All that a man might ask thou hast given me, England,*
> *Yet grant thou one thing more:*
> *That now when envious foes would spoil thy splendour,*
> *Unversed in arms, a dreamer such as I*
> *May in thy ranks be deemed not all unworthy,*
> *England, for thee to die.*

Standon   **By the River Rib**

Tring   **Massive Church Tower and Impressive Nave**

St Paul's Walden   **The Church**

St Paul's Walden A Simple Interior   **St Albans**   Medieval Clock Tower

Mary Stuart and the Casket Letters

SIR RALPH SADLER, born in London in 1507, was trained in the household of Thomas Cromwell, passed into the service of Henry the Eighth, and for the next half century, the most dramatic years of our Tudor dynasty, was active as a Secretary of State and diplomatic agent engaged in affairs with Scotland.

His life was strangely interwoven with Mary Stuart's. In Scotland, at the time of her baptism, he wrote to Henry that "it is as goodly a child as I have seen of her age." He was charged to arrange a marriage between Mary and the future Edward the Sixth, and the Scots desired that he and his wife should educate her for her future position as wife of an English king.

After the accession of Elizabeth he helped to make peace between the two nations, and met Mary under dramatic circumstances. A lovely woman of 26, twice a queen and twice a widow, she had married Bothwell, the murderer of her second husband, and, fleeing to England from her offended subjects, was now a prisoner. Sadler was one of the Commissioners who sat at York to determine whether she was a fit person to meet Queen Elizabeth, whose protection she claimed.

Here it was that the famous Casket Letters were seen for the first and last time in England. Seized in the possession of a servant, the eight letters, with love sonnets, had been written by Mary to the infamous Bothwell, who had enclosed them in a silver casket. Passages in the letters clearly suggested Mary as a party to the murder of Darnley. Mary denounced them as forgeries, but as one of her biographers has said, "If the letters were forged, the forger cannot be identified by any art known to history."

Sadler had no doubt of their authenticity, and sent copies to London condemning her. The letters were taken back to Scotland, where they mysteriously disappeared. Copies are preserved, and they remain the subject of controversy which is unsettled after nearly three centuries.

After her long imprisonment at Sheffield Sadler reluctantly became Mary Stuart's gaoler for nearly a year, and won her gratitude by moderating the rigours of her captivity. They met no more. He was a man of 80 when the queen he had dandled in infancy laid her head on the block at Fotheringhay.

P   209

A Man on the Map

STANSTEAD ABBOTS. Here lies a man whose name is on the map of one of the most romantic spots in the world, but we have a long hill to climb before we find him, for the old village (where the Romans left a pavement 15 centuries ago) is on the northern slope of the Stort Valley, and the church, with its spiked 15th century tower, is at the top of the hill.

As we wind our way up through the trees a group of Elizabethan almshouses comes into view with a cedar and a pine towering beside them on a knoll. They were founded by Sir Edward Beash, son of the man who looked after the food supplies for Elizabeth's navy. He also added a chapel to the 13th century church. There they laid him to rest in Armada Year, and there we see him kneeling in stone facing his wife, with one son in armour and two in black cloaks on a ledge below him, and the royal arms of his queen in the window above. One of his neighbours, William Saxaye, who died in 1581, has his brass portrait here, and three others show an unknown knight in 15th century armour, and a Tudor husband and wife with clasped hands.

We may imagine that these folk of long ago must have smiled at the quaint heads of men and animals outside the windows of the nave; they must have pushed open this medieval door in the 13th century doorway, sheltered by an open timbered porch. There are 500-year-old tie-beams in the roof of the nave and a three-decker pulpit of the 16th century. It has lost its canopy, though the carved support for it still forms a background for the preacher, who may think it just as well that he is so high up, for otherwise he could scarcely see the congregation in the high box pews. Dwarfed by the lofty tower arch is a screen with much Elizabethan ornament on its door and cornice.

Two reliefs showing a sphinx and emblems of war are in memory of a naval captain, Robert Jocelyn, who died at 82 the year after Trafalgar, and his son John, who had already fallen in the hour of victory at Alexandria. Another relief shows a woman gazing on the medallion portrait of Sir Felix Booth, the London merchant who was made a baronet by William the Fourth for fitting out at his sole cost the ship which discovered the Magnetic Pole. The Endeavour set out in 1829 under Sir James Ross to make the North-West Passage, but made this discovery instead on the northernmost point of British North America, which is named Boothia Felix after the man who lies in this Hertfordshire village. Thanks to his generosity a great stride forward was made in geographical science, and in addition to the point Boothia Felix Commander Ross named after his patron a gulf, a cape, an isthmus, and two harbours.

Cromwell's Kinsman and Milton's Friend

STANSTEAD ST MARGARET. It is by the River Lea, which comes down to it from Amwell. On one side of the road is a brick building with an 18th century clock house; on the other is a gabled manor with a painted coat-of-arms on the 18th century gate. The church gate is in the shadow of two great elms. The church is but a fragment of what it was 600 years ago, when the chancel was made new. Two small Norman windows are blocked up over a doorway, and buried in the wall is an arcade of the 14th century, part of it still peeping through. Set against the wall of the modern vestry is a medieval gravestone seven feet long.

Here lies, under a dark stone before the altar, a famous puritan of St Ives, Henry Lawrence, whom they laid to rest here in 1664. He was Cromwell's kinsman and Milton's friend. He was the landlord of the house Cromwell lived in at St Ives, and it was to his Uncle Henry that Cromwell would pay the rent for the barn still standing there. It was while Cromwell was living at St Ives that the trouble over ship money began, and Lawrence sought refuge in Holland during the difficult times that followed. Returning to England, he did much work for the Commonwealth, mediating between England and Scotland, helping in the government of Ireland, but opposing the trial of the king. After Cromwell's death he proclaimed the succession of Richard Cromwell to the Protectorate, and at the Restoration was permitted, like Milton, to continue to live in seclusion, so he came to live at Goldingtons here. It was to a son of Lawrence that Milton addressed one of his sonnets, beginning:

> *Lawrence, of virtuous father virtuous son,*
> *Now that the fields are dank, and ways are mire,*
> *Where shall we sometimes meet, and by the fire*
> *Help waste a sullen day?*

STAPLEFORD. Home came a sailor from sea to be rector for 30 years after the Battle of Waterloo. He was Commander Charles Prowett, and the story of his capture of a Dutch ship of 14 guns is told in the church. Many a parson before him trod the yew-shaded path to this church in the meadows by the River Beane, for though it looks so new its walls were built 800 years ago. The restorers of the centuries have changed it beyond recognition, but all have spared the beauty of the Norman doorway, whose chevron moulding and leafy capitals are still the great attraction of the church. There are some 400-year-old beams in the nave roof, fragments of 15th century glass in one of the windows, and stone heads of a medieval king and a bishop outside. The curious tower of wood and lead was added last century.

The Town of the Six Hills

STEVENAGE. It lies on the Great North Road which widens as it passes by the six little hills which set every motorist wondering. How old they are no man knows, but, Danish, Roman, or Celtic, they were built up here as burial mounds and remain as the town's chief monument, the six hills from which the Saxons named it Stevenage, meaning Hills by the Highway. There are inns from the coaching days which seem young compared with the six graves, but at one of them, the Swan, the first Earl of Minto died in 1814 on his way home after a vigorous rule of India as Governor-General. At one end of the town is the grammar school founded by Thomas Alleyn in 1558. It has, of course, grown greatly, but has one of its oldest buildings still in use. At the other end of the town, near the new church, is a timbered building 400 years old which is used as a workhouse. The main street is bordered with picturesque houses and inns, and any boy you meet in it will tell you that it is the highest street between London and York. We must leave them to settle it with the boys of St Albans.

A fine avenue of limes and chestnuts leads through the fields to where the 15th century spire of the old church rises on a hill, with but a remnant round it of the village which moved down the hill after a fire. The church is Norman and medieval, the Norman tower with little Norman windows remaining after 800 years. The nave arcades have 15th century arches on 13th century pillars, and the chancel arcades are 14th century, so that we have Norman work and the work of our three great building centuries. Above the tower arch is an opening made by the Normans which led into their nave roof, and from the outside we may see another opening made to lead into a roof 600 years ago. There are ancient wooden corbels supporting the nave roof, and stone angels supporting the chancel beams. The 13th century font has an ancient cover still touched with colour. There are six stalls with misereres carved about 1400, and four screens with handsome 15th century woodwork in them.

In one corner of the church is the broken stone figure of a woman in 13th century dress, a priest and an angel supporting her, so that she must have been a great lady, though not too great to have been used for generations as a stone in the floor, face downwards. On a brass of 1500 is the portrait of the rector, Stephen Hellard, in his canon's cope.

At Stevenage was born in the middle of last century, and in this churchyard lies, Harry Bates, whose genius as a sculptor was developed in art classes at Lambeth, where he was a carver's apprentice. He won a South Kensington silver medal and was given a gold medal and a travelling scholarship for his famous relief of Socrates talking to his pupils. His Pandora's Box is one of the most popular English sculptures at the Tate Gallery.

STOCKING PELHAM. It has three good companions, a little church, a barn about twice as big, and the rectory still guarded by part of its old moat. The plain little church has been here about 600 years, and in its belfry hangs a bell which may have rung out the news of Agincourt. Its business, it tells us in Latin, is to drive away all evil things. One other link has this church with the Long Ago, fragments of glass five or six centuries old.

The Two Brothers from Hamburg

TEWIN. It was the Saxons who first penetrated the forest and settled in this clearing. Now, among woods and commons, with sloping fields, narrow lanes, and winding paths, Tewin is a centre for lovely walks in unspoiled country, not an hour's ride from London.

It has two greens, most of the village lying round the lower one, while the church is half a mile away in the fields. The hand of the

Saxon helped to build the walls, but the oldest part of what we see is a Norman nave under a 15th century timber and plaster roof, with one blocked window taking us back nearly to the Conquest, and the remains of two clerestory windows added 700 years ago, when the nave arcade was built. The chancel arch is 14th century. The spiked tower came late in the 15th. Five of the bells are nearly 300 years old, and a sundial from the days before village clocks is scratched on a corner of the chancel. There is an Elizabethan silver chalice.

In front of the altar is a stone carved about 1356 to the memory of a rector, Walter de Louthe, and a small brass shows us Thomas Pygott, who died in 1610, when his family had been in Tewin 300 years. There is a monument to Josephine Sabine, a General who fought under Marlborough and was Governor of Gibraltar. He died out there and was brought home for burial here. His marble monument, 15 feet high, shows the General, dressed in Roman armour, lying in front of a pyramid. Here, too, is a tablet to a queer adventurer, Lady Cathcart, who inscribed on her ring when marrying her fourth husband: "If I survive I'll make it five." Number Four took her to Ireland and kept her a prisoner there for 20 years while he spent her money and sold her lands. He died when she was an old lady of 75 and she went to law, recovered Tewin House and her estates, and died at 97 before she had a chance to make it five.

Her story is true, but not true is Lady Anne Grimston's whose grave is the great sight of Tewin churchyard. It has been split by ash and sycamore trees, which have broken the stones and crumpled the railings. The legend everybody will tell you here is that Lady Anne was an infidel, and that she declared it as likely that she would rise again as that a tree would grow from her grave. It is not true, for Lady Anne was a lady of deep faith and piety; but it is true that trees have grown from her grave, heaving up the great stone, breaking it into fragments, and tearing up the heavy iron railings so that bits of them are now raised high, embedded in the trunks.

The pleasant 18th century rectory makes use of a pretty timbered stable and a thatched wooden tithe barn, both from the 17th century. Beyond the upper green stands Queen Hoo Hall, a stalwart Elizabethan house with wide latticed windows looking over the wooded slopes. Sir Walter Scott recognised in the house a fine setting for one of his tales, but never fully told it.

There have been laid in this churchyard in our own century two very remarkable men who lived in the great house called Tewin Water, Alfred and Otto Beit. "I was one of the poor Beits of Hamburg," said Alfred Beit, meaning that he was a member of a poorer branch of this family of Hamburg merchants. He went to the Cape when he was 22 to qualify himself for a merchant's office, and there he found diamonds selling for much less than their value in Europe. He started as a diamond merchant where Kimberley is, foresaw the rise of that town, and bought up land all round him, on which he put up corrugated iron offices. The time came when he sold the land for £260,000. He met Cecil Rhodes and was fascinated by his great ideas. He lent him a quarter of a million on no security. He joined with him for good and ill, and lost £200,000 by his share in the stupid Jameson Raid. When Cecil Rhodes died he carried on his work, and even while this book was being printed there was opened the Otto Beit Suspension Bridge, spanning the Zambesi and uniting the two Rhodesias. Alfred Beit bought a house in Park Lane, built up a collection of pictures, helped on the Cape-to-Cairo railway, but at last he had a stroke and came home to England a dying man in the summer of 1906. His will was full of public spirit, and he left pictures to the National Gallery and the Berlin Museum. Already he had given away two millions to great causes. He was a simple man, who never gambled and had no selfish ambitions.

His younger brother Otto devoted himself to carrying on his work, succeeding to the estate of Tewin Water, supporting the cause of the Rhodes Scholars, and giving unselfishly for the cause of science and the welfare of the Empire. With all his wealth he, too, was modest and simple; there have been fewer examples in history of brothers so rich, so devoted, so unassuming and unselfish, as these two Jews of Hamburg who made South Africa their dream and England their home.

The Twisted Man and His Two Companions

THERFIELD. It snuggles under deep thatch high on a last spur of the Chilterns, a wide stretch of windswept heath linking it to its neighbour Royston. Some of its timber cottages have been thatched through so many generations that the thatch is three feet deep. The 15th century wing of the rectory is of another world. Cold and austere, with beautiful mullioned windows, it is all that remains of what must have been Therfield's chief building when Baron Berners was born here in 1467. He attended Henry the Eighth at the Field of the Cloth of Gold, and in his quieter hours translated Froissart's Chronicles. In the 16th century the village saw the building of the timbered house with a dormer window in the steep-pitched roof between the gables of the overhanging storey; we found it being used as the village reading room.

In the vestry of the rebuilt church is a mysterious 14th century stone on which the tiny sculptured figure of a bearded man lies twisted most uncomfortably, with his knees crossed. He is only about ten inches high, and has still tinier companions, a woman at his head and another at his feet. No one knows the story of this very curious little group.

From the old church also came the six bells, led by a veteran from Elizabethan England, a plain 14th century font, two silver flagons of 1667, a medieval stone coffin, several stone heads, the wooden angels and bosses decorating the new roof, and three 15th century oak angels in the tower, where is a memorial showing Time with his hourglass and scythe and Death in a shroud, carved in cedar and set here by the rector of 1677 in memory of his wife, Ann Turner. Another rector, who was here for 23 years and died in 1757, is remembered as " of robust constitution, though he lived many years without animal food or any fermented liquor."

To the north-west of the church are the earthworks of a village fortified in medieval days. There is a mound about five feet above a ditch which sends a branch round a courtyard, and other enclosures may be traced. Much older are a group of five burial mounds on Therfield Heath, near a barrow 42 yards long and 32 broad. It is the only long barrow left in the county.

It was at Therfield in 1843 that the great bird man William Yarrell, who lies at Bayford in this county, saw the only rock thrush ever known to have visited this island of its own accord.

Pompous Man

THORLEY. Through the lychgate at the end of the lane we come in the shade of tall pines, limes, and ancient yews to the old church humbled a little by its coat of plaster, but with a 15th century tower, a 14th century chancel, and a 13th century nave. We enter through a Norman doorway with twisted shafts and scalloped capitals; there is another tiny Norman doorway opening to the tower stairs inside, its delicate capitals probably carved by the craftsman who made the font. The piscina and the triple sedilia are both 14th century.

Thorley had as rector the brilliant Samuel Horsley who lies here, his coffin having been brought from St Mary's, Newington Butts, when that church was pulled down to make room for a railway. Born in 1733, he lived till after the Battle of Trafalgar in spite of his quarrelsomeness and eccentricities. He would make bitter speeches at stormy meetings of the Royal Society, attacking Sir Joseph Banks as President, and at one of these meetings, pointing to the mace on the table, he shouted: "when the hour of secession comes the president will be left with his train of feeble amateurs and that toy upon the table, the ghost of that society in which Philosophy once reigned and Newton presided as her minister." He also had a bitter controversy with Joseph Priestley, the discoverer of oxygen, which began in a Good Friday sermon and lasted 12 years. He was clever enough to learn Latin without a master in his youth, and in his old age he would ride about in a coach and four. He believed that Napoleon would set up as a Messiah. As a preacher he was powerful and eloquent and a great force, but he was pompous and irritable.

The Three Acrobats

THROCKING. It seemed to us that this small place was struggling to keep its head above the grass, which we found growing everywhere, even across the lane. It has a farm, a few cottages, a house which was once the rectory, and a church hidden behind the hedges in the shadow of tall elms and a spreading yew. The little wooden angels 300 years old are still holding up the roof, though it has been made new. The font has been here 500 years, ever since the nave and chancel were built. The four-foot thick walls of the tower are 200 years older, though its rather top-heavy upper half of brick was added in 1660 by Sir Thomas Soames, whose stone here tells us that he died aged 88 "or thereabouts." The 17th century added the substantial pews and the choir-stalls with carved heads, on one of which we noticed three acrobats, one man supporting another upside down on his head and swinging the third by the leg—easily the most comical thing to see in Throcking.

There are two monuments by fashionable sculptors of their day to the Elwes family, one by Nollekens showing a woman reading a book, the other by Rysbrack. Round the walls are 11 painted crosses, newly coloured, but marking the spots which the bishop touched with holy oil on consecration day 500 years ago.

A Great Resolve

THUNDRIDGE. Angels spread their wings round the tower of the new church on the hill, and the heads of a medieval king and queen look out from a window on the valley below, as if seeking the lost church from which they and the angels and the four old bells all came. There in the meadows of the Rib, lovely in summer, waterlogged and desolate in winter, the tower of the vanished church stands sentinel among the graves. It has no roof to protect the memorials within it, but its sundial still counts the sunny hours, and a Norman arch built into it when the rest was demolished last century still flaunts its carvings, reward enough for a walk along this flowery valley.

As the tower marks the place of the old church, and a chimney stack marks the ruined manor house within a water-filled moat, so a little obelisk by the roadside at Wadesmill marks a milestone in endeavour. Here, it tells us, Thomas Clarkson resolved to devote his life to ending slavery. Clarkson has told us that in writing an Essay for his University he was excited by the deep interest and importance of his subject. In the daytime he was weary; in the night he had little rest. He sometimes never closed his eyes for grief. It became not so much a trial for academical reputation, as a question of doing something for Africa. He slept with a candle in his room that he could get up at any hour of the night to put down a thought that came to him. Then he sent in his Essay, and one day, as he came in sight of Wadesmill during a walk, he sat down disconsolate on the grass and was seized with the feeling that if his Essay was true it was time somebody should see that these calamities came to an end. It was summer time in 1785; in the autumn he had begun the work which never ceased till the slaves were free.

A Rare Old Lady

TOTTERIDGE. From the sanctuary of a country lane we may look across the valley of the River Brent and see smoky London. It is delightful country, ponds and blackberry bushes sometimes alternating with the gardens of the houses. One of the new estates, Copped Hall, perpetuates the memory of the vanished house where the first Lord Lytton lived and where Cardinal Manning was born. Great elms flank the road by the 18th century church, and a giant yew 27 feet round screens it. In the churchyard lie several members of the Pepys family, among them the first Earl of Cottenham, a Lord Chancellor, and Sir Lucas Pepys, physician to the unhappy George the Third. The church is a plain little place, but has much interest, with a gallery of paintings on the walls, two by the famous Benjamin West showing St John at Patmos and the Woman of the Apocalypse; another by the painter-parson Matthews Peters RA (said to have been won in a raffle by Cardinal Manning's father), and, surpassing all these, a delightful group by the Italian artist Lorenzo Lotto, in which the Madonna and Child are accompanied by Peter and Paul. This little masterpiece was given by Lord Rothermere in memory of his mother, Mary Geraldine Harmsworth, a gracious figure often seen among the worshippers here, though she lies at Finchley with Lord Northcliffe.

She was a rare old lady, mother of a group of brilliant sons, one of whom, Lord Northcliffe, never allowed a day to pass without sending her a greeting. She was Irish but a Protestant, a handsome woman of strong character, and to her it was chiefly due that her big family of sons received a sound education and were sent out into the world determined to do something in it. She was head of the family, and her word was law. She did not approve of wines or spirits, and at a dinner at her house nothing of the sort appeared on the table. Almost every Sunday her house at Totteridge was the scene of gatherings of the Harmsworth family. Her great memorial is in the fine little park just over the Thames from Westminster, with the War Museum rising in the midst of it. The building was once the Bethlem Hospital, or Bedlam as it was called when the lunatics were shown in cages like wild beasts. The hospital has gone out into the country and Lord Rothermere has transformed the site into a park and given it a lovely memory, naming it the Mary Geraldine Harmsworth Park and dedicating it to children.

Under an evergreen tree on a triangular green through which daffodils were thrusting when we called, rises the peace memorial, a tall cross with 26 names on its base. Among them are two Harmsworth boys, sons of Lord Rothermere, and a VAD nurse whose name appears below that of her brother.

The Cardinal of the Poor

CARDINAL MANNING was born at Totteridge in 1808, the son of a West Indian merchant and a governor of the Bank of England. He was educated at Harrow and Balliol and became rector in a Sussex village, where his wife lies. It happened that a notorious case arose of a clergyman who was refused an appointment because of his beliefs on baptism, and Manning was so perturbed that the Church of England could allow such matters to be decided by a court that he resigned and joined the Roman Catholic Church.

His promotion in that Church was rapid. After three years' study in Rome, in intimate contact with the Pope, he returned to high office in London. On the death of Cardinal Wiseman he was made Archbishop of Westminster, and ten years later a cardinal.

Cardinal Manning was nothing if not thorough. The Church of England had not been thorough enough for him. He thought that all its bishops ought to have insisted on regenerative baptism. When he joined the Roman Catholic Church he became and remained an insister on every tenet of the Church that all the Christian world outside that Church, and some Catholics, regarded as extreme. He emphasised the infallibility of the Pope, and the right to temporal as well as spiritual authority.

This rigidity in his beliefs was accompanied by intense labour to extend the influence of Roman Catholicism in England, through educational foundations of various kinds. But there was another aspect of his work which did not equally commend him to some of his fellow Churchmen. His religious activities brought him into touch with the working-class poor, and for them he had acute sympathy, especially those of the casual-labour type, whose earnings were low and precarious. That sympathy took him into the midst of strikes and other labour troubles, and he did not hesitate to appear on public platforms with such men as Joseph Arch, the organiser of farm-labourers' unions, and Charles Bradlaugh, who had no religion at all. His aim was fairplay for the under-dog. Some of his friends felt uneasy respecting the company he kept; but he won the confidence of those he sought to help, and had a wide conciliatory influence. No leading ecclesiastic of his time was in such close touch as he with the life of the unorganised labouring masses. Worn out with work and a rigorously ascetic life, he died in 1892 at the age of 73. He was a popular preacher, an indefatigable worker within the lines of the authority to which he submitted himself, and was full of human sympathy, but he was not an important intellectual force. He showed no signs of constructive thought. The only remedy he suggested for relieving the poverty he deplored was widespread charity. He practised it himself, and though he had command of much wealth available for religious foundations, he died worth only a few hundred pounds. He was a good and useful man, but lacked breadth of outlook and was hampered in thought and purpose by his subservience to the past.

Lord Rothschild's Museum

TRING. Heads should be held high and eyes raised in this small town on the Buckinghamshire border, which has had a market for 600 years and was known as Treung to King Alfred. There is little of beauty in the small houses crowding the winding streets, but in the midst of old and new rises the massive tower of a fine church, and over all are the hills, with Tring Park of 300 acres surrounded by some of the loveliest woods in this countryside so rich in woods. There are many beeches, and in the beautiful park, where we are free to wander, are splendid avenues. Part of the park has been bought by the County Council. The great house has little to remind us of the house in which Nell Gwynn is said to have lived, the old walls having been encased in red brick, and a top storey been added. The stables are said to have been designed by Christopher Wren.

The Rothschilds have done much for Tring from their home in the park. At one of its fine iron gates is a timbered lodge and a little row of gabled dwellings. Near by is a charming row of timbered houses where the estate workers live when their work is done. Here too is the Zoological Museum which Lord Rothschild bequeathed to the British Museum in 1938, with a section for students and galleries crowded with thousands of exhibits for all to enjoy. Beginning with a cottage in which Lord Rothschild housed his marvellous collection of insects, the buildings now cover over half an acre of ground space, accommodating enormous collections on which Lord Rothschild is said to have spent half a million pounds; it includes animals, reptiles, fishes, birds, and two million butterflies and moths.

The thousands of mounted birds range from tiny creatures no bigger than a walnut and of exquisite colouring, humming birds and birds of paradise, to extinct quaint birds like a dodo, the giant moa of New Zealand with its gigantic egg, and the great auk; with the ostrich are the best collection of cassowaries in existence. There are over 4000 bird skins. We see the elephant, the giraffe, the weird armadillo in its formidable suit of armour, and a great cast of the giant sloth. In a room full of antelopes are some small enough to be put in a suitcase. There are gorillas, chimpanzees, and a fine specimen of the extinct South African quagga. There are dolphins, seals, and tortoises, of which some are giants and some are as small as a shilling.

Among the reptiles is a wonderful skeleton of a great python. The great lizard known as the Komodo Dragon looks every inch worthy of its name. Among the crabs and lobsters is a tree-climbing crab with a stretch of nine feet. There are sponges and corals and fishes (dainty and fantastic fish, and fish of gorgeous colour) including the enormous basking shark (the robber of fishermen), the unusual bank oar fish (caught off Flamborough Head), the ribbon fish of New Zealand, a halibut which weighed 450 pounds, and a jewfish of 750 pounds. Attached to the museum is a library of thousands of volumes.

Facing the north entrance of the park, the church stands off the busy road to Aylesbury, in a churchyard we found charming with patches of daffodils under silver birches. Here too is the town's tribute to men who fell in the Great War, a tall cross with a carving of the Crucifixion.

The striking church has a haphazard patchwork of flint and stone in its walls, and great battlements, some of them chequered. Under the battlements are grotesques and faces. Except for Norman masonry, which may remain at the east end of the south aisle, the oldest part of the church is the 13th century north wall of the chancel.

The chancel itself was partly rebuilt in the 16th century, but it has a 15th century arch dividing it from the nave. The tower, with a corner stair turret and a vaulted ceiling, is 14th and 15th century. The clerestory and the arches of the nave arcades are also 15th century, but the clustered pillars are 19th.

There are 14 old figures on brackets at the ends of the beams of the nave roof, perhaps the disciples with Paul and Barnabas. The shafts below them rest on stone corbels between the arches of the arcades, carved with a fox running off with a goose, a monkey with a book and a bottle, a griffin eating a man in armour, a chained bear, an animal eating a woman, and animals fighting. The old rood stairs lead to the gallery of a modern screen. There is an Elizabethan chalice. The peal of bells has one of 1624, and there is a Jacobean carved chest, with two older ones of iron guarding records dating back to 1566. These throw light on the ancestral family of George Washington, for here was buried in 1655 Amphillis, widow of Lawrence Washington, who lies at Maldon in Essex. Her son Lawrence was baptised in this church. Two years after her death her elder son John Washington emigrated to America, and his great-grandson was the famous George. Four golden angels guard the altar, and on the reredos, shining with gold and colour, are scenes of the Crucifixion and the Resurrection, the conversion of Paul, and Paul preaching.

Good Sir William Gore, once Lord Mayor of London, is here with his wife, a little pompous and self-satisfied, in a monument of 1707. Below them, in 13th century simplicity, lie a stone coffin lid and a few old worn tiles. A marble memorial has the portrait of Edward Pope, a doctor in Tring for sixty years.

The Upper Icknield Way runs between the town and the hamlet of Little Tring a mile away, near reservoirs which are frequented by rare birds. One of the reservoirs feeds the Grand Union Canal which, at New Mill close by, reaches its highest point at about 400 feet above the sea. By the Summit, as this spot is called, is an old flour mill made new, and facing it is the miller's charming thatched bungalow; he built it with brick from part of the old wall his father set up round his orchard. It has an interesting gate made of iron in the shape of farm and garden tools—sickles, scythe, forks, spades, hoe, axe, flail, and hayforks. The garden path is made of 11 old millstones (of which two were made in France and cost over

£100), and 28 copies of millstones in concrete. The weathervane in the garden is a cat chasing a rat.

Tring lies nearly two miles from its station, two miles of loveliness, for most of the way is a thick chestnut avenue which some day may draw crowds on Chestnut Sunday from its rival in Bushey Park, or start a poet singing, Come down to Tring in chestnut time.

Paymaster of Europe

NATHAN MEYER ROTHSCHILD was born at Frankfort in 1777, one of the sons of a man who, intended for a rabbi, joined his father in business as a financier and merchant, and sent forth his four sons into four European capitals to carry on the work and extend the operations of the house.

The third son, aged 20, came to England to buy cotton goods in Manchester, but stayed to become a naturalised Englishman and one of the greatest financiers ever known. He had not been long established in London when the Government commissioned him to pay the subsidies due to our continental Allies. This gave him an international status; European princes and powers turned to him for advice, for the raising of loans and the investment of resources.

The English house of Rothschild developed into an institution resembling a cosmopolitan chancellery, with agents everywhere, with its own couriers and news agents, one of whom brought the first news of the Battle of Waterloo to England 24 hours in advance of the Government's messenger. It is not the fact that Rothschild turned this knowledge to account to reap a fortune; he immediately placed the intelligence at the disposal of the Cabinet, which was entirely incredulous until its own courier arrived with dispatches.

From paying England's allies and her Peninsular armies in the war, Rothschild turned to the more profitable promotion of the enterprises of peace, and raised immense loans for England and the Continent. He was powerful enough to devise means for the stabilisation of the currencies in which interest had to be paid and loans repaid, and at short notice to find the 15 millions needed by the Government as compensation to the West Indies when the slaves there were set free.

Rothschild's aim was, by making money circulate, to keep industry so active that men would have neither time nor desire for war. If he helped to finance a war he had more to hope from steady trade in

The Spacious Church of St Mary

On the River Lea
SCENES IN OLD WARE

Watford **In Cassiobury Park**

Westmill **By the Village Green**

gold and stocks and quicksilver of which he once owned the entire world's supplies.

His work was productive and fertilising, and he was a man whose word was his bond. With increasing wealth and power and love of England, he was emboldened to inaugurate the campaign for the removal of Jewish disabilities which denied civil and political rights to his race. He lived to see Jews made freemen of the City of London, allowed to qualify as sheriff, and to vote for Parliament.

His eldest son Lionel, who was born in 1808, was equally notable as financier, philanthropist, and reformer. Following in his father's footsteps, he raised enormous loans for England and other governments, one of the smallest, but most beneficial being the four millions enabling the Government to buy the Suez Canal shares. Elected to Parliament, he was not permitted to serve owing to his inability to take the oath "as a true Christian." Four times he was elected in the course of 11 years, and then at last in 1858 he was admitted a member. He died in 1879, and his son Nathan Meyer Rothschild, who was born in 1840, was created a baron of the United Kingdom. It was Lionel Rothschild who bought Tring.

A Village Sensation

WALKERN. Some of its farms have been dotting the landscape with their timber and plaster fronts for many generations, one of them with a charming dovecot under a cupola. A mile away is the plateau of a hill 400 feet high, moated round in the days of the Magna Carta barons; the ditch is 50 feet wide between the ramparts. Through all these centuries the ancient church has been amassing treasure in brass and stone. We come to it down a lane from the mile-long village street, crossing the River Beane and reaching the rectory in the shade of a noble cedar and the church in the shade of a splendid chestnut tree. The tower, built of flint and chalk, has consecration crosses on the walls and is crowned with a short spire. The walls of the nave are probably older than the Conquest, and it may be that in those Saxon days there was here a rare chalk rood of which we see traces on the south arcade. The arcade was cut in this wall and the south aisle added when the Normans settled down; the north arcade came in the 13th century. The chancel arch is 14th century, the plain roofs and the clerestory 15th. The font is 600 years old, the screen 500, and the pulpit 400; but older than any of these is the remarkable marble figure of a knight lying in a recess clad from head to foot in chain mail. Even his face is hidden by the vizor of his flat-topped helmet, but he is believed to represent one of the ancient Lanvalei family.

After them came the Humbarstons; their portraits are in brass. A 15th century couple are shown with a hand pointing to the words, Learn to die and live ever; and an Elizabethan family group, Edward Humbarston and his wife with eight children, is made from a patchwork of older brasses. In the vestry is a brass to Richard Humbarston, of 1581, which has on the other side an inscription to John Lovekyn, four times Lord Mayor of London, where he was buried in 1370. It is clear that his brass has been stolen and used again 200 years after. There is another Londoner in brass in the chancel, the haberdasher William Chapman and his wife, with their 12 children, all in 17th century dress. Gyles Humbarston and his wife, who died in Charles Stuart's happy days, are kneeling here in stone, and near them kneel another couple on a classical monument, Daniel Gorsnor and his wife, who lived on to see the king at war with his people.

All England was talking of this quiet village 200 years ago, when Jane Wenham, who had been accused of being a witch by a farmer, and had obtained a shilling compensation from him, was declared by the rector's servants to be bewitched, and was at last arrested and ducked in the pond. She was committed to the Assizes by the local magistrate, three clergymen gave evidence against her, and the jury found her guilty. She was sentenced to death by the judge against his will, but he was able to obtain a free pardon from Queen Anne. There was much controversy in Parliament and out, and the case at last led to the repeal of the statute against witchcraft in 1736. The good squire of Gilston, John Plumer, found the poor woman a cottage at Hertingfordbury, and when he died Earl Cowper looked after her.

In hundreds of our villages we have found the staples in the font which were put there to save the holy water from the witches; this village has the distinction of having led to the abolition of this superstition from the Statute Book.

A Friend to the Rescue

WALLINGTON. We climbed its lonely ridge and found a gaunt church falling to pieces, with ivy growing through the roof, and mice tearing holes in the cloth of the rough medieval pews. But we came again and found the roof repaired, the mice gone, and the bells back in a tower made strong enough to hold them, with a new bell in memory of a man who had rung them for over 40 years. The handsome medieval porch alone could almost hold the villagers, and they were not enough to save the old church themselves, but it was good to be told that a man whose ancestors lie here passed this way, saw the valiant wooden angels striving to hold up the broken roof, and came to their rescue. The angels have been here 500 years, and carving of the same age screens the chapel, where are the marks of vanished brasses and a nameless tomb with saints in niches and the arms of the Piggots and Prysots, which appear again in early 16th century glass. Seven fine big windows light the aisle and show up the impressive size of this church which stood for nearly 500 years and then nearly tumbled down. The scent of limes drifts in, and outside queer animal gargoyles watch the swallows under the eaves building their nests of mud from the church pond.

The Great Bed

WARE. It was known to the Danes, who are said to have brought their ships up the River Lea, and to John Gilpin on his famous ride, and was important enough 600 years ago for the county town to be referred to as Hertford-by-Ware. Long associated with malting, its aspect has been spoiled by the cone-shaped cowls of many kilns, but there are quaint survivals of old Ware, looking its best as we come from Hertford and see its clustering red roofs and the fine grey church with a tiny spire. There is a pleasant tree-lined walk along the towpath on this side of the town, and the gardens of the houses have quaint gazebos along the north bank. George Stephenson's iron bridge over the River Lea was cased by a concrete bridge early in our century.

The church stands finely at a corner which is like a paved garden, with a sundial among the flowers. In the narrow streets about it is a sprinkling of old houses, some with overhanging storeys. Facing the church is a big house with creepered walls and a roof of mellow tiles; known as the Priory, it has been much altered since it was built from the remains of a Franciscan friary founded in 1338 by the lord of the manor, Thomas Wake. It has some medieval windows, and in the entrance hall is an arch resting on corbels crudely carved with the heads of men. Here too is a 14th century refectory table of oak and ash and poplar, said to be unique for its time in England. The house and its gardens were given to the town in 1920 by Annie Elizabeth Croft—the gardens small but charming with lawns and flowers, fine trees, and the river flowing through, a weeping willow making an arbour near the bridge to a tree-shaded island. The manor house, north of the church, is believed to stand on the site of a priory founded soon after the Conquest. Gilpin House in High Street, 17th century, keeps green the association of Cowper's John Gilpin with the town. The Bluecoat House, built in 1686 by the Governors of Christ's Hospital, served as a school till the children were removed to Hertford in 1760, and has since been a private house. An 18th century house in the London Road, home of the Quaker poet, John Scott, became part of the grammar school for girls opened in our own time. A curious transformation has taken place at 65 High Street, where the timbered fronts of two 15th century houses (which once faced each other across an alley) now form the walls of a coal cellar. One of the fronts has its original window frame and oak doorway, the curved arches above them having pierced spandrels.

Unspoiled by time or trade, the spacious cross-shaped church of St Mary is a grand tribute to its medieval builders, and to the restorers since the middle of last century, who have made the embattled exterior, including most of the windows, look rather new. Most of the old work is 14th and 15th century, but the chancel (said to have been completed by the mother of Henry the Seventh, Margaret Beaufort) has 13th century masonry and a fragment of an original window. The chancel arch is 15th century. Opening to the lady chapel is a rare 14th century round-headed archway divided into two pointed bays, with straight mullions in the spandrel. The chapel has a sedile and piscina 600 years old, 17th century panelling with a fine border of pierced carving, 15th century screenwork dividing it from the south transept, and a panelled and traceried roof in red and gold, with floral bosses. The 500-year-old doorway to the vestry has slender shafts, and a draped head and the head of a demon peeping from hollow moulding; it frames an old oak door. The 17th century altar rails now enclosing the Children's Corner were cast out of the church last century and served for a time as a garden fence before being brought back a few years ago.

The nave and aisles are from the end of the 14th century, and the tower with double buttresses is a little older. The graceful arches of the arcades, and the big windows of the clerestory (which are partly medieval) carry the eye to the splendid 15th century nave roof, with stout tie-beams and bosses of flowers, shields, and quaint heads, supported by modern stone corbels of saints and apostles. Good heads of medieval folk are between the arches of the arcades. The north transept has two 15th century recesses, and two brass portraits of the same century, showing a woman in flowing robes and ornamented headdress, and Elen Coke of 1454 wearing draped headdress and wide sleeves. There is a remarkable brass in the south transept with 23 people on it—fine small figures of William Pyrey of 1470 in a belted gown, his two wives in horned headdress, and charming groups of 20 children, each wife having given him five sons and five daughters.

The font is magnificent with its vigorous carving of figures under leafy arches round the bowl. We see Gabriel and Mary, St Margaret slaying the dragon, St Christopher carrying the Holy Child over the stream, St Catherine with her wheel, St James with his pilgrim's staff, St John the Baptist, and a bearded St George in armour, slaying the dragon. It is this armour of St George which enables us to date the lovely font at about 1380, for it closely resembles that of the Black Prince in Canterbury. At the corners of the font are angels with musical instruments and Passion symbols; the stem, only a little narrower than the bowl, is carved with quatrefoils, and round the base is a wreath of branchwork and flowers. The traceried and pinnacled cover is modern.

An arresting contribution of our day is the lovely Christopher Whall glass in two windows. In the north aisle is a tribute to the fallen of the South African War, showing St George in golden armour, St Michael and a dragon, and St Alban as a Roman soldier. The other window is a great Te Deum in the north transept, Mrs Croft's memorial to her parents. Angels are by Our Lord in Glory, and in the company of saints and apostles below are David as a boy with his sling and as a king with his harp, Elijah and the raven, Catherine, Agnes, Stephen, Michael, and Joan the Fair Maid of Kent, whom the Black Prince wooed and won. She is holding a model of this church, reminding us of the tradition that it was built largely by her generosity.

Sir Richard Fanshawe's descendants have restored his marble monument in the south transept. Son of Sir Henry Fanshawe, who was a horticulturist and an Italian scholar, Sir Richard was born in 1608 at Ware Park, a domain of over 200 acres west of the town, partly encircled by the River Lea and the River Rib. He was a famous ambassador of Charles Stuart, and his son was taken prisoner at Worcester, and became Latin secretary to Prince Charles at the Hague. Returning at the Restoration, he became a Privy councillor and in 1664 was English ambassador at Madrid, where he died in 1666. His body was brought home and buried here.

Ware Park is now a sanatorium. One of its rooms is said to have been the original home of a piece of furniture that lives in Shakespeare, the Great Bed of Ware, which has lately been bought for the Victoria and Albert Museum. For nearly four centuries this wonderful oak bedstead, nearly 11 feet square and over 7 feet high, has been a byword with English people. It has often been mentioned in literature. Shakespeare makes an amusing allusion to it in Twelfth Night, when Sir Toby gives advice on courtship to Sir Andrew Aguecheek, telling him to write to Olivia, assuring her of his valour, "as many lies as will lie in thy sheet of paper, although the sheet were big enough for the Bed of Ware in England." Early in the 18th century it was in the Crown Inn at Ware, and in 1764 was moved to the Saracen's Head near by. Last century it was taken to a building in the grounds of Rye House in Hertfordshire, renowned for the famous plot against Charles Stuart's two sons, happily discovered before they could be assassinated. The bed is magnificently carved. The head is a work of art, and the canopy and bedposts are also richly decorated. From the moment the idea of this huge bed entered the mind of its maker the Great Bed of Ware must have been a perpetual joke down the centuries. All kinds of travellers stopping at the two inns have slept under its great canopy, and many strange bedfellows it must have seen.

A Gallant Scholar

SIR RICHARD FANSHAWE, poet, linguist, and diplomatist, faithful to the Stuarts in their darkest hours, was one of the most attractive and romantic figures of that period. He was born at Ware in 1608 and when he was 27 became secretary to the English ambassador in Spain and stayed in that country until King Charles made Oxford his capital in the Civil War. At Oxford he met and married Anne Harrison, the nineteen-year-old daughter of a Hertfordshire gentleman. The pair had not twenty pounds between them, but the marriage was a great success.

Fanshawe was appointed secretary to Prince Charles, and when it became necessary for the prince to seek safety from capture the Fanshawes went with him. While in Spain Fanshawe had a baronetcy conferred on him by his fugitive master, whom he accompanied as his secretary to Scotland, and on his advance into England, where he was captured by Cromwell at the Battle of Worcester when Charles escaped. On petition from Lady Fanshawe Cromwell let her husband out on bail, from which he was eventually released. After Cromwell's death Fanshawe rejoined Charles abroad and was appointed his Latin secretary; returned with him for the Restoration; was elected MP for Cambridge; went to Portugal as ambassador; and in 1664 took up the appointment of ambassador to Spain, where he next year signed a preliminary draft of a commercial treaty with which Clarendon, who was then Lord Chancellor, and the great power in England, disagreed. So Fanshawe was superseded at Madrid by Lord Sandwich, and in less than a month after receiving his letters of recall died there of "an inward fever."

It was a sad ending to a life of faithful service. No doubt Fanshawe was precipitate in signing a paper he had not submitted to the home authorities, but Clarendon himself admitted that he was "a gentleman very well beloved; no man knew the Spanish Court better, or was so well versed in the language."

Sir Richard had lived a wandering life, often depending on the hospitality of loyal friends, and spending a small fortune on the Stuarts; he did much fine translation work, and his own memoirs were written by his faithful wife, who had been his companion in nearly all his wanderings, and had borne him 14 children. A gallant, scholarly, and virtuous cavalier was Sir Richard, in a dissolute age.

Burne-Jones Windows

WATERFORD. The happy Barnardo boys have found a fine home here in the great house of Goldings, once the home of the banking family who built the church last century. Windows to their memory make a delightful gallery, especially one to a young daughter of the house showing a girl with an angel hovering over her. Under another are moulded in bronze the nine medals won by Colonel Wilfred Abel-Smith, including the famous Khartoum medal. He lived here in the park before he went out to the war and fell at Festubert in 1915. But it is the Burne-Jones windows that are the chief attraction of the church. They show Mary and Gabriel in the shade of orange trees, Miriam dancing to her timbrel under a pomegranate tree, and David with his harp.

A Hero of the Great War

WATFORD. It is Hertfordshire's biggest town, and though it is fast losing its old buildings, with factories springing up in their place, it has kept something from its ancient days. There are old houses in the narrow High Street, and behind them eight 16th century almshouses with steep gables. Close by is an imposing building of 1704, with a wooden bell turret, once the Free School. Reset in a new timbered inn at the corner of Market Street is a 15th century oak window. Cassiobury Park, though it has seen the last of the home of the Earls of Essex, has not lost all its ancient beauty, serving now partly for golf and partly as a park where all may sit in the shade of the willows of the River Gade. Watford has about 900 acres of parks and playing fields.

The old church is tucked away behind the High Street, where trees struggle with tombs for light and air, and one fig tree is springing from a tomb. Above them all a massive 15th century tower with a tiny spire rises up 100 feet. The wide chancel arch is 13th century; the broad nave and aisles are 15th, with a massive roof of tie-beams supported on a dozen angels and some quaint heads left from the 13th century. The altar table, the ornate chairs, and two chests are Jacobean. There is a chair of Cromwell's time, and a tall chest of the 18th century carved with medallions of the Evangelists and their winged emblems. The 18th century carving on the pulpit is so delicate that its craftsman (Richard Bull) is believed to have been a pupil of Grinling Gibbons. The modern choir stalls are surely unique, for among their elaborate ornament are the portraits of two curates carved as poppyheads by their vicar. On a window-sill we found a fierce-looking dragon which was once the weathervane.

On the wall behind the stalls are portraits in brass of Judge de Hollis (buried here in Agincourt year) and his wife. Kneeling in stone, a serene dignified figure at her prayer desk in the chapel she built in 1595, is the widow of Sir Richard Morrison, and a unique brass tablet on the wall portrays three faithful servants of her son's family. The family themselves, the Morrisons, are here in two elaborate monuments by Nicholas Stone, who himself records that he carved them royally and in the best manner. We see Sir Charles Morrison lying in his armour with his daughter, the Countess of Sussex, and his son Charles kneeling in separate recesses at each end. This same son we see again on the other monument, this time reclining on a ledge above his beautiful wife, who gazes at the canopy. At their feet kneel their two sons, and at their head kneels their daughter Elizabeth, whose own son was the first Earl of Essex of Cassiobury Park. All around are memorials of their descendants.

Remembrances of many other Watford families are in the 15th century chapel of the Heydons of the Grove, a lovely park by the River Gade, with a stately house owned long after them by the Earl of Clarendon. An anchor memorial is to George Pidcock, who fell boarding a pirate's junk off Amoy in 1853. Robert Clutter-buck, the famous historian of Hertfordshire, lies in the churchyard, and his son James is also remembered here; he fell carrying the colours of the West Suffolks at Inkerman. A group of officer friends who died in the Indian Mutiny have a window picturing David and Jonathan. Thomas Bevan, who was organist here for 48 years, has a window with a lovely figure of St Cecilia.

Watford has a group of modern churches of much interest. The great tower rising above the roofs with a spire turret 117 feet high belongs to the Roman Catholic church, a place of much grandeur designed by John Bentley, the architect of Westminster Cathedral. St James's Church received as a contribution from the old church the pedestal of her Norman font, with its wavy mouldings and beaded ornament, and St John's Church received from the old mother church her 18th century font, which stands beside a modern stoup with two delightful cherubs. The pride of St John's, however, is in its dark oak chapel screen with a gilded St Michael on one side and a silvered St George on the other. It is in memory of 47 men who were not here to worship after the war, among them the famous General Maude, who lies far away at Bagdad, where he was struck down in the midst of his triumph. He was one of the bravest soldiers of the Great War, taking part in two masterly operations on Gallipoli, and leading his men with consummate genius to the relief of Kut and on to Bagdad. It was his last great victory. Bagdad was in the grip of cholera, and General Maude drank a glass of milk at a children's party, and in four days was dead of cholera. He was a man of high integrity and deep religious faith, a bitter loss to the Army.

One thing we must note at Watford, a piece of work that might well be an inspiration to many other towns. The walls of the children's section of the public library have been covered with an admirable background for the world of books, the work having been done by the students of the Art School. The scenes are in six panels representing the peoples of the world, their industries and customs and methods of transport. One panel is devoted to each continent, the sixth panel bearing a map of the world. On the panel representing Asia are a junk and a rickshaw, a Chinese with a kite, Tibetan dancers, a deodar, a pagoda, the Forbidden City of Lhasa, and lovely Fujiyama. Next come an Afridi, a Benares brass-worker, and other Indians, including a prince on an elephant. A Persian rugmaker is at work next to a representative of Turkey in Asia, Lawrence of Arabia stands by a camel, and behind him is the Holy Stone at Mecca. It is an excellent example of what may be accomplished by public spirit in education, and we may feel that much more might be done in our towns by an eager co-operation between the civic authorities and the schools.

Medieval Brass

WATTON. In its friendly street are homes 300 years old, and to the north of the church is Watton Place, a good example of a Tudor home. Watkins Hall has been rebuilt but still has the old beam which recorded its change of name in 1636 like this:

Watton Hall alias Watkins Hall.

The village pump has an oak shelter in memory of a Commander of the Bath and General of the Guards, Sir Philip Smith. The little River Beane swells into a wide lake in Woodhall Park. The impressive church is a generous example of 15th century architecture even to the roofs of its aisles, and has a whole collection of medieval folk in brass. First comes a knight in armour of the 14th century, Sir Philip Peletot, sheltering in the only modern addition to the church, the barrel-roofed north chapel. With him is another knight in Tudor armour, probably one of the Butlers, who have several other brass portraits here, and a grand alabaster slab of 1471 inlaid with portraits of Sir John Butler with his two wives and eight children. They lived at Woodhall manor house. Also in brass are a medieval priest and the wife of Edmund Bardolf (who died in 1455). There is a fine ironbound chest 300 years old, good carving on the doorway of the north porch, and out in the great churchyard is a handsome altar tomb 200 years older than the church itself. Away in Well Wood are traces of a moat, and a mile from the village is a 16th century farmhouse, Broom Hall.

Dr Johnson Calls

WELWYN. Within a mile of new Welwyn, the garden city of 20th century colonists, lies this old Welwyn where the Roman colonists settled, probably with a temple where the church now stands on the edge of the Maran valley. Roman tiles have appeared in the churchyard; Roman bricks are in the church walls; but most of the church has been made new. There is a bit of a Norman capital in the vestry walls, and some medieval heads are preserved in the aisle. One of the arcades is 13th century, and from the 15th come two plain roofs, the screen with elaborate tracery and finials, and the porch approached by a grand yew hedge. The piscina is 700 years old.

Under the altar Edward Young was buried in 1765. On the wall is a tablet to this poet, who was rector for 35 years and planted the rectory's fine avenue of limes. Dr Johnson much admired his Night Thoughts, and admired also these lime trees when he called here at the invitation of the poet's son, an invitation manoeuvred by Boswell, who went on ahead leaving Dr Johnson sipping tea at the inn quite ignorant of his friend's intention. Boswell came back with the invitation, and Johnson greeted the poet's son with a very polite bow, saying: "Sir, I had a curiosity to come and see this place; I had the honour to know that great man your father." They sat and talked in the rectory summerhouse, and we may think that Johnson would recall that much-quoted epigram of Dr Young on Voltaire:

> *Thou art so witty, profligate, and thin,*
> *At once we think thee Milton, Death, and Sin.*

In the home of Edward Young there lived for 40 years another famous man, Henry Fynes Clinton, one of the most remarkable classical scholars of the 18th century. It is known that he mastered in eight years 33,000 pages of Greek literature and that he read 69,322 verses of poetry. He kept a journal in Latin and Greek till the day before he died. Few men have ever had a more complete knowledge of Greek poets and prose writers; he lived out the Psalmist's span of life and gave nearly every day of it to scholarship. He lies in a village graveyard in Nottinghamshire.

The rectors of Welwyn are also the lords of the manor, for the manor was given to the church by Edward the Confessor.

The graves of Romans buried here centuries before the Confessor's day have yielded many interesting objects, including glass decanters and a tiny clay statue of a lady of the 1st century. Older finds from the park of Locksleys form a striking group in the Iron Age Gallery of the British Museum. They include an iron frame 42 inches high which may have served as a sacrificial altar, three pairs of fire-dogs ending in fantastic animal heads, and five huge jars for wine or oil. Other finds were some silver cups and bronze vessels, and three bronze masks marked with moustache and hair. They appear to have been imported from the Mediterranean about the time Julius Cæsar first invaded Britain, when his raiders reached the neighbourhood of St Albans, where a critical battle was fought.

WELWYN GARDEN CITY. It may not be a city, but it is surely a garden, a lovely place of lawns and flowers, which has not yet been growing twenty years. It is an ordered village in which the area devoted to gardens and green-verged, tree-lined roads so greatly exceeds the red and white houses that the impression is of light and air everywhere. If it is lovely now, it will be lovelier still when the trees rise to the height of the fine Sherrards Park Wood on its northern boundary, with the pretty village of Digswell close by and old Welwyn village beyond. A branch railway runs through a delightful glade in these woods, and from its beautiful bridge we look down along the great open space through the heart of the Garden City, set out with splendid avenues and beds of flowers; the view continues to the hills beyond the valley of the River Lea. The factory area of the village is spaciously laid out on the eastern side of the main line of the railway; the residential area is on the west.

The red brick church is planned on spacious and striking lines. The nave inside is of mottled brick, the chancel and the chapels are white. The chancel is one of the biggest we have seen, mounting in seven steps to the altar, which is draped with blue and grey. Great grey draperies hanging from the roof take the place of an east window. The roof is timbered and painted.

On a wall by one of the lawns at the shopping centre we read that Ebenezer Howard founded this town. It is, of course, the child of his dreams, like Letchworth, where we come upon him again.

Charles Lamb's Acre

WESTMILL. It is a village of great beauty, treasuring its past and caring for its present. It has a charming little green and a row of old cottages, a giant chestnut shading an inn, an ancient barn, a library, a museum, and stones a thousand years old in its church. One other thing it has which must interest all, a little thatched cottage which belonged to Charles Lamb, though he never lived in it. It is called Button Snap and is a mile away at Cherry's Green, and it has been happily passed into the safe keeping of the Royal Society of Arts for its own sake as a lovely cottage and for its association with Charles Lamb. We saw it in a coat of bright yellow and with more thatch than walls, attractive with little diamond paned windows, and on turning up our Elia we found that in his essay on his first play he speaks with mock pride of this only bit of landed property he could ever call his own:

When I journeyed down to take possession, and planted foot on my own ground, the stately habits of the donor descended upon me, and I strode (shall I confess the vanity?) with larger paces over my allotment of three quarters of an acre with its commodious mansion in the midst, with the feeling of an English freeholder that all betwixt sky and centre was my own.

237

The museum is opposite the inn with the giant chestnut. Here, housed in an ancient thatched cottage, is a small collection of things recalling the old life of the village. Handmade iron implements, a wooden flail, the harvest horn which woke men from their beds, and pots and coins from the days of the Romans, whose Ermine Street runs by and whose bricks are preserved with Saxon stones in the walls of the church; we see them in the gable. The long-and-short stones of the Saxons are at a corner of the nave. An arcade of two great arches was added in the 12th century when the north aisle was built, and most of the rest of the church is 15th. From that time comes the spiked tower with its lofty arch and its newel stairway, the font and the roof, and two rare stone angels with flaming torches guarding the west door. The chalice is Elizabethan; the twisted altar rails are a little later. On the wall of the tower is a stone inscribed in Norman French to Nicol, son of the lord of the manor in 1277. The clock above it strikes on one of the oldest bells in the county; it is 600 years since its maker proudly wrote on it, William Rofforde made me. An old lady who loved to hear this peal of five bells ringing was Mrs Winnington-Ingram, whose son was for so long the popular Bishop of London; her father was rector here before he became a bishop, having the interesting name of Henry Pepys.

One of the curates here gave up his pulpit rather than acknowledge Queen Anne as his sovereign; he was Nathaniel Salmon, who gave up the rest of his life to writing. He paid close attention to the study of Roman remains, wrote a history of Hertfordshire, and made preparations for histories of several other counties. His History of Hertfordshire is in the village library, which is housed in a tiny room of one of the almshouses. The village hall has been made out of an ancient barn, pleasant to look upon but not so noble in its antiquity as the thatched barn of ten bays supported on oak trusses reaching from floor to roof, belonging to the manor house.

The Village Samson

WESTON. Two lanes climb from the Great North Road, one past a smock-mill with broken sails, the other through a delightful little beech wood, both to meet in this village scattered on the top of the gentle Weston Hills. The stone heads of medieval folk greet us from the church windows, but from without the central tower scarcely bears witness to its Norman ancestry, though inside we see its four beautiful rounded arches with simple Norman carvings on two of the piers. The small north transept is wholly Norman; the font is 15th century; the plaster and timber roof of the nave has handsome carved bosses; but it is the extraordinary stone heads on which the nave and aisle roofs rest that astonish us with their ancient distorted faces and arms. There are 30 in all, 500 years old, like strange creatures from a pagan masque, though two are said to represent Henry the Fourth and his queen.

A window of the Good Shepherd is in memory of the Farr family, whose sheep have grazed on these slopes for five generations. A century-old charity bequeaths 16 loaves of bread to "16 poor married men" every Sunday for ever, but the baker's cart now takes them round on Saturday.

The church was given to the Knights Templars by Gilbert Strongbow, father of the Richard Strongbow who captured most of Ireland for Henry the Second. But it is another strong man of the bow who has pride of place here, a legendary fellow called Jack o' Legs; any boy will point out his grave in the churchyard marked by two low stones 12 feet apart. This was a friendly giant, but he would turn highwayman on occasion, robbing travellers on Jack's Hill, and snatching their morning's batch from the Baldock bakers. At last Baldock rose against him, caught him, and bound him like another Samson. When he knew he was to die Jack made one request, that he might be buried where his arrow struck the ground, and the story goes that it flew through the air, glanced off the roof of this church, and fell between these two stones.

Mackery End

WHEATHAMPSTEAD. As we walk about these lanes we may imagine a queer little man clinging close to his Bridget, drinking in the beauty of the countryside, and chatting eagerly in his delight at being here. He was Charles Lamb. Here are 400-year-old cottages he knew, a pleasant inn of the same old age, and a church with stone and brass memorials of no less than 50 folk of medieval days. But the hills looking down on them all, the River Lea cutting its way through, and the wild Heath of No Man's Land carry memories far more ancient than these.

The heath took its name, it is said, from its position as the dividing land between the domains of the abbots of St Albans and the abbots of Westminster. Round about are entrenchments dug before the days of history. A boundary dyke, in places 32 feet deep and 100 feet across the top, runs for a mile from Bernard's Heath to St Albans Road. To the south-east Devil's Dyke and the Slad run nearly parallel. Were these the fortifications where the British tribe turned Cæsar's raiding forces back?

History speaks with more assurance at Mackery End, the 16th century farmhouse delightful with its elegant gables and famous for its place in literature, for here Charles Lamb as a weakly child lived with the Gladmans in the tender charge of his Bridget. His memories of those days, recalled by a visit 40 years later, make one of his most delightful essays:

The oldest thing I remember is Mackery End, a farmhouse delightfully situated within a gentle walk from Wheathampstead. I can just remember having been there; on a visit to a great-aunt, when I was a child, under the care of Bridget, who, as I have said, is older than myself by some ten years. . . . More than forty years had elapsed since the visit I speak of; and who or what sort of persons inherited Mackery End (kindred or strange folk) we were afraid almost to conjecture, but determined someday to explore.

By somewhat a circuitous route, taking the noble park at Luton in our way from Saint Albans, we arrived at the spot of our anxious curiosity about noon. The sight of the old farmhouse, though every trace of it was effaced from my recollection, affected me with a pleasure which I had not experienced for many a year. For though I had forgotten it, we had never forgotten being there together, and we had been talking about Mackery End all our lives.

Bridget's was more a waking bliss than mine, for she easily remembered her old acquaintance again, some altered features, of course, a little grudged at. At first, indeed, she was ready to disbelieve for joy; but the scene soon reconfirmed itself in her affections, and she traversed every outpost of the old mansion, to the woodhouse, the orchard, the place where the pigeon-house had stood (house and birds were alike flown) with a breathless impatience of recognition, which was more pardonable perhaps than decorous at the age of fifty-odd. But Bridget in some things is behind her years.

The only thing left was to get into the house, and that was a difficulty which to me singly would have been insurmountable; for I am terribly shy in making myself known to strangers and out-of-date kinsfolk. Love stronger than scruple winged my cousin in without me; but she

Knebworth   **The Home of the Lyttons**

Wheathampstead   **Charles Lamb's Mackery End**

A Lovely Avenue

An Ideal School
WELWYN GARDEN CITY

soon returned with a creature that might have sat to a sculptor for the image of Welcome. It was the youngest of the Gladmans; who, by marriage with a Bruton, had become mistress of the old mansion. A comely brood are the Brutons. Six of them, females, were noted as the handsomest young women in the county. But this adopted Bruton, in my mind, was better than they all—more comely.

Those slender ties that prove slight as gossamer in the rending atmosphere of a metropolis bind faster, as we found it, in hearty, homely, loving Hertfordshire. In five minutes we were as thoroughly acquainted as if we had been born and bred up together. . . . The fatted calf was made ready, or rather was already so, as if in anticipation of our coming; and, after an appropriate glass of native wine, never let me forget with what honest pride this hospitable cousin made us proceed to Wheathampstead, to introduce us (as some newfound rarity) to her mother and sister Gladmans. . . . When I forget all this, then may my country cousins forget me; and Bridget no more remember that in the days of weakling infancy I was her tender charge, as I have been her care in foolish manhood since, in those pretty pastoral walks, long ago, about Mackery End in Hertfordshire.

In an older Mackery End than this was born John of Wheathampstead, the famous abbot of St Albans who founded the abbey library and whose tomb still graces the abbey church. He was a powerful man in the 15th century. In the church at Wheathampstead his proud parents, Hugh and Margaret Bostock, are portrayed in brass. Other portraits in the north transept picture John Heyworth and his wife, a Tudor couple with their nine children, and another nameless couple of those days are here with eight children not their own, for they do not fit the stone. We may suppose they come from one of the stones in the chancel and the south transept, where are fragments of many other brasses.

The north transept was the chapel of the Garrard family of Lamer Park, where their shields still appear on a 17th century entrance arch and in the window of the dairy, which was once a chapel. From that chapel at Lamer Park (older than the house, which is 18th century) came the church's oak pulpit and two chairs, all 17th century. A whole family of Garrards appear in the transept on a coloured marble monument of 1637, Sir John (one of the earliest of our baronets) in armour with his wife, and below them in relief six sons and eight daughters. Opposite is a white stone cut with a sketch of John Heyworth of 1558 kneeling with his wife and three children, and on their tombs in the south transept lie the alabaster figures of Sir

John Brocket in 16th century armour with his wife. Round the tomb eight mourners stand out in relief. On the chancel walls we read of Nicholas Bristow, servant to the last four Tudor sovereigns, and of Thomas Stubbinger, who in the 17th century seems to have successfully combined the business of a merchant with the life of a rector.

The foundations of an earlier apse show that there was a church here in Norman or perhaps in Saxon days, but the oldest part of the present building is the chancel, with its stringcourse and three lancets of the 13th century. The central tower, with its odd spire and graceful arches, was rebuilt at the end of that century. The tracery of the 14th century builders fills the windows of both transepts and both aisles; theirs are the arcades and the ballflower arch of the west doorway, the font, and the rare stone reredos of seven canopied niches in the north transept, where the sill of the east window is brought low to support this treasure, with all its delicate detail. The screen to this transept was made from the timbers of a gallery of 300 years ago.

Charles Lamb's Country and its Old Cronies

WIDFORD. We may think we hear his laughter echoing, for here he came often to laugh before he came to weep. At the great house of Blakesware his grandmother Mrs Field was housekeeper to the Plumer-Wards, and little Charles played in the park. It was all his, he said—his that gallery of good old family portraits, that marble hall with its mosaic pavements and its twelve Cæsars in marble, that lofty Justice Hall with its high-backed chair of authority, terror of a luckless poacher, and his the costly fruit garden and the ampler pleasure garden rising from the house in terraces. Here Mrs Field was housekeeper for over half a century, and Lamb knew the old house and loved it as his home.

Then came the day when, going north, he turned aside to see the great house coming down; a few bricks lay about representing what was once so stately and so spacious. "Death does not shrink up his human victims at this rate," he wrote, and he was indignant then, as we are now, to see the vandal spirit at work in the countryside. Had he seen these navvies at their destroying work, he said, at the plucking of every panel he would have felt the varlets at his heart, and would have cried out to them to spare him something—at least a plank out of the cheerful storeroom in whose window-seat he used to sit and read Cowley. Every plank and panel of the house had magic in it for him. He had the range at will of every apartment, knew every nook and corner, wondered and worshipped everywhere.

Alas, the old house has gone.

Charles Lamb knew everybody here, all the villagers and the old cronies, some of whom come into his poems:

> Kindly hearts have I known,
> Kindly hearts they are flown.

He tells us in one of his poems of Kitty Wheatley who sleeps in the kirk house, and poor Polly Perkin who had gone to the work-house; of fine gardener Ben Carter, in ten counties no smarter; and Lily postilion with cheeks of vermilion; and in some verses which he afterwards suppressed he told of wicked Dorrell who lies in the churchyard here, declaring that had he mended in time he need not

> Have groaned in his coffin,
> While demons stood scoffing:
> You'd ha' thought him a coughing:
> My own father heard him.

It is thought that Old Dorrell cheated the Lamb family of what would have been to them a small fortune, about two thousand pounds.

Many of these people lie in Widford churchyard, and in one corner lies Mary Field herself. She sleeps on the green hilltop hard by the house of prayer, Lamb tells us in his poem on The Grandame, and this is what he says of her:

> She served her heavenly Master. I have seen
> That reverend form bent down with age and pain,
> And rankling malady. Yet not for this
> Ceased she to praise her Maker, or withdraw
> Her trust in Him, her faith, and humble hope;
> So meekly had she learned to bear her cross—
> For she had studied patience in the school
> Of Christ; much comfort she had thence derived,
> And was a follower of the Nazarene.

Truly poignant were his memories of this small place, for here too he had met Anna Simmons, who lived in a cottage, Blenheim, a mile from Blakesware. It was Lamb's first love, an unrequited one:

> Beloved! I were well content to play
> With thy free tresses all a summer's day.

The time came when in his wanderings he found no Anna here:

When last I roved these winding wood-walks green,
Green winding walks and shady pathways sweet,
Oftimes would Anna seek the silent scene,
Shrouding her beauties in the lone retreat.
No more I hear her footsteps in the shade:
Her image only in these pleasant ways
Meets me self-wandering, where in happier days
I held free converse with the fair-haired maid.
I passed the little cottage which she loved,
The cottage which did once my all contain;
It spake of days which ne'er must come again,
Spake to my heart, and much my heart was moved.
" Now fair befall thee, gentle maid!" said I,
And from the cottage turned me with a sigh.

The churchyard of Widford is speckled with primroses and wood anemones, under elms and chestnuts and ancient yews. Bounding it on the west is a 16th century brick wall with fragments of an old priory to which it is said to have belonged. The round archway in the wall is perhaps 17th century, of which time there are some remains in the timber and plaster house here. Near by is a pigeon house which may be older still, but it has come upon sad days. Facing the lychgate to the churchyard is another set up in memory of men who fell in the Great War, opening to a burial ground.

Attractive with the colouring of its flint walls, red roof, and green copper spire, the simple aisleless church is chiefly 14th and 15th century, though the nave may have some Norman masonry. One of a number of Norman capitals found during restoration is now part of a stone table in the chancel. The 14th century tower has a fine arch widened in the 15th, and the top windows are modern. The pretty oak porch is also modern, but it shelters a doorway of 1370 and an old door; a similar door in the old north doorway opens now to the modern vestry, in which hangs a drawing of the church's finely chased cup and paten of 1562.

The chancel has old wall paintings showing a bishop, a knight, and Our Lord seated on a rainbow, with a sword raised and an angel close by. In the 19th century painting of the chancel roof we see St Francis, St Martin sharing his cloak, and the Crucifixion. Old tie-beams still remain. At the 15th century font (which has heads of a lion and a woman among its carvings) was baptised Richard

Whateley, a vicar's brilliant son, who became Archbishop of Dublin and was one of the founders of the Broad Church Party. The glass in the east window, showing scenes in Our Lord's life, is a tribute to John Eliot, the Widford yeoman's son who left church and country for conscience sake, preached the Gospel to the Red Indians, and translated the Bible for them. His Psalm book was the first book printed in America.

John Eliot, the Red Man's Friend

JOHN ELIOT was born here in 1604, the son of a substantial yeoman. After taking his degree at Cambridge he entered the Church, but, being a Puritan, found his life in danger in the England of Charles Stuart and fled to America, accompanied by three brothers and three sisters. He reached Boston in 1631 and settled as a pastor. Relations between the Red Indians and the Palefaces at that time were much as we find them in the pages of Fenimore Cooper, and to scalp a white invader was quite the proper thing for a brave to do. Nevertheless, Eliot determined to make his life among those fierce sons of the wilds.

He obtained a complete mastery of their language and in 1646 entered on his mission, taking his life in his hands and going boldly among the savages to preach the white man's religion. To the utmost intrepidity of spirit he united a dignity and sweetness of manner that made him seem inspired. Immediate success attended his ministration, and he obtained a grant of land on which to build a town. He established the first settled institutions in which the arts of Civilisation were taught to the Red Indian. The movement grew, helped by funds from London, and Eliot soon had 14 communities of "praying Indians" under his direction, while still retaining his pastorate. His work necessitated repeated journeys through swamps and forest wilds, where his life was constantly in danger from jealous medicine men and suspicious chiefs. Often he travelled for a whole week, soaked with rain.

Having produced a metrical version of the Psalms for his converts he translated the entire Bible into their language, and America's first home-printed version of the Scriptures was given her in the tongue of the Massachusetts Indians. Not only did he carry out this masterly work single-handed; he contributed to the cost of the printing, although all he had in the world was his salary of £50 a year. He founded schools and trained schoolmasters, for whom he wrote a Red Indian grammar, and he taught his protégés to conduct the affairs of their own little townships. War brought disaster to his flocks, but Eliot laboured on, and extended his protection to the Negroes. He was the first man in the world to say a word for the slaves. He died in 1690, aged 80, murmuring, "Welcome Joy." He lives to fame as the Indian Apostle, and posterity has endorsed the saying of those who best knew his career and character, that since the death of St Paul a nobler, truer, and warmer spirit than John Eliot never lived. It was Widford that produced him.

Grim's Ditch

WIGGINTON. Perched on a spur of the Chilterns high above Tring, it can see without being seen, and has a wide view of woods and valleys. It is a tiny village with a friendly little church among trim yews, or so it seemed to us, calling soon after the painters had given it bright blue posts for its red-capped bellcot, more blue round the windows and the porch, and blue rainpipes. We found the effect of this colouring with the red-tiled roof extraordinarily warm and pleasant.

An odd little place inside, it is unhappily dark, with strangely low arches and with floors of all levels. Though much has been made new it has absorbed with its old stones a charm for which we must remember little Wigginton. The handsome roof of the west chamber is 500 years old. The chalice is Elizabethan. A stone set up by the Northamptonshire Regiment marks the grave of James Osborne, who died 50 years after winning the VC in the Zulu Wars, when he rode under heavy fire at Wesselstroom, picked up a wounded man, and carried him safe to camp.

The mysterious Grim's Ditch runs for nearly a mile to the south from Longcroft towards Northchurch, with a break at Clayhill, and a reappearance on Berkhamsted Common. The ditch is sometimes 30 feet across and is banked up in places to ten feet. Nobody knows when or why it was made though it is thought to mark a boundary line.

The Little Elephant with a Howdah

WILLIAN. Many who come on this homely place with its green and its ponds, its tall trees, its medieval church, and its thatched vicarage 400 years old, must think it an endearing English scene, fit to be preserved for ever; and so it is to be, for it stands within the green belt bought by Letchworth's Garden City.

Limes and chestnuts strive to out-top the gargoyles of death and the other dread powers peering out from the 15th century tower. Graver medieval heads, 14 in all, support the chancel roof, and tiny heads below them add to the delicate arcading. The 15th century woodcarvers added their quaint fancies to the posts of the choir stalls, where we see a sphinx-like monster with barbed tail above the Baptist's head on a charger; and strangest of all is a perfect little elephant bearing a howdah with openings carved like medieval church windows. Part of a Tudor screen is left in the 15th century chancel arch, which matches the arch of the tower. The walls of the nave and the chancel are the work of Norman masons.

Two vicars of long ago are here in brass and stone, Richard Goldon having a portrait brass of 1446 on the chancel wall, and John Chapman, who died in 1624, appearing as a small kneeling figure in stone with his wife. By the altar kneel more stone figures, Edward Lacon with his wife and three children. The father, who is in armour, died in the year Charles Stuart came to the throne. Thirty years later, when Cromwell ruled in Charles's place, another monument was set here with the busts of a man and his wife looking out from dark recesses. He is Thomas Wilson, who died while he was serving as Prefect here under Cromwell's military system of local government, when the whole of England was divided into ten areas and each area was ruled by a major-general.

Family Portraits

WORMLEY. Its 17th century manor house on Roman Ermine Street has come down in the world, split into two cottages which share the old chimney stack between them; but at the end of an oak avenue is a church which has grown through the centuries, beginning with a Norman nave and north doorway and ending with a new little bellcot and a south aisle of last century, in which part of a Norman window and a Norman arch have been reset. The old timbers remain in the roofs of the nave and the porch. There is a fine Norman font with ears of corn and cable moulding, a Jacobean oak pulpit with quaint portraits of men and women, and an interesting collection of family groups in brass. One shows an Elizabethan couple with their 12 children, another has 15th century Edward Howton with his wife and three sons, and a remarkable brass shows his contemporary John Cok, with his wife and ten sons, the Trinity appearing above them and dogs chasing a hare below them. Almost reaching the chancel roof is the grand marble and alabaster monument of a Jacobean couple, William and Dorothy Purveye, who are sculptured on ledges one above the other, with Dorothy's child cousin, Honoria Denny, kneeling in a niche below holding a skull. The Pilgrim Trust has in our time restored the monument to its original beauty, and made legible the old inscription which tells us that William Purveye left money for the poor of the parish and "poore schollers in Cambridge." Last of these portrait memorials is the bust of Sir Abraham Hume, who lived at the Bury in the park beside the church and gave the splendid altar painting of the Last Supper by Giacomo Palma, the 16th century Venetian. Sir Abraham died in 1838, the year after his daughter Lady Farnborough, who is also here kneeling at prayer.

Wormley was the last home of Richard Gough, whose 74 years of happy and fruitful industry closed here in 1809. The son of an East India merchant, he was born in London, and before going to Cambridge at 17 was already a good Latin scholar and the author of an elaborate work on world geography. As an undergraduate he planned his British Topography, and on leaving the university spent 20 years in giving effect to his scheme. Inheriting a fortune, he had means and leisure such as few travelling scholars have enjoyed.

For more than 20 years he tramped England, exploring every county, examining its churches and public buildings, sifting and pondering deeds and charters, and making an immense number of notes on sculptures and inscriptions. His Anecdotes of British Topography followed an exhaustive work on Carausius, the third century Roman who made Roman Britain mistress of the narrow seas, and this was succeeded by a masterly edition of Camden's Britannia, a labour of love which cost him 16 years of toil.

These books, like his Sepulchral Monuments of Great Britain, covering the period between the Conquest and the end of the Tudor Age, were brilliantly written, and finely illustrated and printed. Almost to the end of his days he pursued his travels, enriching his collections, maintaining friendships with scholars and antiquaries throughout the country, and blessed at home by unclouded happiness. At his death he bequeathed his books and manuscripts to Oxford.

A Flag from Jutland

WYDDIAL. Among its wide fields, threaded by lanes and grassy tracks, with great thatched barns and little thatched cottages of all shapes and ages, we come on a 15th century church scarcely looking its age, but this is confirmed by a broken brass on the chancel wall telling us that the aisle was added in 1532 by George Cannon. The only seats in his aisle are three enormous box-pews over four feet high. In the windows are eight vigorous little pictures in 16th century Flemish glass showing the approach of Judas, and the Trial, the Scourging, and the Crucifixion. A screen under the tower exactly copies two Jacobean screens, pierced and ornamented with grotesque figures. They enclose the chapel of the Goulstons, whose bygone importance as lords of the manor is marked by numerous memorials, one of 1687 with twisted columns holding up the pompous busts of Sir William and his wife Fredeswyde.

Before the altar are brasses to earlier lords of the manor, one of 1546 showing John Gille with his wife and eight daughters, the sons being missing; but the best portrait brass is a fine head and shoulders of Dame Margaret Plumbe, whose first husband, Sir Robert Southwell, was much occupied in suppressing the monasteries and putting some of their money in his own pocket. It was not his only profitable venture, for he helped to put down Sir Thomas Wyatt's rebellion and secured some of his lands in the process. Another lady, Margery Disney, who died in 1621, has a curious memorial painted on wood and topped by a skull and crossbones. Over the door hangs the white ensign flown by HMS Inflexible at the Battle of Jutland.

Claud Lovat Fraser, the brilliant young artist whose gay decorative work was ended by the after effects of the war (his grave is not far off at Buntingford), is remembered here because he designed the Rectors List, on which we read Charles Maxwell's fine record of 53 years service during last century.

Opposite the church is Wyddial Hall, an 18th century house built over some 16th century cellars; and a mile away is the 17th century house Corney Bury, with three gables and a pillared porch.

HERTFORDSHIRE TOWNS AND VILLAGES

In this key to our map of Hertfordshire are all the towns and villages treated in this book. If a place is not on the map by name, its square is given here, so that the way to it is easily found, each square being five miles. One or two hamlets are in the book with their neighbouring villages; for these see Index.

INDEX

This index includes all notable subjects and people likely to be sought for, and a special index of pictures appears at the beginning of the volume.

INDEX

INDEX

INDEX